Critical Perspectives on Cybersecurity

OXFORD STUDIES IN GENDER AND INTERNATIONAL RELATIONS

Series editors: Rahul Rao, University of St Andrews, and Laura Sjoberg, Royal Holloway University of London

Windows of Opportunity: How Women Seize Peace Negotiations for Political Change
Miriam J. Anderson

Women as Foreign Policy Leaders: National Security and Gender Politics in Superpower America
Sylvia Bashevkin

Gendered Citizenship: Understanding Gendered Violence in Democratic India
Natasha Behl

Gender, Religion, Extremism: Finding Women in Anti-Radicalization
Katherine E. Brown

Enlisting Masculinity: The Construction of Gender in U.S. Military Recruiting Advertising during the All-Volunteer Force
Melissa T. Brown

The Politics of Gender Justice at the International Criminal Court: Legacies and Legitimacy
Louise Chappell

The Other #MeToos
Iqra Shagufta Cheema

Cosmopolitan Sex Workers: Women and Migration in a Global City
Christine B. N. Chin

Intelligent Compassion: Feminist Critical Methodology in the Women's International League for Peace and Freedom
Catia Cecilia Confortini

Hidden Wars: Gendered Political Violence in Asia's Civil Conflicts
Sara E. Davies and Jacqui True

Complicit Sisters: Gender and Women's Issues across North-South Divides
Sara de Jong

Gender and Private Security in Global Politics
Maya Eichler

This American Moment: A Feminist Christian Realist Intervention
Caron E. Gentry

Troubling Motherhood: Maternality in Global Politics
Lucy B. Hall, Anna L. Weissman, and Laura J. Shepherd

Breaking the Binaries in Security Studies: A Gendered Analysis of Women in Combat
Ayelet Harel-Shalev and Shir Daphna-Tekoah

Scandalous Economics: Gender and the Politics of Financial Crises
Aida A. Hozić and Jacqui True

Building Peace, Rebuilding Patriarchy: The Failure of Gender Interventions in Timor-Leste
Melissa Johnston

Rewriting the Victim: Dramatization as Research in Thailand's Anti-Trafficking Movement
Erin M. Kamler

Equal Opportunity Peacekeeping: Women, Peace, and Security in Post-Conflict States
Sabrina Karim and Kyle Beardsley

Gender, Sex, and the Postnational Defense: Militarism and Peacekeeping
Annica Kronsell

The Beauty Trade: Youth, Gender, and Fashion Globalization
Angela B. V. McCracken

Global Norms and Local Action: The Campaigns against Gender-Based Violence in Africa
Peace A. Medie

Rape Loot Pillage: The Political Economy of Sexual Violence in Armed Conflict
Sara Meger

Critical Perspectives on Cybersecurity: Feminist and Postcolonial Interventions
Anwar Mhajne and Alexis Henshaw

Support the Troops: Military Obligation, Gender, and the Making of Political Community
Katharine M. Millar

From Global to Grassroots: The European Union, Transnational Advocacy, and Combating Violence against Women
Celeste Montoya

Who Is Worthy of Protection? Gender-Based Asylum and US Immigration Politics
Meghana Nayak

Revisiting Gendered States: Feminist Imaginings of the State in International Relations
Swati Parashar, J. Ann Tickner, and Jacqui True

Out of Time: The Queer Politics of Postcoloniality
Rahul Rao

Gender, UN Peacebuilding, and the Politics of Space: Locating Legitimacy
Laura J. Shepherd

Narrating the Women, Peace and Security Agenda: Logics of Global Governance
Laura J. Shepherd

Capitalism's Sexual History
Nicola J. Smith

The Global Politics of Sexual and Reproductive Health
Maria Tanyag

A Feminist Voyage through International Relations
J. Ann Tickner

The Political Economy of Violence against Women
Jacqui True

Queer International Relations: Sovereignty, Sexuality and the Will to Knowledge
Cynthia Weber

Feminist Global Health Security
Clare Wenham

Bodies of Violence: Theorizing Embodied Subjects in International Relations
Lauren B. Wilcox

Critical Perspectives on Cybersecurity

Feminist and Postcolonial Interventions

Edited by
ANWAR MHAJNE AND ALEXIS HENSHAW

Oxford University Press is a department of the University of Oxford. It furthers
the University's objective of excellence in research, scholarship, and education
by publishing worldwide. Oxford is a registered trade mark of Oxford University
Press in the UK and certain other countries.

Published in the United States of America by Oxford University Press
198 Madison Avenue, New York, NY 10016, United States of America.

© Oxford University Press 2024

All rights reserved. No part of this publication may be reproduced, stored in
a retrieval system, or transmitted, in any form or by any means, without the
prior permission in writing of Oxford University Press, or as expressly permitted
by law, by license, or under terms agreed with the appropriate reproduction
rights organization. Inquiries concerning reproduction outside the scope of the
above should be sent to the Rights Department, Oxford University Press, at the
address above.

You must not circulate this work in any other form
and you must impose this same condition on any acquirer.

Library of Congress Cataloging-in-Publication Data
Names: Mhajne, Anwar, editor. | Henshaw, Alexis Leanna, editor.
Title: Critical perspectives on cybersecurity : feminist and postcolonial interventions /
Anwar Mhajne, Alexis Henshaw.
Description: New York : Oxford University Press, [2024] |
Series: Oxford Studies in Gender and International Relations |
Includes bibliographical references and index.
Identifiers: LCCN 2023043431 (print) | LCCN 2023043432 (ebook) |
ISBN 9780197695890 (pb) | ISBN 9780197695883 (hb) | ISBN 9780197695913 (epub)
Subjects: LCSH: Women and human security—Developing countries. |
Technology and women—Developing countries. | Computer security—Developing countries—
Case studies. | Computer crimes—Prevention—Developing countries.
Classification: LCC JZ5578 .C75 2024 (print) | LCC JZ5578 (ebook) |
DDC 303.48/34091724—dc23/eng/20231212
LC record available at https://lccn.loc.gov/2023043431
LC ebook record available at https://lccn.loc.gov/2023043432

DOI: 10.1093/oso/9780197695883.001.0001

Contents

List of Contributors ix

Introduction 1
Anwar Mhajne and Alexis Henshaw

PART I. EMERGING ISSUES IN CYBERSECURITY: GENDER, GEOGRAPHY, POLICY, AND PRACTICE

1. A Call for Feminist Insights in Cybersecurity: Implementing United Nations Security Council Resolution 1325 on Women, Peace, and Security in Cyberspace 25
Crystal Whetstone and Luna K.C.

2. Cyberspace and the Nouveau Colonialism 52
Erin Saltman and Dina Hussein

PART II. CYBERSECURITY AND SOCIETY IN THE GLOBAL SOUTH

3. Gendered and Postcolonial Perspectives on Data Weaponization in Armed Conflict: The Case of Afghanistan 81
Julia-Silvana Hofstetter

4. Gendered Transnational Authoritarianism in Cyberspace: A Case Study of Uyghurs 114
Murat Yılmaz

5. Disciplinary Power and Feminism: Nudity as Resistance to Cyberspace Bullying in Kenya 134
Margaret Monyani and Allan Wefwafwa

6. The Application of IHL on Israeli's Cyber Strategies Against the Palestinians: A Feminist Perspective 152
Anwar Mhajne

7. Capacity Building and Cyber Insecurity in Latin
   America: Geopolitics, Surveillance, and Disinformation   173
   Alexis Henshaw

Conclusion   194
   Anwar Mhajne and Alexis Henshaw

Index   201

Contributors

Luna K.C., Assistant Professor in Global and International Studies, University of Northern British Columbia, Canada

Alexis Henshaw, Associate Professor of Political Science, Troy University

Julia-Silvana Hofstetter, Senior Advisor, ICT4Peace Foundation; and Non-Resident Research Fellow, Center for Long-Term Cybersecurity, UC Berkeley

Dina Hussein, Head of Dangerous Organizations Policy Development and Expert Partnerships, Meta

Anwar Mhajne, Assistant Professor of Political Science and International Studies, Stonehill College

Margaret Monyani, Postdoctoral Researcher, University of Johannesburg, South Africa

Erin Saltman, Director of Membership and Programs, Global Internet Forum to Counter Terrorism (GIFCT)

Allan Wefwafwa, Sessional Lecturer of Media Studies, University of the Witwatersrand; and Tutorial Fellow of Journalism, Technical University of Kenya

Crystal Whetstone, Assistant Professor of International Relations, Bilkent University

Murat Yılmaz, Instructor of International Relations, Kastamonu University

Introduction

Anwar Mhajne and Alexis Henshaw

Why apply a critical lens to the study of cybersecurity? In the context of international relations (IR), work on the global politics of cybersecurity and cyberwar can still be called a relatively new field. Much of the literature that exists is aimed at carrying forward dimensions of the longstanding neo-neo debates between the paradigms of neorealism and neoliberalism. True to the roots of these theories, these academic debates focus largely on whether (or to what extent) there is an analogy between war and cyberwar, whether governance by the international community can constrain state behaviors, and how cyberweapons might be used to further geopolitical aims.

Such debates have, unsurprisingly, broken down into two camps. On the one hand, there are those who view prospective cyberwar as an extension of traditional warfighting domains, where traditional ideas about power and strategy apply, with some caveats (Lynn 2010; Nye 2010). On the other hand, there is a camp that expresses far more skepticism of cyberwar as a valid or useful topic of analysis, for various reasons. Some theorists center a critique of cyberwar around the notion that cyberattacks, in and of themselves, are incapable of causing death or long-lasting damage. These authors note that such attacks would likely need to be one of many strategies deployed in the conduct of war (Gartzke 2013; Rid 2012). Others note that concepts of offensive and defensive balance, which are particularly relevant to realist variants of IR theory, do not neatly map onto the use of cyberweapons (Libicki 2011; Valeriano 2022a). Still others base their skepticism on the assessment that cyberwar is unlikely to ever happen, and that the scale of cyberattacks is likely to never move beyond nuisance activities and "shenanigans" like crime, espionage, and service disruptions (Walt 2010).

Valeriano (2022b) has lamented the current state of inquiry regarding cybersecurity and cyberwar. Noting the "lack of novelty" and the failure of the literature to evolve, he asks why scholars can't "develop new and interesting questions" about the field. One conclusion he reaches is that the very concept of cyberwar has become "inflated" to the point that, after over a decade worth of dire warnings and billions of dollars (or more) invested, policymakers and scholars alike are stuck explaining why the anticipated cyberwar hasn't happened (Valeriano 2022b). Others seem to share this discomfort about the state of research. Singer and Friedman (2014) imply that many policy discussions around cybersecurity take on a "fake it 'till you make it" attitude, with policymakers, commentators, and even military experts weighing in on subjects even where they have a poor understanding of what they are talking about.[1] In such an environment, how can the literature meaningfully advance?

Critical Feminist and Postcolonial Perspectives on Cybersecurity

We share Valeriano's (2022b) concern about the lack of interesting questions in the literature on cybersecurity and IR, yet we believe that avenues to advance conversation are already within the discipline's reach. That is to say, we believe that there is an opportunity to substantially enrich conversation by bringing insights from critical theories of IR to bear on the concept and practice of cybersecurity. Following Harding's (1986) observation that all phenomena are gendered and Peterson's (2003) early warning about inequality in the virtual political economy, we argue that feminist IR theory offers underexplored insights about the nature and future of cybersecurity. These insights dovetail with emerging literature examining how race/ethnicity and Global North-South divides shape experiences of cybersecurity (or cyber insecurity).

While some scholars have critiqued the use of the term "cybersecurity," arguing that the word hides the multisited and sociotechnical nature of the subject (Dwyer et al. 2022), we choose to engage with it directly. In similar vein to Mhajne and Whetstone (2024), we use the term cybersecurity in this volume instead of embracing alternatives such as "digital politics" or similar terms. The reason behind this decision is that cybersecurity has left a significant impact not only on the field of IR research but also on the policymakers' domains. By preserving the term cybersecurity while incorporating fresh perspectives, our objective is to steer cybersecurity thinking toward more transformative pathways, thereby enhancing its effectiveness in addressing a wide range of insecurities experienced by vulnerable groups globally

(Mhajne and Whetstone 2024). As we have noted in previous work, a feminist lens can encourage us to question how cybersecurity is defined and who is rightfully the referent of cybersecurity policy (Mhajne and Whetstone 2024; Henshaw 2023). It can question the centrality of states (and state militaries) as practitioners and referents of cybersecurity while asking what a human security-driven approach to cybersecurity might look like (Mhajne and Whetstone 2024; Henshaw 2023; Mhajne 2021). It can urge us to reflect on how neoliberalism in the information age gives the technology industry significant political power. It can also call upon us to question where states have acted as agents of cyber insecurity, particularly toward marginalized groups.

This latter point hearkens back to foundational concepts in feminist international relations. Feminist scholars have long sought to both critique and de-center the state in IR theory. Among other things, feminist theory points out that state governments are generally based on patriarchal social contracts that have failed to adequately represent women while also exposing them to harm (Tickner 2001; True 2018). Even in democratic political systems, women generally remain underrepresented, and their interests are too often sidelined (Dahlerup 2017). What is true of lawmaking institutions is also true of national security communities. Depressingly little has changed since Cohn (1987) explored the dominance of masculine ideals in Cold War era nuclear security. While the nuclear security community itself continues to sideline women,[2] efforts to promote gender mainstreaming (especially via national or regional implementation of the Women, Peace and Security, or WPS, agenda) in security operations have moved slowly. Even in countries that view themselves as norm leaders, like the UK, men in government have sometimes siloed WPS as a women's issue while avoiding hard questions about masculinity, violence, and demilitarization (Wright 2020). In highly militarized spaces like the North Atlantic Treaty Organization (NATO) and the national security community in the United States, the issue is even more complex. Here, the transformative aims of WPS are often coopted to serve logics of masculine protection (Hurley 2018). At the same time, the work of implementation is often left to women officials who are expected to naturally know what "gender mainstreaming" means—despite having little training or background in how WPS came to be (Henshaw 2021, 2022). Throughout, women have remained critically underrepresented in cybersecurity spaces. Despite women's historical contributions to computing they still constitute just 20% of the cybersecurity workforce by some estimates (Kshetri and Chhetri 2022).

To be sure, there has been some destabilization of states in the cybersecurity literature. The attribution problem is an almost ubiquitous question for analyses of cyberattacks and possible cyberwar (Manjikian 2020; Singer and Friedman 2014; Valeriano 2022b). The fact that cyberattacks can be so easily routed through and across countries makes their origin difficult to trace, while the relatively low costs associated with committing a cyberattack mean that a variety of nonstate actors have at least basic disruption capabilities at their disposal. More recently, in the age of social media, we have seen that even the relatively low-tech interventions of posting, sharing, memeing, dogpiling, and spamming other users with disinformation can have real political effects (Davey and Ebner 2017; Singer and Brooking 2018). Still, critical theory would argue that the destabilization of the state can go further. Much of cybersecurity literature still centers on states as both the referents and the default providers of cybersecurity—even as the concept itself has continued to expand.

Singer and Friedman (2014) note that the definition of "cybersecurity" has changed many times over the years, with even the US Department of Defense running through more than a dozen definitions. While early definitions focused primarily on the security of physical computer equipment and digital information systems, there has since been a significant mission creep. Official and academic definitions have now come to include, in various assemblages, both public and private technology infrastructure (including cables, cellular equipment, and satellites), digital networks, telecommunications, the "information environment," and the nebulous space of the "cyber commons" within which we all interact and where (depending on who does the talking) there are rights to be protected and/or laws to be enforced (CISA n.d.; Crowther 2017; Hayden 2018; Lynn 2010; Singer and Friedman 2014). Only the latter two facets of this definition speak directly to the politics of social interactions in cyberspace. Especially in the case of information security, many states of the Global North began to highlight the relationship between mis/disinformation and cybersecurity only after the 2016 US presidential election and the infodemic surrounding COVID-19.[3] The fact that such events occurred years after social media had been used to stoke riots in South and Southeast Asia and after decades where the spread of mis/disinformation on reproductive health, abortion, and vaccines went unchecked (primarily targeting women)[4] are indicative of what we may have missed out on by not fostering a more diverse cybersecurity community.

Feminist IR and the study of cybersecurity have been slow to grow toward each other. One of us has written in the past on the paucity of related publications and conference panels—noting that the feminist academic community (at least, in political science and IR) has lagged behind Global South scholarship and racial/ethnic studies in seeing digital politics as a worthy topic of analysis (Henshaw 2023). Recent studies further suggest that discussions of gender or diversity are largely absent in syllabi and coursework on cybersecurity and conflict (Herr et al. 2020). Our desire to forefront intersectional analyses and voices from the Global South in this volume is a recognition of the fact that feminist IR is a relative latecomer to these debates. To make meaningful contributions, feminist interventions on cybersecurity must build upon existing knowledge about topics like electronic surveillance, algorithmic bias, colonialism in the digital space, and the emergence of a digital rights movement. Much of this work emerges from critical communities like racial/ethnic studies (Benjamin 2019; Browne 2012; Noble 2018; Noble and Tynes 2016), surveillance studies (Dubrofsky and Magnet 2015; Gill 2019), queer theory (Guyan 2022; Moore and Currah 2015), and work by Global South authors (Bhandari 2021; Mukerjee 2016; Prasad 2018). Taken together, this work not only establishes the relevance of gender for cyber and information security—it also further establishes that questions of gender are inseparable from discussions about race/ethnicity, geographic positionality, and other social power relationships. These points have been further underscored by the work of privacy- and digital rights-focused NGOs and social movements, which have consistently and repeatedly highlighted the differential social risks associated with new technologies and the propensity of states to undermine the cybersecurity of their own citizens.

Perhaps the most visible example of this to date has been the abusive deployments of Pegasus spyware by multiple countries against their own citizens, as documented by a community of journalists and researchers. The Pegasus scandal looms large over many of the substantive chapters of this book,[5] where it is discussed in greater detail, but in brief it shows how the development of cyberweapons and cybersurveillance tools under the rubric of counterterrorism can be twisted to suppress dissent and commit egregious violations of human rights. Originally intended as a tool to harvest information from the phones of suspected terrorists and criminals, Pegasus and other tools developed by Israel's NSO Group have ended up in the hands of governments who used them to surveil human rights defenders, women's rights advocates, journalists, political candidates, diplomats, and more. In many instances, these tools were licensed with the support and approval of the US or Israeli government, in decisions based more on political expediency than on any assurances of ethical use (Bergman and Mazzetti 2022).

Postcolonial theories of international relations, which in part explore the material conditions of relations between the Global North and the Global South, can shed light on why the cyber-utopian ideal of a world in which the free flow of information renders authoritarian governance impossible has never materialized (Wilkens 2007). In the 1980s and 1990s, the so-called cyber domain might have been considered something analogous to outer space: An emerging area in which many states wanted to influence policy or exercise power but where few could truly dominate due in part to the high barriers to entry. In the ensuing decades, we have seen that balance of power shift in the digital realm—to an extent. Today, some of the world's largest populations of internet users are in the Global South. Many countries in the postcolonial space have national cybersecurity plans and/or cybersecurity capabilities. Some of the biggest security threats, too, also emerge from developing countries.

Yet critical areas of dependency remain. As the following section shows, major powers like the US, Russia, China, and states of the European Union still largely shape the norms that the rest of the world is expected to follow in cyberspace. They export cyberweapons capabilities, including spyware and censorship tools, while trying to impose their own logic about how such tools should be used. As discussed in Chapter 7, dealing with Latin America, powerful states also influence policy across the Global South by shaping cybersecurity strategy through diplomatic intervention and foreign assistance. All the while, they repeat the mistake of projecting an understanding of "security" that is based in Eurocentric worldviews. Postcolonial IR theorists point out that dominant views about the emergence of modern world order often position the European powers of the colonial era as the facilitators of progress and modernization. This ignores both preexisting networks of international relations across the Global South and the harms imposed by colonialism (Acharya 2007; Barkawi and Laffey 2006; Seth 2011). In the case of cybersecurity, where most historical narratives start with the development of government proto-networks in the United States, one might be tempted to point out the extent to which histories omit the role of the Global South in shaping today's technological landscape. This includes the knowledge extracted from the Global South via brain drain, the labor outsourced to the

Global South (such as training AI systems[6]), the research and development knowledge gained by piloting emerging technologies in the Global South, and the data extracted from these same populations under ethically dubious circumstances. The study of cybersecurity, like IR and security studies before it, has at best downplayed these contributions.

At the same time, adopting a postcolonial lens means seeing spaces for resistance. One theme across the various chapters of this volume is the range of resistance and refusal strategies deployed by populations across the Global South, as they are threatened with new technologies of surveillance, digital authoritarianism, digital colonialism, and so on. Postcolonial interventions in security studies note that Eurocentric perspectives on security have historically de-legitimized certain forms of threat and resistance, especially where these emerge from the postcolonial space (Barkawi and Laffey 2006). While Bertrand (2018), following Spivak (1988), notes the impossibility of having the subaltern speak in security studies, we hope that by centering Global South perspectives on cybersecurity in this volume—alongside other critical contributions—we can move toward a more inclusive literature on cybersecurity.

Governance and Norms, Revisited

A reevaluation of the dominant narratives surrounding norms and laws in cyberspace demonstrates the value of adopting a more critical perspective. Scholarship depicts three main approaches to applying international law to cyberspace. The first is liberal institutionalism (Wu 1997), which focuses on international institutions and multilateralism regulating cyberspace. The second, the statists approach, places states at the center of formulating national and international law to govern cyberspace (Lewis 2010). These approaches are also reflected in international debates on regulating cyberspace. The third approach, cyberlibertarianism, holds that cyberspace should not be regulated (Barlow 2016).

The bulk of existing scholarship on cybersecurity in IR has appealed to statist or institutionalist views. In the statist camp, the United States is viewed as "a norm entrepreneur in seeking to establish the right of all people to have access to the Internet as a universally accepted principle" (Manjikian 2020, 263). US commitments in this area are seen as emerging from the country's own notion of its identity and role as the promoter of democracy and freedom as well as from foundational myths of the internet, which stress that the internet was partially the invention of American computer scientists whose views on "academic freedom and hippie mentality" led them to prioritize the freedom to connect and interact (Singer and Friedman 2014, 253). In this telling, the militarized history of the internet in the United States takes on a secondary role. As such, it becomes easy to contrast a US-led "pro-freedom" camp with a rival, aspiring norm entrepreneurs like Russia and especially China. These countries' views on cyberspace and cybersecurity are more closely associated with territorialization, concerns for sovereignty, and limits on access and content (Mueller 2020). To these states, access and the free flow of information amounts to information warfare. In particular, they see in cyberspace an attempt by the US (and its allies) to undermine their political systems and advocate for regime change (Singer and Friedman 2014). As such, these countries see a valid national security interest in securing cyberspace through measures like censorship, limitations on access, internet shutdowns, and so forth. Alongside these two main camps, some scholars additionally hint at the development of a third normative axis, led by the countries of the European Union (EU), which generally embraces the US interest in online freedom while tempering it through more aggressive privacy laws and restrictions on hate speech (Singer and Friedman 2014).

In many ways, this discussion of norm entrepreneurship is grossly oversimplified. To begin by problematizing the stances of powerful states, roles are more complex than they may seem. In the case of the United States, despite its vision as a champion of rights, access, and information cyberspace is not truly "free" to its own citizens. The COVID-19 pandemic threw into sharp relief how cyberspace was restricted not by censorship but by cost and the lack of infrastructure. As public schools and government services moved rapidly online, it became obvious how many US citizens struggled with fast and reliable access to the internet from home. The Pew Research Center (2021) noted that while the vast majority (93%) of Americans say they use the internet, age, education, income level, and geographic location were all factors that contributed to significant differences in access/use. While nearly all young adults use the internet, only 75% of senior citizens indicated that they were regularly online. Just 86% of the poorest Americans were online, compared to nearly all individuals from households making $50,000 or more. Usage statistics further declined when taking into account who had access to a high-speed internet connection at home. Just 77% of all US users surveyed met these criteria, including only 64% of senior citizens, 57% of the poorest households, and 59% of those who lacked a college education (Pew Research Center 2021). While gender disparities in overall access and high-speed access were small (1% or less in each case), racial disparities were pronounced in the case of high-speed access. While 80% of white Americans indicated they had a home broadband connection, just 71% of Black Americans and 65% of Hispanics answered this question in the affirmative.

Under President Joseph Biden, the United States has attempted to improve connectivity through the Affordable Connectivity Program, which offers discounts for internet service and computers or tablets. Yet despite attempts to lower costs, service is still limited by the lack of appropriate infrastructure in many parts of the country as of this writing. A 2021 report on broadband infrastructure noted that the US government lacks reliable or comprehensive data on broadband connectivity, with data from the Federal Communications Commission (FCC) likely overestimating true connectivity (Joel 2021). Data from private companies shows that a large swath of the rural United States has under 15% of the population accessing high-speed internet. Connectivity is lowest in counties that have a sizable Native American population, especially in the Southwest and Alaska (Joel 2021).

Some have called the existence of socially driven digital divides a "soft issue" in cybersecurity at the international level (Hurwitz and Schaub 2018). Such language is revealing and hearkens back to feminist security studies, which encourages us to see how the designation of "hard" versus "soft" security issues is gendered, racialized, and so forth (Cohn 2014). In this case, US discourse about the need for free access and freedom of information online runs up against the interests of private economic actors, for whom it is not profitable to provide infrastructure or low-cost services to every community. Private interests also contribute to issues with cybercrime and other concerns that impact the free enjoyment of cyberspace. Consider the emerging distinctions between the United States and countries of the EU as they relate to the treatment of hate speech and privacy rights. One of the earliest cases exploring issues of sovereignty and limitations on freedom in cyberspace emerged out of France, where a court in the year 2000 ruled that Yahoo! must comply with French law limiting the exhibition and sale of Nazi artifacts. Following this initial ruling, Yahoo! opened its own case in US courts, seeking to render the French decision unenforceable on the grounds it would violate the First Amendment to the US Constitution.[7] On a much smaller scale, this case presaged the larger debates about jurisdiction, sovereignty, and national security that dominate the geopolitics of cyberspace today.

In the area of data privacy, too, profitability, freedom, and cybersecurity collide. While the EU's General Data Protection Regulation (GDPR) prevents data overcollection, establishes accountability for the secure collection and transfer of personal data, and enshrines a right to be forgotten (i.e., the right for individuals to request the removal of personal data or for data to expire), the United States lacks similar provisions. As of 2021, just three US states had comprehensive laws on consumer privacy. In most jurisdictions, the lack of privacy laws leaves Americans vulnerable to, among other things, data harvesting, having sensitive personal data posted online by data aggregators, having their online data scraped to train AI-based systems (including facial-recognition technologies), and various forms of cybercrime. Even legal requirements regarding when companies must notify citizens of a data breach are unclear, with at least 54 different laws governing practice across US jurisdictions (Klosowski 2021). When a comprehensive data privacy and protection law was proposed in the US Congress in 2021, it was called one of the "most-lobbied" bills of all time, with more than 180 corporate entities seeking to engage in the legislative debate (Klar and Evers-Hillstrom 2022). Among other things, corporate lobbying was seen as responsible for weakening the accountability of telecom carriers and opt-out provisions for targeted advertising (Klar and Evers-Hillstrom 2022). The US Congress still has not, as of this writing, passed the proposed law.

Taking all of this into account, it is possible to downgrade the United States from the standard-bearer for internet freedom to an advocate of not only the relatively free flow of information online but also for the commercialization of access and information. Seeing the role of private actors in shaping this position is relevant because it calls into question state-centric understandings of the nature of cybersecurity and norm entrepreneurship. Many authors have used the analogy of nested clubs or groups to refer to the nature of cyberspace (Raymond 2016, 2018; Singer and Friedman 2014). This reflects an understanding that cyberspace is not simply an extension of territorial space but an overlapping web of infrastructure and goods that is both publicly and privately owned, controlled and/or regulated by states, private actors, international organizations, and the global commons. In this sense, a variety of nonstate actors engage in the creation of governance and norms. These players defy simple categorization as "good" or "bad" actors. Consider the case of tech companies. While some countries (like the US and the UK) view public-private partnerships as integral to cybersecurity strategy (Farwell 2018), some of the same companies that participate in partnerships with US government and law enforcement agencies—players like Cisco, Microsoft, and Google—also help uphold systems of censorship and surveillance in authoritarian regimes. The tolerance of such practices arguably shows the limitation on states' ability to constrain these players and maintain a monopoly—or perhaps even a preponderance—of power in the cyber domain.

Moving away from a statist approach, liberal institutionalist frameworks also interrogate how international organizations take part in the governance of cyberspace. With a few exceptions, such as the Budapest Convention on Cybercrime and the African Union Convention on Cyber Security and Personal Data Protection, there are no overarching international legal frameworks for regulating cyberspace (Hollis 2021). However, international organizations, such as the UN General Assembly's First Committee on Disarmament and International Security, the G20, the European Union, ASEAN, and the OAS, agree that existing international law applies in cyberspace (Hollis 2021). The disagreement, however, is over how it applies. For instance, some states have challenged the applicability of international humanitarian law (IHL) in the cyber realm (Hollis 2021). These are essential debates that shape how states "conduct their cyber operations in armed conflicts, their ability to respond to malicious cyber activity conducted by other states, and what actions they must take to protect the rights of third states from harms originating in their own territories" (Hollis 2021).

Additionally, there are interpretive issues at the core of international law. These issues emerge due to ambiguity and difficulty in defining sovereignty in cyberspace and what constitutes a violation of human rights in the virtual realm. Furthermore, the push of some states, such as Russia and China, for digital sovereignty and information security has contributed to the difficulty of building an international regulatory framework. A focus on information security broadens government control of the data and its flow. Unlike cybersecurity, which is limited to protecting networks, devices, confidentiality, and data integrity, information security includes regulating and filtering content and controlling access to communication tools deemed threatening to the government (Segal 2017). Information security is directly tied to debates on cyber sovereignty, which argues that "states have authority within a fixed boundary to devise rules, laws, and norms about behaviour of individuals, institutions, applications, and other actors and factors in the cyberspace" (Mirza 2021, 598). Still, despite their philosophical differences, efforts led by UN member states to tackle the applicability of international law to cyber issues have increased. For example, moving beyond the original UN Group of Governmental Experts forum, UN processes now also encompass an Open-Ended Working Group in the UN General Assembly's First Committee and a Third Committee process on a UN cybercrime convention.

A New Direction: Centering the Global South and the Global Commons

An understanding of cyberspace rooted in critical feminist and postcolonial theory might call upon us to recognize cyberspace as a global commons. Hurwitz and Schaub (2018) describe the global commons of cyberspace as a common pool resource characterized by polycentric ownership of infrastructure and content that, like the commons of the past, is at risk of overuse and abuse. In this view, the futures of cyberspace are dependent on both the maintenance/expansion of infrastructure and the maintenance of public trust, that is, the willingness to engage in this domain (Schaub and Hurwitz 2018). From the latter perspective, the need to constrain nefarious acts—like cybercrime, cyberterrorism, and other forms of cyberattack—is key.

Returning to the foundational myths of the internet, we see how feminist and postcolonial interventions can redefine key moments in the history of cyberspace and cybersecurity. From the very beginning, the internet was an entity co-constituted by the US Department of Defense and an epistemic community of researchers. Once opened to the public, various nonstate actors played important roles in defining or redefining the possibilities for this space. The International Campaign to Ban Landmines, for example, was one of the earliest examples of how activists could use email and other forms of online communications to coordinate large-scale efforts and influence international law. The Zapatista Army of National Liberation (EZLN) was similarly among the first nonstate armed groups to leverage the power of the internet in the early 1990s, when sympathetic allies turned to listservs and message boards to circulate content produced by the group and amplify their grievances (Cleaver 1998). Such developments rarely appear among the milestones in the history of cyberspace—but perhaps they should, as they point to the role nonstate actors have long played in contesting the territorialization and/or militarization of cyberspace.

Today, we continue to see how global civil society, including movements from the Global South, are challenging the boundaries of cyberspace. An example of such action is the work of the Independent Groups of Experts who crafted the Tallinn Manuals between 2009 and 2012. The first Tallinn Manual addresses the law applicable to armed conflict, whereas the Tallinn Manual 2.0 addresses cyber operations in and out of armed conflict. In the Global South, a digital rights movement is challenging practices of digital colonialism (a matter this volume deals with in Chapter 2). Among the concerns voiced by the activist community are issues of net neutrality (especially a desire to break up the monopolies enjoyed by major Western tech companies in some parts of the world), concerns over data privacy, the right to access relevant information in local languages, and the proliferation of ethnic- and gender-based violence online. As alluded to above, a diffuse cyberlibertarian movement is also mounting its own challenge to the landscape of cyberspace. In the push to create "Web 3.0," or the decentralized web, a diffuse collection of technology afficionados, cyberutopians, conspiracy theorists, criminals, privacy advocates, extremists, and even professionals in international development are working to leverage technologies like blockchain, cryptocurrency, and decentralized models of finance and content sharing in ways that bypass the state (Golumbia 2016). In each of these instances, the results of advocacy and/or action convincingly demonstrate how global civil society can limit or constrain the power of states and private companies in the cyber domain.

At the same time, global civil society is embattled. Issues of gender, race, and sexuality are compelling us to reevaluate our understanding of cybersecurity. The mass movement of a diverse population into cyberspace (beginning, roughly, in the 1990s) has led to both the emergence of new forms of targeted violence and the delivery of old forms of hate by new means. In cyberspace, we can observe racist, sexist, and homophobic/transphobic harassment occurring on a massive scale. However, harassment also manifests in newer and novel forms including revenge porn, deepfake/cheapfake pornography, doxing, zoombombing, deadnaming, and the like. The spread of targeted violence online has been so extensive that Dubravka Šimonovic, UN Special Rapporteur on Violence Against Women, estimated in 2018 that at least one-quarter of all women had experienced online abuse, with 10% experiencing online violence before the age of 15 (Šimonovic 2018). This is in addition, of course, to the near-ubiquitous nature of cybercrime. While comprehensive cross-national statistics on cybercrime are difficult to come by, given variation among local laws and data collection efforts, it is probably safe to say that every individual with an email address, a social media profile, or even a nominal web presence has been the victim of a phishing, hacking, or identity theft attempt.[8] The US Cybersecurity and Infrastructure Security Agency estimates that 47% of U.S. adults have had their personal data exposed by a data breach, while one in three US homes are affected by malware (CISA n.d.). Yet despite these staggering numbers (or, perhaps, because of them), states have largely proven ineffective at preventing or prosecuting cybercrime. The goal of prevention is largely outsourced to individuals, who must undergo a daily security theater of avoiding scams, changing passwords, surrendering biometric credentials, and so on.

Is this an abdication of states' responsibilities vis à vis their citizens? If so, at what point do states begin to lose their legitimacy as providers of security in the cyber domain? Some authors conclude that we have not yet reached a crisis point in the degradation of cyberspace because "there is little evidence of people exiting" the web (Schaub and Hurwitz 2018). But this is not necessarily true. Research on women's experiences of harassment and online violence in particular shows the impact of sustained online attacks. A 2018 study on women's use of Twitter showed that 32% of female users across eight countries surveyed quit the platform or self-censored as a result of harassment (Amnesty International 2018).[9] In most of these countries, at least two-thirds of women indicated that they had somehow changed the way they interact with social media based on their experience of harassment. Research from South Asia further underscores the potentially severe offline consequences of online crimes. Sambasivan et al. (2019) found that nearly three-quarters of women surveyed had experienced online violence, with several experiencing offline sexual violence and/or beatings as a result of these experiences. Some reported being "banished" from social media by their families because of their actions online and/or the crimes they had experienced. While the majority did not leave the online environment entirely, women have discussed using other coping strategies—such as making fake online profiles—that help them avoid abuse while also rendering social media profiles less useful (Sambasivan et al. 2019). Women journalists in Pakistan, for example, have noted that there are professional consequences associated with coping strategies like self-censorship or the use of fake accounts (DRF 2020). Keeping all this in mind, it seems high time to ask what feminist and Global South perspectives can tell us about cybersecurity.

Introducing the Volume

This volume offers a variety of critical perspectives on cybersecurity. Bearing in mind the foregoing discussion, we define "cybersecurity" broadly—referring to the security of digital systems, infrastructure, information, and data as well as the human security of those who interact through and within the digital space. This move, which is inclusive of equal rights to access and the enjoyment of cyberspace, is sure to be contested by some. Yet we contend that states, as explored above, have already opened this dimension of the dialogue by including discussions of human rights and equality in their national cybersecurity strategies.

We further see the value of this definition through the individual contributions made by our authors, who are situated throughout the world and who engage in both the academic and practitioner spheres. Their chapters each represent their own vision of cybersecurity, understood through the contexts in which they work and study. We have, broadly, structured this volume in two parts. The first deals with larger, transnational, or systemic questions around cybersecurity, while the second examines cybersecurity in a series of smaller, regional, and national contexts.

Part I opens with a contribution by Crystal Whetstone and Luna K.C., who explore the relationship between gender and cybersecurity in the context of the Women, Peace and Security (WPS) agenda. While appealing to UN Security Council resolutions on WPS and the National Action Plans (NAPs) developed by individual countries, they argue that human security and the security of women are inseparable from larger discussions about security in the digital space. Their contribution is followed by that of Dina Hussein and Erin Saltman, who discuss the potential risks of "nouveau colonialism" in cyberspace, especially as states, organizations, and other actors of the Global North establish new laws and regulations governing data protection.

In the second part, we turn to individual case studies that illustrate diverse understandings of cybersecurity in the Global South, at the same time exploring how these contexts are racialized and/or gendered. Julia Hofstetter examines the weaponization of data in Afghanistan, calling attention to the need for digital literacy and advocacy in fragile and conflict-affected areas. Murat Yılmaz continues with a case of gendered digital authoritarianism in Central Asia, specifically looking at how China has regulated the Uyghur people through surveillance and censorship. Margaret Monyani and Allan Wefwafwa explore the issue of online harassment in Kenya, looking at how women who share nude photos are subject to disciplining practices as well as how they find spaces for resistance. The final two case studies in the book examine race and gender issues in surveillance and security technologies. Anwar Mhajne looks at how the deployment of such technologies against the Palestinian people represents a challenge to international humanitarian law. Alexis Henshaw similarly looks at the use of security and border technology in Latin America. This latter analysis also approaches mis/disinformation as a transnational problem and one that is gendered, especially with regard to health disinformation and the proliferation of anti-feminist conspiracy theories.

Though the contributions of these authors engage with different contexts, technologies, and actors, we conclude the book with a discussion of some shared themes that we believe should form the framework of a human-centered approach to cybersecurity. This includes a need to move beyond the academic literature's somewhat narrow focus on cyberwar and/or cyberattacks as a tool of traditional warfare. While many individual authors in this volume touch upon how cybersecurity (or the lack thereof) shapes conflict dynamics, cybersecurity also exists in a much broader context. Data politics, for example, is a cross-cutting concern for many of these authors. Insofar as data is being used every day throughout the world to surveil, to control, to commodify, and to police, the contributions in this volume call upon us to reflect on how scholars and policymakers alike should engage with data protection and data privacy as elements of security. Similarly, the differential impacts of technology discussed by many authors in this volume—impacts that fall particularly upon women, racial/ethnic minorities, people of the Global South, LGBTQ+ communities, and other marginalized communities—call for greater engagement with the roles that individuals, experts, communities, and civil society actors can play in cybersecurity practice and policy. Though international humanitarian law and international law and governance on cybersecurity often talk past each other, broadening cybersecurity beyond state-centric conversations can arguably only happen when different and diverse perspectives are brought to the table.

Taken together, it is our hope that the chapters in this volume demonstrate an expansion of our understanding of cybersecurity, highlighting especially how the daily lived experience of cybersecurity looks for populations whose voices are often excluded from policy discussions. We hope to expose the shortcomings in existing international (and national) law and policy and to bring the focus of cybersecurity back to people and community rather than states and systems. Finally, we hope these chapters also offer some template for resistance and/or innovation, showing that critical perspectives on this issue need not be technophobic. As the technologies discussed in this volume—including but not limited to surveillance systems, biometrics, social media, information and communication technologies (ICTs)—are bound to play a role in our daily lives, we hope to provide insight on how to create norms that incorporate diverse voices and how to promote an ethic of responsibility.

Notes

1. See also Hayden (2018).
2. See Hurlburt et al. (2019).
3. As an example, the 2003 US National Strategy to Secure Cyberspace contained no mention of misinformation or disinformation and went so far to assert that "information flows continuously and seamlessly across political, ethnic, and religious divides" in cyberspace (White House 2003).
4. On the role of Facebook in ethnic/religious violence incidents prior to 2016, see Fuller (2014). The anti-vaccine movement has a long history, but the emergence of anti-vaccine discourse online has been traced to the publication of the now-discredited Wakefield study in 1998. In terms of the spread of reproductive health mis/disinformation, pro-life literature as early as 2000 was boasting about and encouraging the spread of pro-life talking points online, including the false claim that abortion enhances breast cancer risk (Alcorn 2000). Hitt (2006) further documents how the internet was used by women in Latin America to find/circulate information on inducing abortion in the early 2000s.
5. See Chapters 6 and 7.
6. For example, refer to OpenAI's use of Kenyan labor in the development of ChatGPT (Perrigo 2023).
7. For a more complete discussion, see UNODC (n.d.).
8. Indeed, even having a web presence is no longer a prerequisite for becoming a cybercrime victim. Data breaches can expose the personal information of anyone whose data is stored on electronic systems. In 2020, experts concluded that poor information security practices at Brazil's Ministry of Health left the data of over 243 million Brazilians potentially accessible to criminals for a period of six months. Those affected included anyone who had engaged with Brazil's national health system (Peters 2020). El Salvador's rollout of bitcoin as a national currency was similarly marred by large-scale fraud as a result of poor information security practices. While the government-sponsored Chivo wallet system promised the equivalent of US$30 in bitcoin to anyone who registered, it only required basic, publicly available information for anyone to "prove" their identity. As a result, the equivalent of millions of dollars were lost to

fraud, and an unknown number of Salvadorans had their identity stolen by criminals who created fake wallets in their names (Alvarado 2022).
9. The countries included the US, UK, New Zealand, Spain, Italy, Poland, Sweden, and Denmark. See also Amnesty International (2017).

References

Acharya, Amitav. 2007. "The Emerging Regional Architecture of World Politics." *World Politics* 59: 629–652.
Alcorn, Randy. 2000. *Pro-Life Answers to Pro-Choice Arguments*. Crown.
Alvarado, Moisés. 2022. "US$12 millones fueron hurtados de Chivo Wallet en El Salvador." *No-ficción*.https://www.no-ficcion.com/project/us12millones-hurto-chivo-wallet.
Amnesty International. 2017. "Amnesty Reveals Alarming Impact of Online Abuse Against Women." Press Release. https://www.amnesty.org/en/latest/press-release/2017/11/amnesty-reveals-alarming-impact-of-online-abuse-against-women/.
Amnesty International. 2018. *Toxic Twitter—A Toxic Place for Women*. London. https://www.amnesty.org/en/latest/research/2018/03/online-violence-against-women-chapter-1/.
Barkawi, Tarak, and Mark Laffey. 2006. "The Postcolonial Moment in Security Studies." *Review of International Studies* 32: 329–352.
Barlow, John Perry. 2016. "A Declaration of the Independence of Cyberspace." Electronic Frontier Foundation. https://www.eff.org/cyberspace-independence.
Benjamin, Ruha. 2019. *Race After Technology: Abolitionist Tools for the New Jim Code*. Medford, MA: Polity.
Bergman, Ronen, and Mark Mazzetti. 2022. "The Battle for the World's Most Powerful Cyberweapon." *New York Times*, January 28. https://www.nytimes.com/2022/01/28/magazine/nso-group-israel-spyware.html.
Bertrand, Sarah. 2018. "Can the Subaltern Securitize? Postcolonial Perspectives on Securitization Theory and Its Critics." *European Journal of International Security* 3, no. 3: 281–299.
Bhandari, Vrinda. 2021. *What's Sex Got to Do with It? Mapping the Impact of Questions of Gender and Sexuality on the Evolution of the Digital Rights Landscape in India*. Delhi: Internet Democracy Project. https://internetdemocracy.in/reports/whats-sex-got-to-do-with-it-mapping-the-impact-of-questions-of-gender-and-sexuality-on-the-evolution-of-the-digital-rights-landscape-in-india/.
Browne, Simone. 2012. "Race and Surveillance." In *Routledge Handbook of Surveillance Studies*, ed. Kirstie Ball, Kevin Haggerty, and David Lyon, 72–80. Florence, KY: Taylor & Francis Group.
CISA. n.d. "The Facts." Cybersecurity & Infrastructure Agency. https://www.cisa.gov/be-cyber-smart/facts.
Cleaver, Harry M. 1998. "The Zapatista Effect: The Internet and the Rise of an Alternative Political Fabric." *Journal of International Affairs* 51, no. 2: 621–640.
Cohn, Carol. 1987. "Sex and Death in the Rational World of Defense Intellectuals." *Signs* 12, no. 4: 687–718.

Cohn, Carol. 2014. "Women and Wars: A Conceptual Framework." In *Women and Wars*, ed. Carol Cohn, 1–35, Cambridge: Polity Press.

Crowther, Glenn Alexander. 2017. "The Cyber Domain." *The Cyber Defense Review* 2, no. 3 (Fall): 63–78.

Dahlerup, Drude. 2017. *Has Democracy Failed Women?* Cambridge, UK and Malden, MA: Polity.

Davey, Jacob, and Julia Ebner. 2017. *The Fringe Insurgency—Connectivity, Convergence and Mainstreaming of the Extreme Right*. London: Institute for Strategic Dialogue. https://www.isdglobal.org/wp-content/uploads/2017/10/The-Fringe-Insurgency-221017_2.pdf.

DRF. 2020. *Addressing Online Attacks on Women Journalists in Pakistan*. Pakistan: Digital Rights Foundation. https://digitalrightsfoundation.pk/wp-content/uploads/2020/11/Policy-1.pdf.

Dubrofsky, Rachel E., and Shoshana Magnet, eds. 2015. *Feminist Surveillance Studies*. Durham, NC: Duke University Press.

Dwyer, Andrew C., Clare Stevens, Lilly Pijnenburg Muller, Myriam Dunn Cavelty, Lizzie Coles-Kemp, and Pip Thornton. 2022. "What Can a Critical Cybersecurity Do?" *International Political Sociology* 16, no. 3: olac013.

Farwell, James P. 2018. "Strengthening Private-Public Partnerships in National Cybersecurity." In *Understanding Cyber Security: Emerging Governance and Strategy*, ed. Gary Schaub Jr., 205–232. Lanham, MD: Rowman & Littlefield.

Fuller, Thomas. 2014. "Mandalay's Chinese Muslims Chilled by Riots." *New York Times*, July 13. https://www.nytimes.com/2014/07/13/world/asia/mandalays-chinese-muslims-chilled-by-riots.html.

Gartzke, Erik. 2013. "The Myth of Cyberwar." *International Security* 38, no. 2: 41–73.

Gill, Rosalind. 2019. "Surveillance Is a Feminist Issue." In *Routledge Handbook of Contemporary Feminism*, ed. Tasha Oren and Andrea Lee Press. Abingdon, Oxon and New York: Routledge.

Golumbia, David. 2016. *The Politics of Bitcoin: Software as Right-Wing Extremism*. Minneapolis, MN: University of Minnesota Press.

Guyan, Kevin. 2022. *Queer Data: Using Gender, Sex and Sexuality Data for Action*. London, UK: Bloomsbury.

Harding, Sandra. 1986. *The Science Question in Feminism*. Ithaca, NY: Cornell University Press.

Hayden, Michael V. 2018. "The Future of Things Cyber." In *Understanding Cyber Security: Emerging Governance and Strategy*, ed. Gary Schaub Jr., xi–xv. New York: Rowman & Littlefield.

Henshaw, Alexis. 2021. "Gendered Labor in the Making of U.S. Policy on Women, Peace, and Security: An Interagency Perspective." *International Feminist Journal of Politics* 24, no. 5: 767–789.

Henshaw, Alexis. 2022. "'Women, Men, Boys, and Girls': Analyzing the Implementation of Women, Peace, and Security in the United States." *Foreign Policy Analysis* 18, no. 4: orac024.

Henshaw, Alexis. 2023. *Digital Frontiers in Gender and Security*. Bristol, UK: Bristol University Press.

Herr, Trey, Arthur P. B. Laudrain, and Max Smeets. 2020. "Mapping the Known Unknowns of Cybersecurity Education: A Review of Syllabi on Cyber Conflict and Security."

Journal of Political Science Education 17: 503–519. https://www.tandfonline.com/doi/full/10.1080/15512169.2020.1729166.
Hitt, Jack. 2006. "Pro-Life Nation." *New York Times*, April 4. https://www.nytimes.com/2006/04/09/magazine/prolife-nation.html.
Hollis, Duncan. 2021. "A Brief Primer on International Law and Cyberspace." Carnegie Endowment for International Peace. https://carnegieendowment.org/2021/06/14/brief-primer-on-international-law-and-cyberspace-pub-84763.
Hurlburt, Heather, Elizabeth Weingarten, Alexandra Stark, and Elena Souris. 2019. *The "Consensual Straitjacket": Four Decades of Women in Nuclear Security*. Washington, DC: New America. http://newamerica.org/political-reform/reports/the-consensual-straitjacket-four-decades-of-women-in-nuclear-security/.
Hurley, Matthew. 2018. "The 'Genderman': (Re)Negotiating Militarized Masculinities When 'Doing Gender' at NATO." *Critical Military Studies* 4, no. 1: 72–91.
Joel, William. 2021. "This Is a Map of America's Broadband Problem." *The Verge*. https://www.theverge.com/22418074/broadband-gap-america-map-county-microsoft-data.
Klar, Rebecca, and Karl Evers-Hillstrom. 2022. "Corporate Lobbying Could Imperil Sweeping Data Privacy Bill." *The Hill*. https://thehill.com/business-a-lobbying/3585322-corporate-lobbying-could-imperil-sweeping-data-privacy-bill/.
Klosowski, Thorin. 2021. "The State of Consumer Data Privacy Laws in the US (And Why It Matters)." *Wirecutter: Reviews for the Real World*. https://www.nytimes.com/wirecutter/blog/state-of-privacy-laws-in-us/.
Kshetri, Nir, and Maya Chhetri. 2022. "Gender Asymmetry in Cybersecurity: Socioeconomic Causes and Consequences." *Computer* (February): 72–77.
Lewis, James A. 2010. "Sovereignty and the Role of Government in Cyberspace." *The Brown Journal of World Affairs* 16, no. 2: 55–65.
Libicki, Martin C. 2011. "Cyberwar as a Confidence Game." *Strategic Studies Quarterly* 5, no. 1: 132–147.
Lynn, William. 2010. "Defending a New Domain: The Pentagon's Cyberstrategy." *Foreign Affairs* 89, no. 5: 97–108.
Manjikian, Mary. 2020. *Introduction to Cyber Politics and Policy*. Los Angeles: CQ Press.
Mhajne, Anwar. 2021. "A Human Rights Approach to U.S. Cybersecurity Strategy." Carnagie Council. https://www.carnegiecouncil.org/publications/articles_papers_reports/a-human-rights-approach-to-us-cybersecurity-strategy.
Mhajne, Anwar, and Crystal Whetstone. 2024. "Unveiling Invisible Cyber Violences and Challenging Protectionism: A Feminist Approach to Addressing the Crisis of Cyber(in)security." *International Affairs*. Forthcoming.
Mirza, Muhammad Nadeem. 2021. "Conceptualising Cyber Sovereignty and Information Security: China's Image of a Global Cyber Order." *Webology* 18: 598–610.
Moore, Lisa Jean, and Paisley Currah. 2015. "Legally Sexed: Birth Certificates and Transgender Citizens." In *Feminist Surveillance Studies*, ed. Shoshana Magnet and Rachel E. Dubrofsky, 58–78. Durham, NC: Duke University Press.
Mueller, Milton L. 2020. "Against Sovereignty in Cyberspace." *International Studies Review* 22, no. 4: 779–801.
Mukerjee, Subhayan. 2016. "Net Neutrality, Facebook, and India's Battle to #SaveTheInternet." *Communication and the Public* 1, no. 3: 356–361.
Noble, Safiya Umoja. 2018. *Algorithms of Oppression: How Search Engines Reinforce Racism*. Illustrated edition. New York: New York University Press.

Noble, Safiya Umoja, and Brendesha M. Tynes, eds. 2016 *The Intersectional Internet: Race, Sex, Class, and Culture Online*. Lausanne, Switzerland: Peter Lang.

Nye, Joseph. 2010. *Cyberpower*. Cambridge, MA: Harvard Kennedy School, Belfer Center. https://www.belfercenter.org/sites/default/files/legacy/files/cyber-power.pdf.

Perrigo, Billy. "Exclusive: The $2 Per Hour Workers Who Made ChatGPT Safer." *Time*, January 18. https://time.com/6247678/openai-chatgpt-kenya-workers/.

Peters, Jay. 2020. "Leak Left 243 Million Brazilians' Medical Records and Personal Info Ripe for the Picking." *The Verge*. https://www.theverge.com/2020/12/3/22150973/brazilian-ministry-of-health-leak-medical-records-personal-information.

Peterson, V. Spike. 2003. *A Critical Rewriting of Global Political Economy: Integrating Reproductive, Productive and Virtual Economies*. New York: Routledge.

Pew Research Center. 2021. "Internet/Broadband Fact Sheet." Pew Research Center, Internet, Science & Tech. https://www.pewresearch.org/internet/fact-sheet/internet-broadband/.

Prasad, Revati. 2018. "Ascendant India, Digital India: How Net Neutrality Advocates Defeated Facebook's Free Basics." *Media, Culture & Society* 40, no. 3: 415–431.

Raymond, Mark. 2016. "Managing Decentralized Cyber Governance: The Responsibility to Troubleshoot." *Strategic Studies Quarterly* 10, no. 4: 123–149.

Raymond, Mark. 2018. "Managing Decentralized Cyber Governance." In *Understanding Cyber Security: Emerging Governance and Strategy*, ed. Gary Schaub, Jr., 25–48. New York: Rowman & Littlefield.

Rid, Thomas. 2012. "Cyber War Will Not Take Place." *Journal of Strategic Studies* 35, no. 1: 5–32.

Sambasivan, Nithya et al. 2019. " 'They Don't Leave Us Alone Anywhere We Go': Gender and Digital Abuse in South Asia." CHI, Glasgow, Scotland. https://www.classes.cs.uchicago.edu/archive/2020/winter/20370-1/readings/GenderSouthAsia.pdf.

Schaub Jr., Gary, and Roger Hurwitz. 2018. "Tragedy of the Cyber Commons?" In *Understanding Cyber Security: Emerging Governance and Strategy*, ed. Gary Schaub Jr., 49–76. Lanham, MD: Rowman & Littlefield.

Segal, Adam. 2017. "Chinese Cyber Diplomacy in a New Era of Uncertainty." Hoover Institution. https://www.hoover.org/research/chinese-cyber-diplomacy-new-era-uncertainty.

Seth, Sanjay. 2011. "Postcolonial Theory and the Critique of International Relations." *Millennium—Journal of International Studies* 40: 167–183.

Šimonovic, Dubravka. 2018. *Report of the Special Rapporteur on Violence Against Women, Its Causes and Consequences on Online Violence Against Women and Girls from a Human Rights Perspective*. New York: United Nations.

Singer, Peter W., and Emerson T. Brooking. 2018. *Like War: The Weaponization of Social Media*. Boston: Eamon Dolan/Houghton Mifflin Harcourt.

Singer, Peter W., and Allan Friedman. 2014. *Cybersecurity: What Everyone Needs to Know*. New York: Oxford University Press.

Spivak, Gayatri Chakravorty. 1988. "Can the Subaltern Speak?" In *Marxism and the Interpretation of Culture*, ed. C. Nelson and L. Grossberg, 271–313. Basingstoke, UK: MacMillan Education.

Tickner, J. Ann. 2001. *Gendering World Politics*. New York: Columbia University Press.

True, Jacqui. 2018. "Bringing Back Gendered States: Feminist Second Image Theorizing of International Relations." In *Revisiting Gendered States: Feminist Imaginings of the State in International Relations*, ed. Swati Parashar, J. Ann Tickner, and Jacqui True, 33–48. New York: Oxford University Press.

UNODC. n.d. "Yahoo! Inc v UEJF and LICRA." Sherloc, Case Law Database.//sherloc.unodc.org/cld/en/case-law-doc/cybercrimecrimetype/usa/2006/yahoo_inc_v_uejf_and_licra_.html.

Valeriano, Brandon. 2022a. "The Failure of Offense/Defense Balance in Cyber Security." *The Cyber Defense Review* 7, no. 3: 91–102.

Valeriano, Brandon. 2022b. "Why Can't Cyber Scholars Move Beyond the Basics?" Cato Institute. https://www.cato.org/commentary/why-cant-cyber-scholars-move-beyond-basics.

Walt, Stephen M. 2010. "Is the Cyber Threat Overblown?" *Foreign Policy*, April 30. https://foreignpolicy.com/2010/03/30/is-the-cyber-threat-overblown/.

White House. 2003. *The National Strategy to Secure Cyberspace*. Washington, DC. https://www.energy.gov/sites/default/files/National%20Strategy%20to%20Secure%20Cyberspace.pdf.

Wilkens, Jan. 2007. "Postcolonialism in International Relations." In *Oxford Research Encyclopedia of International Studies*. New York: Oxford University Press (online). https://oxfordre.com/view/10.1093/acrefore/9780190846626.001.0001/acrefore-9780190846626-e-101.

Wright, Hannah. 2020. "'Masculinities Perspectives': Advancing a Radical Women, Peace, and Security Agenda?" *International Feminist Journal of Politics* 22, no. 5: 652–674.

Wu, Tim. 1997. "Cyberspace Sovereignty?—The Internet and the International System." *Harvard Journal of Law and Technology* 10: 647.

PART I
EMERGING ISSUES IN CYBERSECURITY: GENDER, GEOGRAPHY, POLICY, AND PRACTICE

1

A Call for Feminist Insights in Cybersecurity

Implementing United Nations Security Council Resolution 1325 on Women, Peace, and Security in Cyberspace

Crystal Whetstone and Luna K.C.

Introduction

Since the late 1990s, the cyber realm has proliferated, offering new digital opportunities through information and communication technologies (ICTs). ICTs refer to a range of digital platforms, including "mobile phones, smartphones, laptop computers, and tablets" (Aceng et al. 2020, 1; Brown et al. 2018, 209). As feminist scholars of comparative politics and international relations (IR) working at the nexus of women, peace, and security, we see a need to bring feminist scholarship to bear on cybersecurity. Furthermore, with the rise of the cybersphere worldwide, and given the specific cyber violence faced by women, girls, and sexual and gender minorities (SGM) living in conflict-affected and postconflict countries, we bring attention to the urgent need to promote human rights in the cyber realm and highlight conflict-affected countries as a starting point.

Specifically, this chapter is a call for the United Nations Security Council Resolution 1325 on Women, Peace, and Security (hereafter, UNSCR 1325) to recognize the disproportionate effects of cybercrime and other forms of cyber violence against women and girls and to advocate the position that cyber insecurity is a key issue in UNSCR 1325 and the Women, Peace, and Security (WPS) agenda. UNSCR 1325 was passed in 2000 to promote women's equal participation in peacebuilding, peacekeeping, and conflict resolution activities and decision-making, as well as to address women's special needs. It has led to the development of the WPS agenda, which promotes women's

Crystal Whetstone and Luna K.C., *A Call for Feminist Insights in Cybersecurity* In: *Critical Perspectives on Cybersecurity*. Edited by: Anwar Mhajne and Alexis Henshaw, Oxford University Press. © Oxford University Press 2024.
DOI: 10.1093/oso/9780197695883.003.0002

inclusion in peace and security governance. Countries are encouraged to develop National Action Plans (NAPs) to implement the priorities outlined in UNSCR 1325 (Basu 2016). Given the extent of cyberspace, we argue that applying UNSCR 1325 and the WPS agenda to the virtual sphere will facilitate attention and resources to better address women's security from a holistic perspective. We focus our chapter on conflict-affected countries that experience increases in gender-based violence in war environments and fragile postwar states where cybercrime is pervasive due to populations' vulnerabilities (Pinto-Jayawardena and Guthrie 2016; Adesina 2017).

We are aware of critiques of securitization (the rendering of issues traditionally seen as outside of military and other national security matters to be seen as security issues) in the context of UNSCR 1325 and the broader WPS agenda. On the one hand, 1325 and related policies bring attention and resources to women; the role of gender and women's issues in peace and security matters and help broaden what constitutes wartime violence. However, securitization does not end the "gendering, racialization, classing, and sexualizing" that permeates security discourses, which often result in targeting marginalized and vulnerable peoples in the name of security (Runyan 2019, 88). Securitization often leads to the justification of war and militarization that can harm women while also depoliticizing gender power differentials rather than working to disrupt political processes that uphold gender hierarchy (Jansson and Eduards 2016). We acknowledge this conundrum, but given the popularity of 1325, we seek to make use of this resolution to bring attention and resources to gender-based violence in cybersphere. However, we are careful to emphasize the need to use 1325 critically as a measure against the negative side of securitization.

While cybersecurity is a growing area of IR, feminist IR has yet to give significant attention to cyber issues. Throughout this chapter, we bring feminist and human rights perspectives to cybersecurity studies through a critical rereading of UNSCR 1325 and a broadening of the WPS agenda to the cyber realm. This exploratory chapter outlines a theoretical framework that builds on the work of previous feminist IR scholars who have called for the expansion of UNSCR 1325 in innovative ways, embedding our work in current feminist debates. This chapter contributes to the WPS agenda, feminist IR scholarship, and human security scholarship by addressing women's security in the cybersphere, with a focus on finding means to undermine online violence against women and secure women's rights.

This chapter proceeds as follows. First, we describe the cyber violence that women and girls as well as SGM are at a greater risk of facing through a review of the scholarship on cyberfeminism. The second section overviews the theoretical precepts outlined in feminist IR that we take as applicable to the digital realm, including the lenses of human security, human rights, and intersectional analysis, which are also often associated with the application of UNSCR 1325 and the WPS agenda. In the third section, we review UNSCR 1325 and WPS scholarship and make linkages from recent innovations in this area as a jumping-off point for our argument. The fourth section details our critical rereading of UNSCR 1325 and the WPS agenda to apply to cyberspace before we offer a short conclusion that outlines the implications of our argument.

Cyber Gender-Based Violence Grows as Access to ICTs Grows

Cyberfeminism is a growing area of research mainly investigated by women, gender, and sexuality studies scholars as well as media and mass communications scholars. In this section, we review two key takeaways from this rich area of interdisciplinary knowledge. The first takeaway is the problem of cyber violence against women and girls as well as SGM. The second takeaway is the violence seen online is rooted in gendered (as well as racialized and other systems of) power relations that mirror the structures of the physical world.

Cyber Violence Is a Problem for Women and Sexual and Gender Minorities

A clear trend indicates that more women, men, and other gender categories are entering cyberspace, raising concerns about human rights in the cybersphere. As of January 2021, globally, there were 4.66 billion active internet users, 4.32B active mobile internet users, 4.2B active social media users, and 4.15B active mobile social media users (Statistica 2021). However, only 48.4% of women worldwide have access to the internet versus 58.3% of men. This gender digital gap is most pronounced in the Global South (see table 1.1).

Table 1.1 Global Gender Gap

Access to the Internet		
	Women	Men
Worldwide	48.4%	58.3%
Africa	22.6%	33.8%
Asia and the Pacific	41.3%	54.6%
Arab states	44.2%	58.5%

Source: International Telecommunications Union (2021).

In this context where men outnumber women in digital access, evidence indicates that cyberspace is a hotbed for proliferating and mainstreaming online misogyny, hatred, and violence against women and girls as part of online gender-based violence (GBV) (APC 2017; Aceng et al. 2020; UN Women 2015; SIDA 2019; Amnesty International 2018; Vogels 2021; Laxton 2014; Khoo 2021; Lomba et al. 2021).

GBV refers to all forms of violence—physical, psychological, economic, sexual, and otherwise—perpetrated against an individual due to their gender identity. Such violence may occur in the public or private sphere and stems from structural gender inequalities and power relations. While GBV may impact men and boys, it is women, girls, and gender nonconforming people who are more likely to endure GBV (Britton 2020, 13; UN Population Fund n.d.). GBV encompasses violence against women, yet it is also an umbrella term that notes how all individuals are gendered (Brown and Pytlak 2020, 3–4). Online, or cyber, GBV refers to any forms of GBV "committed, abetted or aggravated, in part or fully, by the use of" ICTs "such as mobile phones, the internet, social media platforms, and email" (Association for Progressive Communication 2017, 3).

Cyber GBV includes a range of behaviors that ultimately result in silencing women and girls—particularly women from minority groups and women of color—who fear physical repercussions because of their digital engagement (Ferrier and Garud-Patkar 2018; Madden et al. 2018). While trolling refers to those who engage in intentionally disruptive behavior in online environments for the sheer amusement of being argumentative and/or aggressive toward others, gender trolling includes gender-based insults such as "cunt, whore, slut" (Mantilla 2013, 564). Gender trolling also tends to include vicious language, threats and threats made real, including "doxxing," which is when a person's offline identity is shared online, even disclosing home addresses that allow potential attackers to find online users and physically harm them (Mantilla 2013, 564). Doxxers—a term that derives from "dropping documents"—peruse widely available information online to uncover personal identification numbers and sensitive passwords, often working in concert with others (Calabro 2018, 57). People of color and women are most likely to be victims of doxxing (Calabro 2018).

While statistics are only rough estimates, according to research conducted by the Networked Intelligence for Development, women are 27 times more likely to be abused by men and 61% of online harassers are men (UN Women 2015, 15). Moreover, in Europe alone, 9 million women report undergoing online harassment before the age of 15 and women-identified individuals ages 18 to 24 years old are at a high risk of experiencing online GBV (UN Women 2015, 15). Globally, sexual violence has been bolstered using cyberspace. Since becoming mainstream, pornography has undergone a transformation in the ubiquity of increasingly violent and misogynistic depictions of sexual acts. Moreover, sex trafficking—which impacts more women and girls than men and boys—is facilitated through cyberspace, where traffickers can more easily evade detection by authorities and civil society groups who seek to end sex trafficking (UN Women 2015). Cyberfeminists point out that digital technologies have made it easier to engage in intimate partner violence (IPV), which affects more women than men, by providing new pathways to monitor, stalk, harass, humiliate, and threaten (former) partners (Woodlock 2017; Brown et al. 2018). Women are generally more likely than men to report being cyberstalked whether by intimate partners, acquaintances, or strangers, and men are more likely to admit being perpetrators of cyberstalking behavior (Paullet et al. 2009; Woodlock 2017).

Additionally, women are more likely than men to experience negative consequences from sexting, or the sharing of explicit photos online, even as women in cishetero relationships experience social pressure to share such images. When women and girls sext, their images traverse cyberspace greater distances than images of men and boys, often shared without consent. A survey revealed that 23.3% of women claimed that any violence they endured was a consequence of sexting (UN Women 2015, 22). Many nonconsensual shared images fall under the concept of "revenge porn," which refers to "non-consensual pornography" in which a victim's explicit image is shared by a perpetrator (without permission) with the intention of humiliating the victim (Ruvalcaba and Eaton 2019, 1). Most perpetrators of revenge porn have had a relationship with the victim. In a recent survey of 3,044 aged 18 and older Americans, 31.15% of perpetrators of revenge porn had been a current romantic partner of the victim and 39.75% had been a previous romantic partner (Ruvalcaba and Eaton 2019, 4). The study also supports the notion that those in relationships with men are more vulnerable to revenge porn (Ruvalcaba and Eaton 2019). In many countries, lax regulation of sexual exploitation leaves victims of revenge porn and others of nonconsensual sharing few legal means for women and girls to address violations of their private images (UN Women 2015).

Power Relations Are at the Core of Online GBV

The second critical takeaway from cyberfeminism scholarship is that the violence against women, girls, and SGM in online spaces is not different from the violence that occurs in the physical world. Rather, cyber GBV mirrors the same structures of discrimination and oppression based on gender, racialized, and other forms of power hierarchies found in the nonvirtual world. The sexist and misogynistic ideologies that have proliferated in online forums do not stay contained within these virtual spaces but rather enter mainstream political discourse (Khoo 2021). This impacts women's access to online political and public spaces and dampens their political participation as they fear for their lives (Olson and LaPoe 2018). Such fears indicate that the borders between the online and physical worlds are blurry and that what takes place in the virtual world has physical world consequences; laws against cyber GBV remain inadequate and most members of law enforcement fail to see how threatening online violence is (Stroud and Cox 2018; Asian School of Cyber Laws 2021; Brown et al. 2018). In part, this is due to the advancement of digital technology that makes it easy to delete evidence of a cybercrime permanently, which makes it difficult to file a case against online crimes.

There are real-world consequences to online harassment. In 2016, after taking on cyberbullying in her political work, Congresswoman Katherine Clark (D-MA) became a victim of "swatting," which is linked to doxxing. Online harassers sent a fake tip to the police that Clark's residence was being attacked by an active shooter. Swatting aims to rouse a highly armed police response (SWAT teams) to frighten the target. Clark and her children suffered a major scare when barricades blocked both ends of her street and police holding large guns stood outside her home (Calabro 2018). Gender trolling and other forms of gendered harassment are common when women speak online about their experiences of sexism. Attackers are largely—although not always—men (Mantilla 2013).

Online harassment of women, girls, and gender nonconforming individuals is often related to people's appearances and behavior that are based on socially conservative gender norms and respectability politics. Women are vulnerable to online attacks for not conforming to Western, white ideals of female beauty or for not conforming to other idealized views of womanhood that demand women act submissively or serve men (Kim 2018; Vickery and Everback 2018). Cyber GBV reflects the unequal power relations among women, men, and SGM, as well as the power relations among other hegemonic and nonhegemonic groups, whether these are based on racial, ethnic, and/or religious factors (Blauner 1969; MacKinnon [1984] 1991; Vickery and Everback 2018).

While online spaces provide opportunities for mobilization in human rights and related progressive causes—including women's rights—the cybersphere simultaneously provides online opportunities for supporters of sexism, misogyny, white supremacy, racism, and other hate-based communities that support heteronormativity, transphobia, Islamophobia, and similar hierarchies (Daniels 2008; Jenkins and Wolfgang 2018; Vickery and Everback 2018). For example, during the global Women's March of 2017, women activists tweeted such slogans as #mybodymychoice and #No means No. These hashtags were countered by anti-women's rights proponents with messages such as #pro-life #mybordermychoice, #Deplorables. Growing voices in cyberfeminism have raised the issue of the marginalization of women of color in feminist scholarship and activism, noting that "feminism continues to ignore racism in problematic and oppressing ways" (Vickery and Everback 2018, 6; Kendall 2020). These cyberfeminists call for intersectional feminist analysis to understand the conjunction of gender, race, and other intersecting forms of oppression as they implicate online GBV (Hackworth 2018; Madden et al. 2018).

The implications of this second takeaway have increasingly led cyberfeminists to call for the application of intersectionality (Hackworth 2018; Madden et al. 2018), which is a major area of feminist scholarship that emphasizes that all people have multiple layers of identity that are linked and impact their varying experiences of oppression (Crenshaw 1989; McCall 2005). For example, a Muslim Palestinian woman living in Israel will likely experience sexism as well as Islamophobia and anti-minority forms of discrimination that are not experienced separately but rather as compounding oppressions. The emphasis on both violence against women and SGM, as well as the importance of intersectionality in feminist analysis that is found in cyberfeminism, is echoed in feminist IR scholarship. We turn now to feminist IR to examine how this area of IR has emphasized human security, human rights, and intersectionality.

Feminist IR Approaches to Cybersecurity: Human Security, Human Rights, and Intersectionality

Cybersecurity as an area of scholarly inquiry remains ill-defined, with varying definitions in operation depending on the discipline, even subdiscipline. Notably, those focused on cybersecurity in industry, government, and civic organization groups likewise hold multiple views of cybersecurity (Craigen et al. 2014). We prefer the following construction of cybersecurity, which comes from the Internet Free and Secure Initiative, a collective that represents 30 governments dedicated to promoting global internet freedom that takes a human rights approach to cybersecurity:

> Cybersecurity is the preservation—through policy, technology, and education—of the availability, confidentiality and integrity of information and its underlying infrastructure so as to enhance the security of persons both online and offline. (Internet Free & Secure Initiative n.d.b.)

While there are increasing critical perspectives in cybersecurity studies—much of this scholarship lies outside of IR, in related social sciences fields and legal studies, as well among rights advocates working in non-governmental organizations (NGOs)—that emphasize the need to approach cybersecurity using international humanitarian law (IHL) and human rights law (HRL) or other ethics frameworks (Brown and Esterhuysen 2019; Lubin 2020; Christen et al. 2020; Internet Free & Secure Initiative n.d.a.). While feminists working in IR have yet to enter cyber studies en masse, there is growing recognition of the need for feminist and gender perspectives from an international perspective (Slupska 2019; Brown and Pytlak 2020).

We outline how feminist IR has amassed significant insights since its development as a separate area of IR in the 1980s by highlighting human security, human rights, and intersectionality. We call attention to an important feminist IR cybersecurity study, which has begun to embrace these components of feminist IR to show that there are critical contributions to be made to cybersecurity from feminist IR perspectives and that influences our argument in this chapter. This includes Slupska's (2019) groundbreaking article draws attention to the lack of threat models in cybersecurity that take domestic and intimate partner violence into account through an examination of the August Smart Lock, part of a home security system. Slupska explores the victim blaming that takes place when users are targeted by (former) intimate partners, who wield the security system to harass and threaten, rather than focusing on how to promote people's security in cyberspace.

Human Security and Human Rights

A feminist approach to cybersecurity takes people as its starting point, following a human security framework, which is in stark contrast to most IR cybersecurity scholarship that emphasizes national security and the security of private businesses in terms of information security (Slupska 2019, 84). Human security understands security as encompassing the security of people, not simply national security, and it works to disrupt binary thinking, such as pointing out that violence exists in countries that are not at war, a notion that contrasts with typical approaches to security that see peace and war as distinct from one another (Tripp 2013). Feminist human security approaches draw on the work of peace scholar Galtung (1969), who developed the notion of embedded violence, but have added to this theorizing how gender-based violence such as intimate partner violence are forms of structural violences (Alexander 2019). In terms of cybersecurity, Slupska (2019) points out that while information protection is important, it is so only because of the humans whose security is threatened by the misuse and abuse of data.

Human security is linked with human rights as proponents of human security assert that it is "the right of people to live in freedom and dignity, free from poverty and despair" (UN Trust Fund for Human Security 2017, 6). Scholars and advocates of human security seek to make these rights of living in freedom and dignity through "people-centered, comprehensive, context-specific and prevention-oriented responses [to security] that strengthen the protection and empowerment of all people and all communities" that acknowledge "the interlinkages between peace, development and human rights, and equally considers civil, political, economic, social and cultural rights (UN Trust Fund for Human Security 2017, 6). Human rights advocates Brown and Esterhuysen (2019), who work in NGOs promoting digital rights, emphasize the need to bring human rights into the cybersphere. Brown and Esterhuysen (2019) point to cyberattacks that have led to hospital closures, kicking electrical grids offline, and disrupting democratic elections. Yet even with the human rights problems that cyberattacks often launch, the human security and human rights aspects of cybersecurity are often ignored by policymakers and researchers working in cybersecurity in favor of national and business security.

Intersectionality

Slupska (2019) surmises that it is the lack of diversity within the realm of cybersecurity that has resulted in the consistent overlooking of specific needs of social groups concerning their human security and human rights in virtual spaces. Similarly, in Brown and Pytlak's (2020) recent report on gender and cybersecurity, the authors stress how gender—and other social factors—impact people's varying experiences in the cyber realm. Brown and Pytlak document the lack of women in cyberspaces "including cyber security policy and diplomacy," in what is another angle of the gender digital divide (Brown and Pytlak 2020, 15). The UN Group of Governmental Experts (GGE) on advancing responsible state behavior in cyberspace has been meeting over the previous 15 years to formulate norms and standards in cybersecurity. Yet on average, participants at such meetings have included only 20% women. It was only the sixth GGE meeting (held in 2020–2021) that included gender parity of experts at the gathering. This is an important step. However, as recently as September 2019, at the UN Open-Ended Working Group (OEWG) on Developments in the Field of Information and Telecommunications in the Context of International Security, only 32% of the participants identified as women. While women's participation in cybersecurity policymaking is abysmal, this also says nothing of the gender discrimination that women face working as cybersecurity professionals and the fact that women are severely underrepresented in these positions, making up only 15% to 20% of cyber professionals globally (Brown and Pytlak 2020).

An intersectional approach to studying cybersecurity and engaging in cybersecurity policymaking that is often advocated by feminist IR and other feminist scholars emphasizes how people are impacted in different ways by their various social identities in online GBV (Noble 2018). A greater diversity of perspectives in cybersecurity policymaking would better ensure more inclusive perspectives of women, girls, and SGM to ensure human security and human rights. While there are commonalities around cyber GBV, there are regional differences that will require contextualized policies to fit a locale. For example, sub-Saharan Africa (SSA) is seeing a dramatic rise in cybercrimes, particularly in Nigeria, Kenya, and South Africa, and it is through mobile phones that most cyber violence against women occurs. Cases of viral rape videos making the rounds have been a growing problem in South Africa. These videos are shared widely on mobile devices through various social media platforms (UN Women 2015, 15). An infamous case in 2012 was the viral gang rape of a 17-year-old living with mental disabilities in Soweto by a group of men and boys, one as young as 13 years old (Holtzhausen 2012). Understanding the various backgrounds of the actors and the overall political environment can help researchers, policymakers, and members of the community to find ways to address this violence.

Bringing feminist analysis to the cybersphere from a comparative and international politics perspective sheds light on how gender and other inequalities exist in cyberspace. More work remains to be done to expose globally how people are impacted differently through their complex social identities. There are likely regional differences in terms of forms and impact of cyber GBV. Such comparisons can highlight the need for locally specific approaches to cyberpolicy that promotes cyber civil rights to better protect women, girls, and SGM. We begin to articulate our recommendations of implementing UNSCR 1325 and the WPS agenda through a local lens.

Our Theoretical Framework Rooted in Innovative Work on UNSCR 1325 and the WPS Agenda

This section overviews the scholarship on UNSCR 1325 and the WPS agenda, examining how, since its launch, the resolution has evolved beyond the UN Security Council's initial lip service toward women's rights in armed conflicts to become a major area of scholarship and advocacy. We draw on the studies of UNSCR 1325 scholars who have documented increasingly innovative uses of UNSCR 1325 and the WPS agenda, which have inspired our argument for the application of these principles for the cybersphere.

UNSCR 1325 and the WPS Agenda

Following considerable advocacy work by women's rights proponents in NGOs, governments, and academia, UNSCR 1325 was launched in 2000 via the UN Security Council (Basu 2016). The resolution outlined four major areas to promote women's rights in armed conflicts. These areas have become known as the four pillars, and include participation, prevention, protection, and relief and recovery. UNSCR 1325 promotes human security by encouraging the participation of women in peace and security governance as well as by including a gender perspective in peace and security matters. Furthermore, UNSCR 1325 emphasizes the need to prioritize women's protection in armed conflicts. Women's rights advocates ran with UNSCR 1325, using it as a policy tool to justify the expansion of this resolution (Tryggestad 2009). Over the two decades since UNSCR 1325's inception, several follow-up resolutions have ensued in its wake (i.e., 1820, 1888, 1889, 1960, 2106, 2122), reemphasizing UNSCR 1325's priorities. The resolution launched an area of scholarship, activism, and advocacy widely known as the WPS agenda (Kirby and Shepherd 2016).

From 2005 and onward, the UN has encouraged countries to adopt UNSCR 1325 National Action Plans (NAPs) to see the implementation of 1325 and the WPS agenda. Because UN members are countries, the Security Council relies on them to enact NAPs to ensure the policy principles of UNSCR 1325 and the broader WPS agenda to support the four pillars of participation, prevention, protection, and relief and recovery regarding women and girls in armed conflicts. The UN promotes the role of civil society collaboration in the design and implementation of 1325 NAPs, although the design and implementation of NAPs may not be inclusive of local actors (Women's International League of Peace and Freedom 2020a; Basini and Ryan 2016). The NGO Working Group on Women, Peace, and Security and other women's NGOs working in peace and conflict, such as the Women's International League for Peace and Freedom (WILFP), track NAPs and offer support to local peace groups globally, as well as support and promote related development projects that work to expand women's decision-making roles in government and economics (NGO Working Group on Women 2019; Women's International League of Peace and Freedom 2020b).

Scholarship on UNSCR 1325 and the WPS agenda continues to grow with a recent search on Google Scholar for the WPS agenda and 1325 yielding over 200 relevant results for 2021 alone. Nevertheless, the WPS agenda has been both applauded and critiqued by feminists in terms of how it impacts women. Some suggest that the WPS agenda and UNSCR 1325 offer a basis on which women can assert their right to participate in decision-making (as long as there is an adequate budget) (Tryggestad 2009; Yadav 2020). Others counter that UNSCR 1325 and the broader WPS agenda limit women to stereotypical roles such as "peacemaker" (Otto 2006; Shepherd 2011), ignore intersectionality by depicting women solely as victims, and overlook other factors of women's identity such as sexuality (Cook 2016; Hagen 2016); moreover, the WPS agenda and UNSCR 1325 NAPs often consist of a colonizing process in which the international community dismisses local preferences and participation (Basini and Ryan 2016). A deep rethinking of the WPS agenda is required to see the full localization of UNSCR 1325 and to transform the WPS agenda to support a local women's views.

Finally, more voices are calling for intersectionality to be applied to UNSCR 1325 and the WPS agenda projects and NAPs to ensure inclusivity of all women (Nesiah 2012; K.C., and Whetstone 2022). Although UNSCR 1325 and the WPS has been groundbreaking by highlighting the need to prioritize women's needs and interests in armed conflicts and given the move toward intersectional understandings of human security in armed conflict, we suggest that there is more work needed to understand how cyber (in)security functions as a barrier to women's and girls' empowerment in conflict-affected countries and postwar societies, as well as how the cybersphere affects the aims of the WPS agenda. Weaponizing a civilian space such as the cyber realm has enormous implications for human rights, especially for women who are already disadvantaged in conflict settings. Before engaging in a critical rereading of UNSCR 1325, we first explore how scholarship on UNSCR 1325 and the WPS agenda has evolved in creative ways.

Innovative Uses of UNSCR 1325 and the WPS Agenda

UNSCR 1325 NAPs have been typically thought to apply to countries experiencing war or to postconflict countries. When NAPs have been adopted by non-war countries, the plans address countries abroad experiencing war or look at a country's internal state security forces, such as seeking to promote women's participation and advancement in national militaries, police, and other security forces (Kirby and Shepherd 2016). However, Shepherd (2020) has made the case that since no country is violence-free or has full gender equality, NAPs may be legitimately applied to non-armed conflict countries as much as armed conflict countries and that internally focused NAPs have more to address than only women's participation in national security forces. Shepherd calls for the application of UNSCR 1325 beyond conflict-affected and postwar countries, arguing that each country needs to address GBV within its borders.

In a recent study by Paula Drumond and Tamya Rebelo (2020), the authors point out how some UNSCR 1325 NAPs in Latin America have already begun to focus internally, moving beyond promoting the WPS agenda abroad. Argentina's NAP, for example, mentions the issue of GBV in Latin America, as well as human trafficking, which impacts more women and girls than men and boys. Likewise, Brazil's NAP outlines a gendered response to refugees within its borders, whose numbers have grown in the context of Venezuela's status as a fragile state that has led to an outpouring of refugees across the region of Latin America (Drumond and Rebelo 2020). Building on this innovative work around UNSCR 1325 and the WPS agenda, we argue for the application of UNSCR 1325 to cyberspace, to ensure full peace. We envision UNSCR 1325 as protecting women, girls, trans, queer, and other SGM from online GBV as a tool to promote equitable access for marginalized groups to cybersecurity both in terms of access to cyber technologies and participating in cybersecurity governance and policymaking.

Critically Rereading the UNSCR 1325 and WPS Agenda to Apply in Cyberspace

We argue that there is an urgent need for cyber safety for women and girls as well as SGM in conflict-affected countries that could be addressed in part through UNSCR 1325 and the WPS agenda, which promotes attention to, and the protection of, women and girls in conflict and postconflict contexts. Given the disproportionate impact of cyber GBV against women, girls, and SGM, these populations are already at risk of cyber violence (UN Women

2015). In conflict-affected countries, we suggest that the risks are even greater for overlapping reasons. First, war-torn economies leave conflict-affected countries with few resources to address GBV in general, much less GBV occurring specifically online, as overwhelming poverty exists (Pugh 2005). Providing an avenue to funnel resources and attention toward cyber violence will be a benefit. Second, armed conflicts tend to impact fragile countries, where populations are vulnerable to being exploited in cybercrimes due to limited circumstances (Adesina 2017). UNSCR 1325 arose out of the ongoing issue that women impacted by armed conflicts are regularly forgotten or ignored, and women's needs and interests remain at best afterthoughts, at worst unconsidered, in international crisis-management policymaking.

In this section, we perform a critical rereading of UNSCR 1325 to unpack how it applies through its four pillars of participation, prevention, protection, and relief and recovery to the cyber realm. We advocate that UNSCR 1325 and the WPS agenda be applied to the cyber realm where appropriate. We see a need to extend the WPS agenda, including 1325 NAPs, which are the mechanisms the UN promotes to see the measures contained in 1325 actualized, to the cyber realm to achieve sustainable and full peace. The WPS agenda, based on UNSCR 1325, promotes human security by encouraging the participation of women in peace and security governance. We first explore why cyber GBV (and other forms of online violence) pose a particular problem in preconflict societies, conflict-affected countries, and postconflict societies.

Cyber GBV and Other Digital Violences in Preconflict, Conflict-Affected, and Postconflict countries

In conflict-affected countries and preconflict countries, cyberspace can pose serious threats to marginalized groups such as women, girls, and SGM. For example, violent and terrorist organizations that engage in misogyny and sexism, such as ISIS and Boko Haram, use cyberspace—such as online videos, blogs, and social media messaging—to recruit young girls to their organizations, often luring youths of all genders through false and misleading information (Ogbondah and Agbese 2017; Windsor 2020). In general, cyberspace offers fertile ground to escalate tensions, propaganda, and misinformation that exacerbate conflicts globally in both pre-armed and armed phases. The cyber realm provides easy access for recruiting paramilitaries, including foreign fighters, and planning attacks once the barrier of access to ICTs is reached. It is a fiscally prudent avenue for daily organizational needs (Goodman et al. 2007; Weimann 2015; Choi et al. 2018).

Moreover, in conflict-affected and postconflict countries, there is often a rise in GBV that takes place in both the public and private spheres, as well as in the online and physical realms that is linked to armed violence (Pinto-Jayawardena and Guthrie 2016). For example, in Myanmar's internal conflict between the military government and democracy-supporting citizens, cyberspace has worsened the ongoing conflict by spreading fake news, disinformation, and propaganda; and the armed conflict has led to a rise in sexual violence against women and girls (Kleiner and Šupka 2020; Oo and Davies 2021). For example, a recent study found that many young girls have encountered online harassment by individuals unknown to them, while other young women have online accounts created under their names without their consent, including having photoshopped "sexy" photos circulated over social media, most commonly on Facebook. The girls' personal security was threatened when strangers sent the girls inappropriate social content in response to these fraudulent accounts that engaged in name calling and slut-shaming, a form of gender trolling and online harassment (Save the Children 2019).

Similar examples of online GBV exist in postconflict countries. In postwar Nepal, nearly 70% of GBV complaints made to the police over two months in 2019 were cybercrimes, meaning that they were committed in digital spaces, and some women and girls even faced death threats online (Dhungana 2019). For example, in 2020, a 24-year-old Nepali woman's photo circulated online on Facebook, Twitter, and private chats without her consent. The young woman received misogynistic and sexist messages regarding the photo (Aryal 2020). Similarly, recently in Sri Lanka, another postconflict country, a new report shows that women and people of the LGBT community are targets of online hate crimes such as the nonconsensual dissemination of intimate photos and videos (Perera and Wickrematunge 2019). One of UNSCR 1325's early aims was to address these sexual and gender-based violences that women face in armed conflicts and their aftermath, focusing on how rape can be used as a weapon of war to terrorize entire populations and inflict misery on women through humiliation, trafficking into forced labor and/or sex work, and compelling women to give birth to unwanted children (Bernard 1994; Nordstrom 1996; UN Securiy Council 2000; Barrow 2010).

Protection

Over time, the emphasis on violence against women, particularly sexual violence, has been critiqued in UNSCR 1325. Some point out how this approach misses that SGM often face even worse levels of violence compared to hetero, cis women in armed conflicts and that it portrays women in essentializing ways, singularly as victims (Pratt and Richter-Devroe 2011; Hagen 2016). Furthermore, the emphasis on violence against women and girls misses how men and boys are victims of violence—including sexual violence—and it ignores how women are also perpetrators of violence (Cook 2016). Nevertheless, ending GBV remains an ongoing issue. We would like to see the adoption of UNSCR 1325 and the WPS agenda—perhaps better rendered as the gender, peace, and security (GPS) agenda—as focusing attention on cyber GBV as it impacts all individuals, but given the overwhelming evidence we have discussed, most harms women, girls, and SGM (UN Women 2015).

Additionally, there is an urgent need to promote coordinated legislation that works within and beyond country borders to regulate cyber GBV of all forms. Laws on the books against cyber GBV are not enough to protect victims and too many members of law enforcement do not recognize cyber GBV as dangerous (Stroud and Cox 2018; Asian School of Cyber Laws 2021; Brown et al. 2018). The WPS agenda can be used to bolster legal demands for regulations that will ensure women and girls and SGM have legal recourse if they suffer cyber GBV and will have any such threats treated seriously by law enforcement. Protection through regulation will not be enough on its own, but it will give victims further means to address a violation through legal recourse.

Participation

The WPS agenda could be used in cyberspace to advocate increasing the participation of women from diverse backgrounds in decision-making positions in cybersecurity governance, such as the UN Group of Governmental Experts (GGE) on advancing responsible state behavior in cyberspace and the UN Open-Ended Working Group (OEWG) on Developments in the Field of Information and Telecommunications in the Context of International Security. This is where cyber policymaking is formed and having representation from (diverse) women is critical. As Brown and Pytlak (2020) argue, participation in cybersecurity is necessary for women's representation in cyber policy. Without women's full and equal participation, their perspectives are unlikely to be represented within cyber policy. Similarly, expanding the number of women in cybersecurity in the business sector, as well as working to ensure women's equal access to cyber technologies, is necessary to ensure that women have the equitable means of participating in cybersecurity. At a minimum, we seek to promote access to ICTs to end the gender digital divide in terms of access. We also seek to promote women's movement into cyber jobs in government and the private sector, as well as into policymaking. Efforts should be made to recruit women across social sectors, with an emphasis on the most marginalized. This will vary by society but will include those women made vulnerable by ethnic, racial, caste, religious, sexual orientation, and/or gender identity.

Prevention and Relief and Recovery
A broad literature on crisis management in the subfields of IR and public administration emphasizes the need to empower people and communities who have experienced a crisis such as an armed conflict (Walters and Gaillard 2014; Berke et al. 2021) and both sub-areas are moving toward embracing an intersectional approach to understand how marginalized populations are more vulnerable than more privileged sectors of a society but that vulnerable groups differ greatly from one another (Vickery 2018; Whetstone and Demiroz 2023, 18–37; K.C., and Whetstone 2022). Prevention, as well as relief and recovery, will be most effective and efficient if done in ways that allow participation by diverse sectors of a community (Vickery 2018; Kuran et al. 2021).

UNSCR 1325 and the WPS agenda justify gender-disaggregated data collection of cyberspace tools and resources that countries and businesses in the private sector (such as Facebook, Twitter, TikTok) have already launched to make cyberspace safer. These tools and resources offer mechanisms for protecting the data privacy and security of marginalized groups, including women and girls as well as trans, queer, nonbinary, and other SGM. Making these widely available through the transnational WPS networks that connect NGOs, the UN and governments interested in promoting UNSCR 1325 and the WPS agenda could spread the word on how more people can stay safe online. Similarly, offering training for cybersecurity professionals, scholars, and policymakers on gender-specific issues in cybersecurity will promote preventative measures against online GBV and it can help get out the message that achieving sustainable peace requires achieving a safe cyberspace. Likewise, ensuring a gender perspective is brought into cyber policy will go far in helping to innovate solutions to prevent, or at least mitigate, online GBV.

In terms of relief and recovery, UNSCR 1325 and the WPS agenda can facilitate strategies that promote relief and recovery for women, girls, and

SGM who have experienced online GBV that will allow these marginalized groups to be empowered by using tools and resources to protect themselves online. Likewise, bringing those who have experienced online GBV to share with state security forces the seriousness of cyber GBV will help at least some to take action to make a difference and can help law enforcement and related agencies recognize the seriousness of cyber GBV. Globally, cyber violence against individuals is frequently not seen as a "real" threat by law enforcement (Stroud and Cox 2018). Furthermore, the international community and national governments should prioritize relief and recovery resources to help women, girls, trans, queer, and other SGM to ensure their needs are met after they experience cyber GBV, including counseling and other legal protections to ensure their physical safety.

Additional Measures: WPS Scholarship
In addition to the four pillars we viewed above, the WPS agenda could further provide for the application of a feminist intersectional approach regarding cyberspace to understand how women, girls, and diverse gendered categories experience cyberspace differently. Cyberspace is not equal, and a one-size-fits-all policy does not work for everyone, particularly, women and girls and SGM in conflict-affected contexts, who might face unique challenges while using the cyber realm due to weak cyber laws. While considerable work remains to understand how people are differently impacted through their complex social identities in the cyber realm, feminist analysis can shed light on how gender and other inequalities operate in cyberspace and impact human rights. We see the WPS agenda as a starting point for scholarly and policy-focused feminist cyber engagement. Further, we must develop concrete policy and action plans to fight online racism, sexism, and misogyny using intersectional feminist approaches. Our focus must be on bringing meaningful progressive change that can provide a foundation to confront the growing threat of cyber insecurity.

Conclusion: The Implications of Expanding UNSCR 1325 and the WPS Agenda into the Realm of Cybersecurity

Expanding UNSCR 1325 and the broader WPS agenda offers a new avenue to ensuring a human-centered approach to cybersecurity. We have suggested that there is a critical need for an international legal framework to regulate and address the insecurities women, girls, and other marginalized groups face in the cyber realm, which could, for instance, provide awareness and training programs on cybersecurity to combat cybercrimes that impact women and girls. Weaponizing a civilian space has enormous implications for human rights, especially for women and others from marginalized communities who are already disadvantaged in conflict settings. While national security matters, we suggest that cybersecurity needs to take human rights seriously by centering people's empowerment and well-being. UNSCR 1325 and the WPS agenda offer a tangible way forward on this, serving as tools to advocate for women, girls, and other marginalized groups' rights online to promote human security.

Specifically, we highlight five areas where UNSCR 1325 and the WPS agenda can move forward scholarship, advocacy, and policymaking to better secure women, girls, SGM, and other minorities in cyberspace.

1. Protection: Given the ongoing, if not growing, rate of cyber GBV and cybercrimes, UNSCR 1325 and the WPS agenda highlight the need to provide basic security online for all persons, especially among vulnerable populations who are experiencing a buildup toward armed fighting, are in the midst of ongoing armed conflict, or living in a postconflict period, as well as bring attention to marginalized social groups and communities. Where populations are facing war or are living during war, vulnerabilities from structural inequalities render many people susceptible to cybercrimes. Further, the links between armed fighting and GBV are well noted, and thus societies enduring conflict appear to see an increase in GBV not only in the physical realm but also in the cyber realm.
2. Participation: Increasing the participation and representation of women, girls, SGM, and other minority groups as outlined in UNSCR 1325 and the WPS scholarship is critical to better ensuring security. The involvement of marginalized individuals in cyber policy can help international and state policymakers and representatives—especially law enforcement within states—to realize that online violences and threats are valid dangers to people's security. Further, having input from those in marginalized communities in developing policy will lead to better fitting policies for these communities since these communities best know their issues and interests.

3. Prevention: UNSCR 1325 and the WPS agenda advocate preventing—or at least mitigating—GBV. The lack of regulation within the cybersphere leaves everyone less secure, especially those living in conflict-affected countries and those from marginalized communities. As this chapter points out, lack of regulation in the digital realm has led to rising propaganda and misinformation that has had corrosive effects on all societies, including those in preconflict stages, as well as those undergoing armed fighting and in postconflict countries. Although a danger to all societies in terms of potential violence and the rollback on human rights, the immediate consequences are most dire in conflict-affected states. We have suggested that by increasing the regulation of the cyber realm, cyber GBV and misinformation could be better contained.
4. Relief and recovery: The cybersphere is a space that can bring people together to engage in activism and social transformation that avoids the costs of in-country and cross-country travel. Online, people can gather to discuss, debate, and make real the UNSCR 1325 pillar of relief and recovery based on locally derived initiatives that—as long as they are inclusive of all sectors of a society—can have a positive impact on people's lives during war and in the postconflict and reconstruction period.
5. Scholarship: UNSCR 1325 and the WPS agenda scholarship has expanded beyond drawing attention to sexual violence and promoting women's participation in peacebuilding, peacekeeping, and postwar reconstruction. Recent calls for introducing internally focused WPS NAPs in all countries, regardless of whether they are postconflict or conflict-affected, point to new horizons for the WPS agenda. Understanding how the cyber realm influences women's and girls' insecurities (as well as the insecurities of other marginalized groups) must be a part of 1325 NAPs and WPS policymaking and on-the-ground work in implementation. This requires more theorizing from scholars working in WPS-related areas.

This chapter provides a start to how UNSCR 1325 and the WPS agenda relate to cybersecurity from a human security perspective that emphasizes human rights, including the right to development and the right to engage in digital spaces without fear of threat. At this preliminary stage, the relevance of protecting vulnerable populations in conflict-affected societies, particularly marginalized communities, is acute, but there is much more work to be done in this area.

References

Aceng, S., J. Katambi, F. Grandolfo, and G., andrew. 2020. "Online Gender-Based Violence: An Assessment of Women's Safety in the Digital Space." Brief, part of 16 Days of Activism Against Gender-Based Violence Campaign in 2020. https://www.feministhub.org/wp-content/uploads/2021/01/SayNoToOnlineOBV.pdf.

Adesina, O. S. 2017. "Cybercrime and Poverty in Nigeria." *Canadian Social Science* 13, no. 4: 19–29.

Alexander, R. 2019. "Gender, Structural Violence and Peace. In *The Routledge Handbook of Gender and Security*, ed. C. Gentry, S. Laura, and L. Sjoberg, 27–36. New York: Routledge.

Amnesty International. 2018. "Troll Patrol Findings." https://decoders.amnesty.org/projects/troll-patrol/findings.

Aryal, A. 2020. "For Nepali Women, Rampant Objectification and Sexualisation on the Internet." *Kathmandu Post*, May 7, 2020. https://kathmandupost.com/national/2020/05/07/for-nepali-women-rampant-objectification-and-sexualisation-on-the-internet.

Asian School of Cyber Laws. 2021. Global Cyber Law Database. https://www.asianlaws.org/gcld/index.php.

Association for Progressive Communication. 2017. *Online Gender-Based Violence: A Submission from the Association for Progressive Communications to the United Nations Special Rapporteur on Violence Against Women, Its Causes and Consequences.* https://www.apc.org/sites/default/files/APCSubmission_UNSR_VAW_GBV_0_0.pdf.

Barrow, A. 2010. "UN Security Council Resolutions 1325 and 1820: Constructing Gender in Armed Conflict and International Humanitarian Law." *International Review of the Red Cross* 92, no. 877: 221–234.

Basini, H., and C. Ryan. 2016. "National Action Plans as an Obstacle to Meaningful Local Ownership of UNSCR 1325 in Liberia and Sierra Leone." *International Political Science Review* 37, no. 3: 390–403.

Basu, S. 2016. "The Global South Writes 1325 (Too)." *International Political Science Review* 37, no. 3: 362–374.

Berke, P. R., S. M. Quiring, F. Olivera, and J. A. Horney. 2021. "Addressing Challenges to Building Resilience Through Interdisciplinary Research and Engagement." *Risk Analysis* 41, no. 7: 1248–1253.

Bernard, C. 1994. "Rape as Terror: The Case of Bosnia." *Terrorism and Political Violence* 6, no. 1: 29–43.

Blauner, R. 1969. "Internal Colonialism and Ghetto Revolt." *Social Problems* 16, no. 4: 393–408.

Britton, H. E. 2020. *Ending Gender-Based Violence: Justice and Community in South Africa*. Urbana: University of Illinois Press.

Brown, D., and A. Esterhuysen. 2019. "Why Cybersecurity Is a Human Rights Issue, and It Is Time to Start Treating It Like One." Association for Progressive Communications.

https://www.apc.org/en/news/why-cybersecurity-human-rights-issue-and-it-time-start-treating-it-one.
Brown, D., and A. Pytlak. 2020. *Why Gender Matters in International Cyber Security*. Women's International League for Peace and Freedom and the Association for Progressive Communications. https://www.apc.org/en/pubs/why-gender-matters-international-cyber-security.
Brown, M. L., L. A. Reed, and J. T. Messing. 2018. "Technology-Based Abuse: Intimate Partner Violence and the Use of Information Communication Technologies." In *Mediating Misogyny: Gender, Technology, and Harassment*, ed. J. R. Vickery and T. Everback, 209–228. Basingstoke, UK: Palgrave Macmillan.
Calabro, S. 2018. "From the Message Board to the Front Door: Addressing the Offline Consequences of Race- and Gender-Based Doxxing and Swatting." *Suffolk University Law Review* 51, no. 1: 55–76.
Choi, K.-s., C. S. Lee, and R. Cadigan. 2018. "Spreading Propaganda in Cyberspace: Comparing Cyber-Resource Usage of al Qaeda and ISIS." *International Journal of Cybersecurity Intelligence & Cybercrime* 1, no. 1: 21–39.
Christen, M., B. Gordijn, and M. Loi. 2020. *The Ethics of Cybersecurity*. Cham, Switzerland: Springer Open.
Cook, S. 2016. "The "Woman-in-Conflict" at the UN Security Council: A Subject of Practice." *International Affairs* 92, no. 2: 353–372.
Craigen, D., N. Diakun-Thibault, and R. Purse. 2014. "Defining Cybersecurity." *Technology Innovation Management Review* 4, no. 10: 13–21.
Crenshaw, K. 1989. "Demarginalizing the Intersection of Race and Sex: A Black Feminist Critique of Antidiscrimination Doctrine, Feminist Theory and Antiracist Politics." *The University of Chicago Legal Forum* 139: 139–167. https://scholarship.law.columbia.edu/faculty_scholarship/3007
Daniels, J. 2008. "Race, Civil Rights, and Hate Speech in the Digital Era." In *Learning Race and Ethnicity: Youth and Digital Media*, ed. A. Everett, 129–154. Cambridge, MA: MIT Press.
Dhungana, S. 2019. "Online Violence Against Women in Nepal on the Rise." *Kathmandu Post*, October 1, 2019.https://kathmandupost.com/national/2019/10/01/online-violence-against-women-in-nepal-on-the-rise.
Drumond, P., and T. Rebelo. 2020. "Global Pathways or Local Spins? National Action Plans in South America." *International Feminist Journal of Politics* 22, no. 4: 462–484.
Ferrier, M., and N. Garud-Patkar. 2018. "TrollBusters: Fighting Online Harassment of Women Journalists." In *Mediating Misogyny: Gender, Technology and Harassment*, ed. J. R. Vickery and T. Everback, 311–332. Basingstoke, UK: Palgrave Macmillan.
Galtung, J. 1969. "Violence, Peace and Peace Research." *Journal of Peace Research* 6, no. 3: 167–191.
Goodman, S. E., J. C. Kirk, and M. H. Kirk. 2007. "Cyberspace as a Medium for Terrorists." *Technological Forecasting and Social Change* 74, no. 2: 193–210.
Hackworth, L. 2018. "Limitations of 'Just Gender': The Need for an Intersectional Reframing of Online Harassment Discourse and Research." In *Mediated Misogyny: Gender, Technology, and Harassment*, ed. by J. R. Vickery and T. Everback, 51–70. Basingstoke, UK: Palgrave Macmillan.
Hagen, J. 2016. "Queering Women, Peace, and Security." *International Affairs* 92, no. 2: 313–332.

Holtzhausen, L. 2012. "Thirteen Year Old Boy Implicated in Gang Rape of Seventeen Year Old Mentally Disabled Girl from Soweto—A Case of Criminal Capacity." *Article 40* 14, no. 2: 1–5. https://journals.co.za/doi/pdf/10.10520/EJC125604.

Internet Free & Secure Initiative. n.d.a. "About the Internet Free & Secure Initiative." https://freeandsecure.online/about/.

Internet Free & Secure Initiative. n.d.b. "A Human Rights Respecting Definition of Cybersecurity." https://freeandsecure.online/definition/.

International Telecommunications Union. 2021. *The Digital Gender Gap Is Growing Fast in Developing Countries.* https://itu.foleon.com/itu/measuring-digital-development/gender-gap/.

Jansson, M., and M. Eduards. 2016. "The Politics of Gender in the UN Security Council Resolutions on Women, Peace, and Security." *International Feminist Journal of Politics* 18, no. 4: 590–604.

Jenkins, J., and J. D. Wolfgang. 2018. "A Space for Women: Online Commenting Forums as Indicators of Civility and Feminist Community-Building." In *Mediating Misogyny: Gender, Harassment, and Technology*, ed. R. Vickery and T. Everback, 247–268. Basingstoke, UK: Palgrave Macmillan.

K.C., L., and C. Whetstone. 2022. "Rethinking Women, Peace, and Security Through the Localization of United Nations Security Council Resolution 1325 & National Action Plans: A Study of Nepal and Sri Lanka." *Women's Studies International Forum* 92, (online). https://doi.org/10.1016/j.wsif.2022.102575.

Kendall, M. 2020. *Hood Feminism: Notes from the Women That a Movement Forgot.* ebook. Viking.

Khoo, C. 2021. *Deplatforming Misogyny: Report on Platform Liability for Technology-Facilitated Gender-Based Violence.* Women's Legal and Education & Action Fund. https://www.leaf.ca/wp-content/uploads/2021/04/Full-Report-Deplatforming-Misogyny.pdf.

Kim, J. 2018. "Misogyny for Male Solidarity: Online Hate Discourse Against Women in South Korea." In *Mediating Misogyny: Gender, Technology, and Harassment*, ed. J. R. Vickery and T. Everback, 151–169. Basingstoke, UK: Palgrave Macmillan.

Kirby, P., and L. Shepherd. 2016. "The Futures Past of the Women, Peace, and Security Agenda." *International Affairs* 92, no. 2: 373–392.

Kleiner, J., and O. Šupka. 2020. "The Myanmar Conflict: A Role of Cyberspace in Counterinsurgency." *International Journal of Cyber Criminology* 14, no. 1: 254–266.

Kuran, Christian Henrik Alexander, Claudia Morsut, Bjørn Ivar Kruke, Marco Krüger, Lisa Segnestam, Kati Orru, Tor Olav Næverstad, Merja Airola, Jaana Keranen, Friederich Gabel, Sten Hansson, and Sten Torpan. "Vulnerability and Vulnerable Groups from an Intersectionality Perspective." *International Journal of Disaster Risk Reduction* 50 (2020): 1–8. https://doi.org/10.1016/j.ijdrr.2020.101826

Laxton, C. 2014. *Virtual World, Real Fear: Women's Aid Report into Online Abuse, Harassment and Stalking.* Women's Aid. https://1q7dqy2unor827bqjls0c4rn-wpengine.netdna-ssl.com/wp-content/uploads/2015/11/Women_s_Aid_Virtual_World_Real_Fear_Feb_2014-3.pdf.

Lomba, N., C. Navarra, and M. Fernan. 2021. *Combating Gender-Based Violence: Cyber Violence: European Added Value Assessment.* European Parliament: 1–231. https://www.europarl.europa.eu/RegData/etudes/STUD/2021/662621/EPRS_STU(2021)662621_EN.pdf.

Lubin, A. 2020. "The Rights to Privacy and Data Protection Under International Humanitarian Law and Human Rights Law." In *Research Handbook on Human Rights and Humanitarian Law: Further Reflections and Perspectives*, ed. Robert Kolb, Gloria Gaggioli and Pavle Kilibarda, 463–492. Edward Elgar.

Mackinnon, C. [1984] 1991. "Difference and Dominance: On Sex Discrimination." In *Feminist Legal Theory*, ed. K. T. Bartlett and R. Kennedy, 381–392. New York: Routledge.

Madden, S., M. Janoske, R. B. Winkler, and A. N. Edgar. 2018. "Mediated Misogynoir: Intersecting Race and Gender in Online Harassment." In *Mediating Misogyny: Gender, Technology, and Harassment*, ed. J. R. Vickery and T. Everback, 71–90. Basingstoke, UK: Palgrave Macmillan.

Mantilla, K. 2013. "Gendertrolling: Misogyny Adapts to New Media." *Feminist Studies* 39, no. 2: 563–570.

McCall, L. 2005. "The Complexity of Intersectionality." *Signs: Journal of Women in Culture and Society* 30, no. 3: 1771–1800.

Nesiah, V. 2012. "Uncomfortable Alliances: Women, Peace, and Security in Sri Lanka." In *South Asian Feminisms*, ed. A. Loomba and R. A. Lukose, 139–161. Durham and London: Duke University Press.

Noble, S. U. 2018. *Algorithms of Oppression: How Search Engines Reinforce Racism*. New York: New York University Press.

NGO Working Group on Women. 2019. "About." http://www.womenpeacesecurity.org/about/.

Nordstrom, C. 1996. "Rape: Politics and Theory in War and Peace." *Australian Feminist Studies* 11, no. 2: 147–162.

Ogbondah, C. W., and P. O. Agbese. 2017. "Terrorists and Social Media Messages: A Critical Analysis of Boko Haram's Messages and Messaging Techniques." In *The Palgrave Handbook of Media and Communication Research in Africa*, ed. B. Mutsvairo, 313–345. Cham, Switzerland: Palgrave Macmillan.

Olson, C. C., and V. LaPoe. 2018. "Combating the Digital Spiral of Silence: Academic Activists Versus Social Media Trolls." In *Mediating Misogyny: Gender, Technology and Harassment*, ed. J. R. Vickery and T. Everback, 271–291. Basingstoke, UK: Palgrave Macmillan.

Oo, P. P., and S. E. Davies. 2021. "Supporting the Victims of Sexual Violence in Myanmar." Lowy Institute. https://www.lowyinstitute.org/the-interpreter/supporting-victims-sexual-violence-myanmar.

Otto, D. 2006. "A Sign of 'Weakness'? Disrupting Gender Certainties in the Implementation of Security Council Resolution 1325." *Michigan Journal of Gender and Law* 13, no. 1: 114–175.

Paullet, K. L., D. R. Rota, and T. T. Swan. 2009. "Cyberstalking: An Exploratory Study of Students at a Mid-Atlantic University." *Issues in Information Systems* 10, no. 2: 640–649.

Perera, S., and R. Wickrematunge. 2019. *Opinions, B*tch: Technology-Based Violence Against Women in Sri Lanka*. Centre for Policy Alternatives: 1–54. https://drive.google.com/file/d/16ohQ7P2K08qz-kgiQUfSr0JCGvxDLHNR/view.

Pinto-Jayawardena, K., and J. Guthrie. 2016. "Introduction." In *The Search for Justice: The Sri Lanka Papers*, ed. K. Jayawardena and K. Pinto-Jayawardena, xix–lii. New Delhi: Zubaan.

Pratt, N., and S. Richter-Devroe. 2011. "Critically Examining UNSCR 1325 on Women, Peace, and Security." *International Feminist Journal of Politics* 13, no. 4: 489–503.

Pugh, M. 2005. "The Political Economy of Peacebuilding: A Critical Theory Perspective." *International Journal of Peace Studies* 10, no. 2: 23–42.

Runyan, Anne Sisson. 2019. *Global Gender Politics*, 5th edition. New York: Routledge.

Ruvalcaba, Y., and A. A. Eaton. 2019. "Nonconsensual Pornography Among US Adults: A Sexual Scripts Framework on Victimization, Perpetration, and Health Correlates for Women and Men." *Psychology of Violence* 10, no. 1: 1–11. https://www.cybercivilrights.org/2019-publication/.

Save the Children. 2019. *Myanmar Youth Especially Vulnerable to Online Abuse, Hate Speech and Fake News on Social Media*. November 7. https://www.savethechildren.net/news/myanmar-youth-especially-vulnerable-online-abuse-hate-speech-and-fake-news-social-media.

Shepherd, L. J. 2011. "Sex, Security and Superhero(in)es: From 1325 to 1820 and Beyond." *International Feminist Journal of Politics* 13, no. 4: 504–521.

Shepherd, L. J. 2020. "Situating Women, Peace, and Security: Theorizing from 'the Local.'" *International Feminist Journal of Politics* 22, no. 4: 456–461.

SIDA. 2019. "Gender-Based Violence Online: Gender Tool Box Brief." Swedish International Development Cooperation Agency: 1–6. https://cdn.sida.se/publications/files/sida62246en-gender-based-violence-online.pdf.

Slupska, J. 2019. "Safe at Home: Towards a Feminist Critique of Cybersecurity." *St Antony's International Review* 15, no. 1: 83–100.

Statistica. 2021. "Global Digital Population as of January 2021." https://www.statista.com/statistics/617136/digital-population-worldwide/.

Stroud, S. R. and W. Cox. 2018. "The Varieties of Feminist Counterspeech in the Misogynistic Online World." In *Mediating Misogyny: Gender, Technology and Harassment*, ed. J. R. Vickery and T. Everback, 293–310. Basingstoke, UK: Palgrave Macmillan.

Tripp, A. M. 2013. "Toward a Gender Perspective on Human Security." In *Gender, Violence, and Human Security: Critical Feminist Perspectives*, ed. A. M. Tripp, M. M. Ferree, and C. Ewig, 3–32. New York: New York University Press.

Tryggestad, T. L. 2009. "Trick or Treat—The UN and Implementation of Security Council Resolution 1325 on Women, Peace, and Security." *Global Governance* 15: 539–557.

UN Population Fund. n.d. "What Is Gender-Based Violence (GBV)?" https://www.friendsofunfpa.org/what-is-gender-based-violence-gbv/.

UN Security Council. 2000. Resolution 1325. http://daccess-ods.un.org/access.nsf/Get?Open&DS=S/RES/1325(2000)&Lang=E.

UN Trust Fund for Human Security. 2017. "Human Security Handbook: An Integrated Approach for the Realization of the Sustainable Development Goals and the Priority Areas of the International Community and the United Nations System." https://www.un.org/humansecurity/wp-content/uploads/2017/10/h2.pdf.

UN Women. 2015. *Cyber Violence Against Women and Girls: A World-Wide Wake-Up Call*. https://www.unwomen.org/~/media/headquarters/attachments/sections/library/publications/2015/cyber_violence_gender%20report.pdf?d=20150924T154259&v=1.

Vickery, J., 2018. "Using an Intersectional Approach to Advance Understanding of Homeless Persons' Vulnerability to Disaster." *Environmental Sociology* 4, no. 1: 136–147.

Vickery, J. R., and T. Everback. 2018. "The Persistence of Misogyny: From the Streets, to Our Screens, to the White House." In *Mediating Misogyny: Gender, Technology, and Harassment*, ed. J. R. Vickery and T. Everback, 1–27 Basingstoke, UK: Palgrave Macmillan.

Vogels, E. A. 2021. *The State of Online Harassment*. Pew Research Center. January 13, 2021. https://www.pewresearch.org/internet/2021/01/13/the-state-of-online-harassment/.

Walters, V., and J. C. Gaillard, 2014. "Disaster Risk at the Margins: Homelessness, Vulnerability and Hazards." *Habitat International* 44: 211–219.

Weimann, G. 2015. *Terrorism in Cyberspace: The Next Generation*. Washington, DC: Woodrow Wilson Center Press with Columbia University Press.

Women's International League of Peace and Freedom. 2020a. "Build the Movement." https://www.wilpf.org/work-areas/build-movement/#whatwedo.

Women's International League of Peace and Freedom. 2020b. "Member States." http://www.peacewomen.org/member-states.

Windsor, L. 2020. "The Language of Radicalization: Female Internet Recruitment to Participation in ISIS Activities." *Terrorism and Political Violence* 32, no. 3: 506–538.

Woodlock, D. 2017. "The Abuse of Technology in Domestic Violence and Stalking." *Violence against Women* 23, no. 5: 584–602.

Yadav, P. 2020. "When the Personal Is International: Implementation of the National Action Plan on Resolutions 1325 and 1820 in Nepal." *Gender, Technology and Development* 24, no. 2: 194–214.

2
Cyberspace and the Nouveau Colonialism

Erin Saltman and Dina Hussein

Introduction

We often take for granted that the internet is both transnational and cross-platform by design. It has transformed global connectivity in a way that allows for fast, free, international communication and information sharing for anyone with access to a smartphone, computer, or internet café. At its core, the internet is built with equitable global access in mind, a feature that has been a core tenant of its growth and lauded by advocates of free expression. The UN has gone on to emphasize that access to the internet can increasingly be viewed as a human right (UNHRC 2011).

With the global expansion of internet access, protections given to users and their data are increasing concerns, with geographical divides between how nation-states and regions apply regulations, policies, and varying degrees of protections to the online space. As an example, while the introduction of the General Data Protection Regulation (GDPR) initiated by the European Union (EU) set a high bar for personal data protection laws, its protections are jurisdictionally limited to users in the EU. Legislation on user-data protections online remains hyper-localized and fragmented. This is increasingly turning into a form of nouveau colonialism between what protections are legally given to users residing in more liberal democratic countries versus countries leaning more toward authoritarianism where governments are mandating access to user data under the guise of security measures, such as counterterrorism efforts. The term "nouveau colonialism" is used within this chapter to describe the evolving impact of the intersection of data colonialism viewed through the lens of feminist theory and data protection fragmentation.

Tech companies are having to decide how to apply national laws where their platforms are used, despite the transnational nature of information sharing and communications online. The data of users in the Global South is

Erin Saltman and Dina Hussein, *Cyberspace and the Nouveau Colonialism* In: *Critical Perspectives on Cybersecurity*. Edited by: Anwar Mhajne and Alexis Henshaw, Oxford University Press. © Oxford University Press 2024.
DOI: 10.1093/oso/9780197695883.003.0003

afforded limited protection, with minority communities and women facing greater risks, real-world repercussions, and restrictions in their online freedoms or protections. This chapter explores three main pillars of inquiry:

1. The lack of a unified global approach to data protection—leading to national or regional legislations that are increasingly contradicting one another.
2. Authoritative regimes prioritizing security, as well as access to user data, over privacy online, leading to vulnerable communities becoming further susceptible to nefarious targeted attacks online.
3. The obstacles faced by global tech companies in adjudication of localized cyberspace laws while trying to apply equitable global company policies.

This chapter argues that the current trend in nationally and regionally applied legal protections is placing already vulnerable communities further at risk in the real world. At the same time, private tech companies are having to navigate developing policies that are international while also trying to comply with local laws, which are increasingly clashing. There is, therefore, a fundamental need for global baseline standards for data protection and privacy of internet users that apply across online user-interfacing platforms. While there is no real existing international body that could currently house standards of this nature, there is a need for this to be developed in the near future to mitigate further divides in the Global North and South.

Moreover, this chapter argues that frameworks for solutions can be found in feminist theory literature. The core obstacle faced in balancing protections for users globally is about a fundamental imbalance of power between users and government legislators. Feminist theory, therefore, provides a useful lens through which to view the challenges and vulnerabilities intrinsic to the current state of play to develop paths forward for solution building. Due to the nature of the current structural systems, power imbalances that have resulted from the heavy concentration of policy and regulatory decision-making being situated in the US and EU have borne an equivalent imbalance in the protections that have been developed. In addressing this, the conceptual toolkit provided by postcolonial theory allows us to unpack the imperialist approach to privacy that has developed among state regulations of data. Finally, the chapter frames solutions built around tenants of representation, resourcing, and intersectionality, tenants pulled from feminist postcolonial and global international relations.

The Escalation of Increased and Conflicting National and Regional Online Legislations

Legal obligations on tech companies are almost entirely dictated within national and sometimes regional legislative frameworks. Despite internet companies and platforms being utilized by global audiences, there is no unified global approach to data protection, obligations for data disclosure from tech companies, or obligatory protections for online users. Often a tech company must make delicate decisions and develop internal processes for how they comply (or potentially decide not to comply) with requests or demands made by different governments' legal frameworks concerning removals and access to user data. Traditionally, an internet company starts with legal compliance based on the country they are headquartered or founded in, and then it works with internal legal teams or external counsel as and when external legal bodies make requests or demands that seem contradictory to the companies' status quo for legal compliance. Much of a company's ability to navigate these legal demands depends on the size of a company along with its resources and access to experts.

The contradictory or conflicting demands being made by various countries on tech companies have been escalating in recent years as public demand to legislate tech companies has mainstreamed. Cultural norms and political posturing play a large role in how these policies and legal frameworks are being developed. There is also a natural divide in how legal frameworks are prioritized based on larger goals at the leadership level and the relation between national leadership and wider society. The more a country operates within a democratic framework, tied to fundamental human rights, the more legal frameworks tend to focus on protections to online users at a citizen level. These often focus on privacy and speech protections for citizens. These frameworks also often include protections to private companies to ensure independence and the ability to innovate, creating global commerce. The more a country fits within a more authoritarian political culture, or when democratic backsliding occurs, the more legal frameworks emphasize a government's increased access to user data and increased liability on internet service providers, usually under the auspices of safety and security.

The three pillars that are beginning to naturally contradict one another are legal obligations solving for issues around (1) privacy, (2) security, and (3) free speech. This section looks at the range of legal obligations aimed at tech companies and online users that have been developed or are in development in recent years. While hundreds of policies and laws could be within scope internationally, this chapter focuses on legislation that directly or indirectly impacts efforts to counter terrorism and violent extremism online.

In October 2021, the Legal Frameworks Working Group of the Global Internet Forum to Counter Terrorism (GIFCT) identified 24 countries and regions with legislation that was either recently instated or was in the process of being debated for implementation concerning counterterrorism and counter-extremism goals by governments. Table 2.1 highlights these legislative efforts and builds off substantial mapping and analysis work done by Tech Against Terrorism (2021) through their Online Regulation Series. While some legal frameworks questioned in the table explicitly focus on counterterrorism as core to the legal mandate, others focus on wider "harmful content," "illegal content," "hateful content," or, increasingly, "misinformation" that has been linked to societal instability and increasingly violent extremism. Table 2.1 gives a brief overview of the legislations in question in each country or region and where they are in the process of implementation.

Differing Government Measures to Drive Change and Industry Dilemmas

It is well within the rights of governments to identify potential national and regional threats in all their forms and to create measures, through policy and legislation, to counter those threats. Concerns about safety and security of both citizens and the government infrastructure tend to be at the core of legislation for countering terrorism, violent extremism, and related topics that lead to potential violence, such as hate speech and misinformation. The mechanisms these legislative frameworks are using to drive change fit primarily in three categories.

1. Increasing government bodies' ability to legally require the removal of more online content in an expedited manner.
2. Increasing government access to user data.

Table 2.1 International Legislation Affecting Counterterrorism and Counter-Extremism Efforts Online

Country	Legislation/Timing	Primary Purpose
Australia	Online Safety Act (June 2021).[1]	The act largely looks to limit online material that promotes, incites, instructs, or depicts "abhorrent violent conduct." It gives government extended powers to demand content removal within given time frames regardless of platform size.
Brazil	Internet Freedom, Responsibility and Transparency Act, or Law PLS2630/2020, known as the "fake news" bill (June 2020 passed in the Senate but not yet approved by the Chamber of Deputies).[2]	The law looks to restrict certain types of speech and association regardless of the user's location. The act focuses on "fake news" making it a crime, punishable by 1–5 years in prison, and to create or share content that allegedly poses a serious risk to "social peace or to the economic order." The terms are not well defined. The new bill makes social platforms responsible for everything published on them, focusing liability on the platforms rather than users posting harmful content.
Burkina Faso	Amendments largely under Title I of Book III of the Penal Code of 2018, which deals with "Crimes and Minor Offenses against the Security of the State" (adopted by Parliament June 2021, but still needs presidential approval).[3]	Penal Code amendments aim to criminalize certain kinds of online content, including fake news and requirements on terrorism reporting. The law calls for up to 10 years jail time and up to 2 million CFA francs ($3,457) fines for anyone who "participates in an initiative to demoralize the defense and security forces." It also imposes sentences of up to 5 years and fines of up to 10 million CFA francs for the publication of information that could compromise security operations, false information about rights abuses or destruction of property, or any images or audio from the scene of a "terrorist" attack.
Canada	Online Harms Bill, amending Canadian Human Rights Act, Criminal Code, and Youth Criminal Justice Act (federal government consultation closed September 2021).[4]	The categories of "harmful content" focus on terrorist content, content that incites violence, hate speech, nonconsensual sharing of intimate images, and child sexual exploitation. The bill aims to put greater liability on "online communication service providers." A formal definition of "hatred" is also to be added to the Criminal Code to clarify the scope of the bill. There are concerns that the amendment could potentially violate Canada's constitutional and privacy rights, such as the Canadian Charter of Rights and Freedoms.
Ethiopia	Hate Speech and Disinformation Prevention and Suppression Proclamation/ Proclamation No. 1185/2020 (March 2020).[5]	The bill includes mandatory removal of certain types of content within given time frames dictated by the Ethiopian Broadcast Authority but does give certain exemptions for academic study, news, religious teaching, and artistic creativity.

European Union	Regulation 2021/784 on addressing the dissemination of terrorist content online/TCO (2022).[6]	The Terrorist Content Online (TCO) Regulation 2021/784 on addressing the dissemination of terrorist content online goes into effect June 2022. It compels companies to remove terrorist content within one hour from it being flagged by a EU country's designated "competent authority," and to introduce a range of measures to prevent terrorist content spreading on their platforms. TCO financial penalties are proportionate to the size of a platform.
European Union	Digital Services Act (DSA) (adopted December 15, 2020).[7]	The DSA sets the "horizontal rules" covering all services and types of illegal content across Europe. It aims to "harmonise rules for addressing illegal content online." It is meant to complement sector-specific legislation and should "not affect the application of rules resulting from other acts of Union law regulating certain aspects of the provision of intermediary services." Under the DSA, the concept of "illegal content" is defined broadly, covering "information relating to illegal content, products, services and activities"—and pulls out "terrorist content [irrespective of its form]." Due diligence obligations differ across very large online platforms, other online platforms, hosting services, and all intermediaries. The regulatory burden attempts to be proportionate.
France	Countering online hate law, aka the Avia law (adopted in May 2020 and then declared unconstitutional by the French Constitutional Council June 28, 2020).[8]	The law was drafted to apply to online platforms and search engines that reach a certain threshold of user activity. The law was meant to enforce greater restrictions on broad harm categories of content including slander; provocation to discrimination, hatred, or violence against individuals or groups based on protected categories; glorification of criminal offences; denial or trivialization of crimes against humanity (genocide, war crimes, or crimes of enslavement); and sexual harassment content or content related to child pornography. The law focused on algorithmic oversite, mandatory time-based removals, and tooling requirements.
Germany	The Network Enforcement Act, aka NetzDG (implemented June 2017).[9]	The NetzDG applies to companies with more than 2 million users in the country. It compels content removals based on select provisions from the German Criminal Code and imposes high fines for noncompliance with existing legal obligations. It includes removal time frames and fines of up to 50 million euros ($59 million).

(continued)

Table 2.1 Continued

Country	Legislation/Timing	Primary Purpose
Germany	The Repair Act (effective April 2021 amendment).[10]	The Repair Act amends the NetzDG to proactively include pathways for action against right-wing extremist activity online. It changes 5 relevant laws, including the Criminal Code (which defines "illegal content"), the law on Criminal Procedure, the NetzDG, the Telecommunications Act, and the law of the Federal Criminal Police Authority. The Repair Act adds further requirements to the NetzDG—to assess whether users express prohibited types of expression and actions that silence other users by intimidation, incitement to hatred, preparation of violent action against the state, and dissemination of propaganda and symbols from anti-constitutional organizations. Under the act, police can request user passwords.
India	I.T. (Intermediary Guidelines and Digital Media Ethics Code) Rules (implemented May 2021).[11]	While the code does not overtly address terrorism and violent extremism, there is vague language under national security rules that penalize things such as threats to the sovereignty and integrity of India and/or the broad security of the state, incitement to violence, and disturbance of public order. Particularly Section II of Chapter VI, which addresses content that "threatens the unity, integrity, defence, security or sovereignty of India, friendly relations with foreign States, or public order, or causes incitement to the commission of any cognisable offence or prevents investigation of any offence or is insulting other nations." The rules include time-based removal requirements and tool usage by companies. It also puts liability on in-country employees of a given company.
Indonesia	Regulation of the Minister of Communication and Informatics Number 5 of 2020 on Private Electronic System Operators, aka Ministerial Regulation 5.[12]	Regulation 5 governs certain functioning of private electronic systems operators (ESOs) that are accessible to users in Indonesia. This includes social media platforms, search engines, ecommerce, gaming, and communications services. Put into effect November 2020, the regulation grants the government authority to regulate private ESO activity, gives authorities the right to request access to user data, and provides for sweeping notices and takedown orders. Regulation 5 requires ESOs to register with the government and designate a contact person in Indonesia, putting liability on in-country company representatives. It also introduces penalties for noncompliance, from fines to full shutdown of services in Indonesia.

Kenya	Kenya Information and Communication (Amendment) Bill 2019 (proposed), dubbed Social Media Bill.[13]	The bill targets content that might "degrade or intimidate a recipient of the content," as well as content prejudicial against a person based on protected categories, and tries to ensure that online disseminated content is "fair, accurate, and unbiased." Obligations fall on group administrators of social media platforms (with potential fines and imprisonment penalties). It allows the government to mandate that bloggers officially register. The bill places more agency and onus on online users posting content, rather than the platforms being used to host content.
Lesotho	Proposed changes to the Lesotho Communications Authority (Internet Broadcasting) Rules, 2020 Sections 5(1)(c) and 38(2) of the Communications Act No. 4 of 2012 (proposed 2020).	The proposed amendment to the Internet Broadcasting Rules would affect social media users with more than 100 followers and posts by users with more than 100 followers in the country. Social media users would be required to register as "internet broadcasters." The rules would put agency and onus on the online users posting content with the same level of scrutiny, oversight, and potential repercussions as other "broadcasters."
Morocco	Draft law no. 22.20, aka the social media law (leaked in 2020 but suspended during the COVID pandemic).[14]	The law targets the possession of illegal electronic content; it aims to tackle "the various forms of cybercrimes, in particular those which affect general security, public economic order, the publication of fake news, promotion of behavior harming the dignity and spirit of others, as well as certain crimes that target minors." It also penalizes users who post "false information" online. Article 8 language has been cited as vague by critics, as the law targets "any electronic content which clearly constitutes a dangerous threat to security, public order or which would be likely to undermine the constants of the Kingdom, its sacredness and its symbols" with time-based removal requirements.
New Zealand	Films, Videos, and Publications Classification (Urgent Interim Classification of Publications and Prevention of Online Harm) Amendment Act 2021 (2021/43) (to come into force February 1, 2022).[15]	This amendment of the Classification Act aims to allow "the urgent prevention and mitigation of harms by objectionable publications," referring to content that is prohibited under New Zealand's Classification Act. The act makes livestreaming objectionable content a criminal offense. Censorship calls could be made immediately and takedown notices would be backed by law. This amendment expands the scope of the Classification Act to cover livestreamed content online and to allow judicial authorities in New Zealand to issue fines to noncompliant platforms.

(continued)

Table 2.1 Continued

Country	Legislation/Timing	Primary Purpose
Nigeria	National Commission for the Prohibition of Hate Speech bill, aka the Hate Speech Bill (2019).[16]	The Hate Speech Bill allows for penalties against "a person who uses, publishes, presents, produces, plays, provides, distributes and/or directs the performance of any material, written and/or visual, which is threatening, abusive or insulting or involves the use of threatening, abusive or insulting words or behavior, commits an offence, if such person intends thereby to stir up ethnic hatred, or having regard to all the circumstances, ethnic hatred is likely to be stirred up against any person or person from such an ethnic group in Nigeria." It includes penalties for anyone who "subjects another to harassment on the basis of ethnicity for the purposes of this section where, on ethnic grounds, he unjustifiably engages in a conduct which has the purpose or effect of (a) violating that other person's dignity or (b) creating an intimidating, hostile, degrading, humiliating or offensive environment for the person subjected to the harassment." The bill focuses on a wide range of online engagements, introduces fines for companies hosting content if not removed, and allows possible imprisonment (up to life) of those found guilty.
Nigeria	Protection from Internet Falsehoods and Manipulation and other Related Offences bill, aka the Social Media Bill (2019).[17]	The Social Media Bill takes large and broad measures to prohibit statements on social media deemed "likely to be prejudicial to national security" and "those which may diminish public confidence" in Nigeria's government. The bill gives law enforcement the power to shut down access to the internet and social media (without recourse to a court or the National Assembly). The bill introduces fines to companies found violating the bill with possible imprisonment of offenders.
Pakistan	Citizen Protection Against Online Harm Rules (2020).[18]	The rules mandate that the ruling of the Pakistan National Coordinator takes precedence over the terms of service or community guidelines of a social media company. Specifically, Rule 4(4) requires social media companies to deploy proactive enforcement mechanisms to prevent livestreaming "online content related to terrorism, extremism, hate speech, defamation, fake news, incitement to violence and national security." The rules include proactive enforcement of tools for social media platforms and time requirements for removals as well as personal data retention and legal liability for employees of the tech companies while mandating that the social media companies must have physical employee presence in Pakistan.

Philippines	Republic Act No. 10175, Anti-Terrorism Act (implemented July 2020).[19]	The Anti-Terrorism Act to regulate social media includes making tech platforms liable for content hosted. Criticism has included a focus on a vague definition of "terrorism" as "Engaging in acts intended to cause death or serious bodily injury to any person or endangers a person's life; Engaging in acts intended to cause extensive damage or destruction to a government or public facility, public place, or private property; Engaging in acts intended to cause extensive interference with, damage, or destruction to critical infrastructure; Developing, manufacturing, possessing, acquiring, transporting, supplying, or using weapons; and Releasing dangerous substances or causing fire, floods or explosions when the purpose is to intimidate the general public, create an atmosphere to spread a message of fear, provoke or influence by intimidation the government or any international organization, seriously destabilize or destroy the fundamental political, economic, or social structures in the country, or create a public emergency or seriously undermine public safety." The act grants the government excessive powers and allows suspects to be detained without a judicial warrant of arrest for 14 days and surveillance of suspects for 60 days both with possible extensions.
Poland	Protection of the Freedom of Speech on Social Media bill (February 2021).[20]	The bill was inspired by legislation developed in Germany, France, and the EU Data Services Act. The bill states that when a social media platform blocks access to content or blocks a user, the user will be entitled to file a complaint with the platform and appeal it. Users will also be able to request content posted on the platform removed if they think it is illegal under Polish law. In contradiction with GDPR and other data protection laws, it requires companies to hold personal data for 12 months to be made available to law enforcement upon request. In each case, the platform will have 48 hours to examine the complaint. Critics of the bill have focused on poorly defined parameters for what "unlawful content" means, including topics of disinformation, content infringing on personal rights, and "public decency".

(continued)

Table 2.1 Continued

Country	Legislation/Timing	Primary Purpose
Russia	Federal Law No. 405-FZ, On Amendments to Certain Legislative Acts of the Russian Federation (December 2, 2019).[21]	The law sets higher fines for noncompliance with a variety of regulations such as data localization requirements, requirements for messaging apps to handover encryption keys, requirements for search engines to connect to Roskomnadzor's proscribed list, and requirements for "information dissemination organizers" to retain user data and provide them to the authorities. The law also raised financial penalties on users for disseminating calls for extremist or terrorist activities, along with other categories of prohibited information. These amendments have been criticized for damaging user-privacy protections and giving more authority to the government to target, fine, and incarcerate antigovernment voices.
Singapore	The Protection of Online Falsehoods and Manipulation Bill (implemented October 2019).[22]	While the bill does not target online terrorist content directly, it does prohibit "online content that incites or endorses hatred and strife" that can justify the removal of what the government might dictate as terrorist material. The bill applies to wider social media communication as well as to encrypted messaging platforms. The mandate on *breaking* end-to-end encryption is particularly controversial leading to heightened privacy concerns. The bill justifies amendments under national security and public safety concerns, targeting communications that "incite feelings of enmity, hatred or ill will between different groups of persons" (Section 7). Section 16 states that "an internet access service provider that does not comply with any access blocking order shall be guilty of an offence and shall be liable on conviction to a fine not exceeding $20,000 for each day during any part of which that order is not fully complied with, up to a total of $500,000." This puts time-based financial penalization parameters in place on service providers without well-defined definitions of violative content.

Turkey	Law No. 7253, aka the Social Media Bill (implemented October 2020).[23]	The law specifically targets social media companies that have over a million daily users. The law compels these companies to adhere to regulations increasing storage and retention of user data locally. It also applies mandatory removal of content within 24 hours where there are "violations of personal rights" or judicial orders to remove content. If the content is not removed, platforms are fined and access to a given app or site is rendered inaccessible within 4 hours inside the country. Platforms are also meant to have a local representative in Turkey to be able to liaise with courts and officials. Turkish authorities have compared their law to NetzDG in Germany and say it is like regulation coming into force in Germany and France.
United Kingdom	Online Safety Bill (draft 2021).[24]	The bill brings in increased removal requirements around a variety of "harmful" content types. The bill also mandates that service providers should increase use of technology "to identify public terrorism content present on the service and to swiftly take down that content (either by means of the technology alone or by means of the technology together with the use of human moderators to review terrorism content identified by the technology)." The bill also proposes legal liability for senior managers at a service provider if the platform cannot show reasonable steps taken to remove illegal and terrorism content. The bill mandates that companies produce annual transparency reports in specified formats submitted to the UK Office of Communications.
United States	Communications Decency Act 1996, Section 230 reform (proposal).[25]	While Section 230 is not specific to terrorism and violent extremism, it is included in this table because of increased pressure and numerous proposals to update and modify the act. The act is the primary regulatory framework that protects platforms from certain liabilities based on user-generated content. Suggested reforms of Section 230 aim to increase liability directly on tech companies for "illegal content," including terrorist content, generated by users. Section 230 is considered by many to be the bedrock for protecting free expression online. While both Democratic and Republican representatives feel that reforms to this act are needed, they have very different opinions why they feel the act is inadequate and what they would offer up as reform (Anand et al 2021).

(*continued*)

Table 2.1 Continued

Country	Legislation/Timing	Primary Purpose
Zimbabwe	Cyber Security and Data Protection Bill, dubbed social media law.[26]	The bill punishes those deemed to have abused social media via activities such as spreading misinformation against the state and citizens. Clause 164 of the proposed bill states: "Any person who unlawfully and intentionally by means of a computer or information system makes available, broadcasts or distributes data to any other person concerning an identified or identifiable person knowing it to be false with intent to cause psychological or economic harm shall be guilty of an offence and liable to a fine not exceeding level 10 or to imprisonment for a period not exceeding five years, or to both such fine and such imprisonment." The bill increases the government's ability to fine and/or sentence up to 5 years jail time to users whose content falls under these parameters.

[1] Parliament of Australia (2021).
[2] Federal Senate of Brazil (2020).
[3] Burkina Faso, Assemblée Nationale (2018).
[4] Government of Canada (2021).
[5] Federal Democratic Republic of Ethiopia (2020).
[6] Official Journal of the European Union (2021).
[7] European Commission (2020).
[8] Assemblée Nationale (2019).
[9] German Government (2017).
[10] Bundesgesetzblatt (2021).
[11] Indian Ministry of Information and Broadcasting (2021).
[12] Manurung et al. (2021).
[13] Republic of Kenya (2019).
[14] Khamlichi (2020).

[15] New Zealand Parliamentary Counsel Office (2021).
[16] National Assembly of the Federal Republic of Nigeria (2019).
[17] National Assembly of the Federal Republic of Nigeria (2019).
[18] Government of Pakistan Ministry of Information Technology and Telecommunication (2020).
[19] Congress of the Philippines Eighteenth Congress (2020).
[20] Polish Ministry of Justice (2021).
[21] Russian Federation (2019).
[22] Republic of Singapore (2019).
[23] Official Gazette of the Republic of Turkey (2007).
[24] Department for Digital, Culture, Media and Sport (2021).
[25] US Government Publishing Office (1996).
[26] Government of Zimbabwe (2019).

3. Increasing liabilities for online content resulting in financial punishments or imprisonment.

While all three of these mechanisms used to increase a company's or user's compliance with national or regional legal frameworks could be applied within reasonable and human rights compliant frameworks, there has been a lot of scrutiny around how these regulations are being introduced and the vague language and definitions concerning the online content legislation it is meant to apply to. It is also the case that legal requirements of one country or region are increasingly contradictory when compared to another country or region's approach. With a highly transnational online space, this clash will become increasingly apparent, with companies forced to make decisions about which legal framework(s) to adhere to.

Mandatory Removal of Content

The newer regulations that have been or are in the process of being introduced in the EU, UK, France, Germany, Australia, New Zealand, India, Pakistan, Singapore, Canada, Ethiopia, Lesotho, Morocco, and Turkey all include increased content removal requirements by internet service providers based on the type of harmful content a government body identifies. In some cases, such as the EU Terrorist Content Online Regulation, the new regulation gives authority to mandate wider removals from numerous national "competent authorities" that might include judicial bodies, policing bodies, or regulatory bodies within a given European country. These regulations, apart from Singapore, the UK, and Lesotho, include time requirements for the removal of the government-flagged content ranging between one hour and 24 hours. Failure to comply with removal requests within the given time frame can incur increasingly severe fines and other legal repercussions for platforms or internet service providers.

It is understandable that governments look to the expedient removal of "terrorist and violent extremist content" as something considered illegal content online. However, many civil society and academic critics have pointed to the dangers of time-pressured removals, particularly given the lack of common definitions of what constitutes terrorist content and the capacities of smaller and medium tech companies. Legislation that focuses on expedited removal of content without context or nuance has been criticized for pushing companies toward overcensorship and threatening journalists, human rights defenders, and academics who preserve and use this content to highlight global abuses. As an example, 61 human rights organizations, journalists associations, and research institutes came out to urge members of the European Parliament to vote against the EU Terrorist Content Online Regulation.[1] The primary opposition cited the regulation's continued push for automated removals breaching into user privacy without nuanced oversight, the lack of independent judicial oversight, and the expanded remit for member states to issue cross-border removals without proper checks and balances.

This final point of contention about giving a country or region more powers to enforce the removal of "terrorist content" beyond national boundaries is of particular concern to human rights activists and journalists who fear this legislation imposes greater censorship on already marginalized or persecuted groups based on loose national definitions of what terrorism means. It can also be used to censor journalists or human rights groups that document atrocities to hold powers to account. The legislation raised in Pakistan (Karanicolas 2020), Singapore (,[2] Brazil (Nojeim 2020), Canada, and France aim to increase the remit for removal orders beyond national boundaries in the name of security measures. However, this is also where we start seeing a divide in the implementation of such laws between more democratic versus authoritarian-leaning regimes. In the French and Canadian cases, where higher levels of democratic oversight and division of power exist, both laws have had significant push back. In the Canadian case, as the law remains pending at the time of writing this chapter, many experts are already saying the law would violate Canadians' constitutional and privacy rights, with direct criticism from the Canadian Privacy Commission (Karadeglija 2021). In France, the Avia law was adopted in May 2020 and then brought by the French Senate to the Constitutional Council where it was ultimately deemed unconstitutional in June 2020 (Berthélémy 2020). These cases begin to highlight a divide in how legislation is being implemented around the world, with fewer structural mechanisms to ensure legal frameworks are necessary, appropriate, and proportionate in less democratic countries.

Increasing Government Access to User Data

Several legislative frameworks listed also move to give governments increased access to user data under the umbrella of increasing security efforts online. As the offline-online interplay in all aspects of life has increased, so has the need for law enforcement efforts to work in the online space to assist in detecting, analyzing, and acting upon online signals of crime, including terrorism and violent extremism. Laws being put forward in Brazil, the EU, India, Kenya, Pakistan, the Philippines, Poland, Russia, and Turkey put in place increased mandatory data retention time and often demands for localized data retention. This is a point where legislation to protect privacy begins to clash with legislation to increase security. As a prime example, the General Data Protection Regulation 2016/679 (GDPR) is a regulation in EU law on data protection and privacy in the European Union and the European Economic Area. It mandates that data must be stored for the shortest time possible, considering the reasons why a company needs to process the data, as well as any legal obligations to keep the data for a fixed period of time.[3] Companies are asked to establish time limits to erase or review data stored.

Many of the laws reviewed for this research include mandatory data retention periods showing disparities in what a reasonable holding period might be. In the listed legislations, data must be held for at least three months for Brazil, six months for the EU and India, and 12 months for Poland. There is little evidence for why these time frames are chosen, but companies often attempt to hold global policies since disentangling online activity to one country is difficult, if not impossible, depending how users operate on a platform. For example, if there is a piece of content created by an online user in Australia and that content is shared by a user in Pakistan to a user in France, which jurisdiction does the one post sharing this piece of content fall under? While many companies have looked to expand GDPR compliance to a global remit, there are few standardized or internationally recognized parameters about what reasonable data retention time frames should be and what government access to data is permissible. For example, while many privacy laws, such as GDPR and E-Privacy, look to safeguard personally identifiable information (PII), Brazilian legislation includes the increased retention of traceability requirements on messaging platforms, storing of login details for any user that has over a 5,000-person reach, and mandatory identification verification (Alimonti 2020).

Data localization is also a newer trend in legal frameworks to increase government access to source data. Data localization is when the law dictates that servers housing company data must physically exist in the country of operation. Laws mandating server-side data localization are apparent in the Russia, Turkey, and Pakistan legislations listed in Table 2.1. Human rights concerns remain over the potential to use the physical presence of data servers to increase government access to user data without due oversight. Data localization rules can make data vulnerable to security threats and undue government surveillance while imposing barriers to international trade and commerce online (Komaitis 2017). While, as mentioned before, the French law was dismantled by the Constitutional Council in France, other countries do not have the checks and balances to prevent the misuse of server localization as a means of increasing government access to user data.

Increasing Liabilities for Online Content: Financial Punishments or Imprisonment

India, Pakistan, Brazil, Kenya, and Turkey have legislation that requires a physical staff from companies to reside in the country of operation. Mandating the physical presence of employees has been criticized as a means for using human leverage to force companies into wider compliance as these employees can be jailed or fined if their company is seen as not optimally complying with the government (Horwitz and Purnell 2021). Critics have warned that in countries with less democratic oversight and heightened executive powers, having physical offices in a country means the company will face the same constraints as traditional media, making it difficult to defy government requests for data or online content removals (Yackley 2021).

There are clear divides and gaps when looking globally at the various approaches to developing legal frameworks and implementation to counter terrorism and violent extremism. There is a continual clash between safeguards for free speech, concerns for user privacy, and government strengthening of safety mechanisms. While there are those that argue free speech is too important to be regulated by private companies, human rights advocates equally argue that a range of new laws targeting social media highlight some of the dangers of leaving it to individual governments (Keller 2019).

The Provision of Feminist-Driven Solutions

Feminist theory literature has built a strong catalogue of resources to analyze the balancing needs between privacy and equity that impact gender in our experiences online. However, there has been less discourse directed at unpacking the engagement of feminist critical theory on wider power imbalances of data protection through the lens of protection imbalance as a manifestation of nouveau data colonialism. Looking at the previously mapped legislations, only touching on one umbrella area of "online harms," the impact of internet fragmentation and the splintering of previously universally applied protections is palpable. This transition is moving the online sphere into a new frontier where portions of the globe's population are afforded a higher caliber of protections compared to other populations who have little to no control over their data privacy due to where they are physically based.

Analyzing Data Colonialism Through a Feminist Critique

In conceptualizing a framework to adequately address the challenges presented by the increasing imbalance of protection provided to internet users, it is useful to lean in on the lens of data colonialism. Initially introduced by Thatcher et al. (2016), the term "data colonialism" effectively encapsulates the interplay of tech influence with the motifs of choice, resource, and disparity. In their work framing the concept, Couldry and Mejias (2021, 2–3) ask what would happen if we interpreted data and technology today in terms of not just historical but also contemporary relations between colonialism and capitalism? Viewed from this lens, the question becomes less historically comparative and moves closer to an evaluation of the power dynamics implicit in today's operationalization of data capitalism. Historic colonization had severe impacts on national resources and disparate depletion of opportunities for affected populations for generations. Seeing a potentially similar trend in data colonization means that applying a feminist critique through the lens of a feminist assessment of power structures is fitting.

While, currently, the concern is on US-based tech companies with Western and US-focused policy structures, there is an increasing shift away from the original US-based platform dominance. In a 2021 OECD analysis, 15 of the top 50 social media companies with the largest user bases are based in China (OECD 2021). This trend marks a shifting imbalance in the infrastructure intrinsic to internal platform-specific policies, the implicit cultural assumptions made, and the core financial beneficiaries. While this is an important portion of the discussion, it presents a partial image of harm.

Hill Collins (2009) outlines themes of dominance within society, including the structural sphere. Utilizing this framing, we posit that, on the one hand, the presence of protection of some users is, in and of itself, a positive action. However, when viewed through the lens of selective protectionism, the very absence of protections in countries where there exists a "matrix of domination" (Collins 2009) makes the community lacking protections further vulnerable and creates a level of progressive harm that ties closely to the historical process of colonization and resource relocation. Adding to this imbalance, the surging fragmentation of protections outlined in the previous section and the intrinsic contrast in the legislative safeguards in place in the Global South present a unique opportunity to assess this challenge and provide solution-oriented suggestions from a feminist lens.

Global Application of Protections and Balancing Representation in Cyberspace Protection

Global legislative fracturing has, in turn, led to a varied spectrum of legal protections for online users. While most of the legislation reviewed pertains to cybercriminality and counterterrorism efforts, the subset of legislation aimed at addressing data protection is still lacking in geographic parity. To help unpack this, we can pull from the theory that our interaction with power must be placed within a framework of the many paradigms of power, including the intersecting forms of privilege and oppression that sit at the core of feminist theory (Crenshaw 1989). To push back on further power imbalances and inequities for online users, in managing data protection and cybersecurity online, approaches to legislative frameworks will benefit from three main shifts:

1. Ensuring global baseline internet user-protection standards are developed by a set of geographically diverse stakeholders with thematic representation.
2. Building safeguards so that protections are global and equitable so they are not selectively applied to communities or jurisdictions.
3. Housing these standards within a globally recognized body that tech companies or civil society representatives can lean in on if they need to push back on attempts by governments to backslide on baseline protections.

A keen assessment and questioning of established power relations is fundamental to feminist and postcolonial theory. MacKinnon's critique of gender dynamics highlights the need to unpack structural, societal, and legal power dynamics (MacKinnon 1987). Forums built around the understanding and development of these legislations have so far aimed to include a wide variety of technical perspectives. Yet this approach is limited and lacks a consistent engagement with the varied technical and, importantly, geographic reach of social media and big-tech tools.

Beyond this, the limited engagement around the imbalances presented in data colonialism can sometimes fall into the trap of categorizing the global legislative landscape into Western or non-Western groupings when assessing the efficacy of such legal frameworks. Here, an engagement with postcolonial literature outlines a more nuanced assessment of the issues at play, as Swati Parashar (2016, 371) notes, "we now know [the] difference is not just between the West and non-West but within these geographies and temporalities as well and any universalism is discursive violence that writes out histories and mutes voices."

Through this lens, we can more granularly unpack the legislative needs of the wider global user base without the assumption that Western legislation is the most optimal or ineffective approach. In fact, a move toward a more global and diverse input structure allows these protections to better assess the needs of a variable, global user base where the majority of data, innovation, and first adopters are based in the regions categorized by tech platforms as Sub-Saharan Africa and Asia Pacific.

Building non-performative forums that allow for meaningful global representation can ensure robust and tangible engagement (Spelman 1988). Sectoral diversity is also key. Government, tech companies, and civil society representation each bring expertise and perspective about necessary problems and solutions.

Finally, at the core of the imbalance created by data colonialism is the growing body of legislation that, intentionally or otherwise, creates jurisdictional imbalances in the online protections afforded to users. While this fragmentation is only now starting to be unpacked, the broader implications of continuous inaction by states and international bodies is allowing increased isolationist policies by individual countries, leading to a foundational imbalance that will be very difficult to correct over time. Guidelines and standards for baseline protections of global internet users need to be housed by an international body, like the United Nations, so that stakeholders have resolutions and mandates to look to when flagging data abuses to users or when pushing back on pending national legislation that will lead to undermining user-data protections.

Feminist-Driven Solutions

Feminist theory provides the key to conceptualizing a solution to address the imbalances faced when considering more expansive global protections for online user data. This chapter argues that producing an equitable playing field of data protection for users on a global scale will require the framework to be built on three main tenants: representation, intersectionality, and resourcing. In considering these three tenants, we begin with the basic premise that representation around this issue must, at its very core, be inclusive and requires a global inclusion of multistakeholder voices. As we move forward toward a globally balanced protection of rights, active efforts of inclusion must be at the forefront of our approach. Ensuring that there is a global scale of participation from countries on all points of the spectrum of legislative protections will allow for a more holistic understanding of the challenges faced by others grappling with the production of effective, scalable, and operational guidance.

Similarly, as we aim to progress representation of experiences from a global perspective, it behooves us to also apply an intersectional framework to assess the myriad of issue-based challenges facing governments, civil society, and tech platforms. Considering the triple axis approach of holistically assessing (1) privacy, (2) safety, and (3) voice to create a more nuanced understanding of how these legal frameworks create and enshrine modes of discrimination and privilege. Moreover, we propose that the assessment of the issue through an intersectional lens allows for a greater awareness of regional and/or national issues and an application of policies by platforms. Thus, we can solve national issues through means that have a magnified global impact.

Finally, at the core of discussions on legal framework imbalances is the need for all stakeholders to have equal access to the resourcing required to build scalable and operational data protections. While most partners are well versed in the legal parameters of the discussion around data protection, as posited and tied to privacy, the core tenants of data privacy are built on complex, quickly evolving, and highly technical infrastructure. To fully grasp the scope of the challenge and to effectively build with that design in mind, partners need access to resourcing, including academic insights, an understanding of the evolving threat landscape, and the limitations and frontiers around how data manifests. This is a potentially resource-heavy endeavor in the short term, with great benefits and resource saving in the long term. This effort requires a multistakeholder approach, with benefactors from better resourced international bodies, countries, and tech companies.

Notes

1. Liberties EU (2021).
2. Tech Against Terrorism (2021).
3. European Union (2020).

References

Alimonti, Veridiana. 2020. "Brazil's Fake News Bill Would Dismantle Crucial Rights Online and Is on a Fast Track to Become Law." Electronic Frontier Foundation, 24 June. https://www.eff.org/deeplinks/2020/06/current-brazils-fake-news-bill-would-dismantle-crucial-rights-online-and-fast.

Anand, Meghan, et al. 2021. "All of the Congressional Proposals to Change Section 230." *Slate*, March 23. https://slate.com/technology/2021/03/section-230-reform-legislative-tracker.html.

Assemblée Nationale. 2019. "Proposition de loi n° 1785 visant à lutter contre la haine sur internet." French Government, March 20. https://www.assemblee-nationale.fr/dyn/15/textes/l15b1785_proposition-loi.

Berthélémy, Chloé. 2020. "French Avia Law Declared Unconstitutional: What Does This Teach Us at EU Level?" *European Digital Rights (EDRi)*, June 24. https://edri.org/our-work/french-avia-law-declared-unconstitutional-what-does-this-teach-us-at-eu-level/.

Búndesgesétzblatt. 2021. "Gesetz zur Änderung des Netzwerkdurchsetzungsgesetzes." *Búndesgesétzblatt* (Federal Law Gazette), June. https://www.bgbl.de/xaver/bgbl/start.xav?startbk=Bundesanzeiger_BGBl&jumpTo=bgbl121s1436.pdf.

Burkina Faso, Assemblee Nationale. 2018. *Projet de Loi: An Portant Modification de la Loi No. 025-2018/ An du 31 Mai 2018 Portant Code Penal* (Modifications to Laws 025-2018 and to May 2018 Penal Codes). 7th Legislature. https://perma.cc/VZ3T-NS3V.

Collins, Patricia Hill. 2009. *Black Feminist Thought: Knowledge, Consciousness, and the Politics of Empowerment*. Routledge.

Congress of the Philippines Eighteenth Congress. 2020. "Senate S. No. 1083: The Anti-Terrorism Act of 2020." Senate of the Philippines 18th Congress. http://legacy.senate.gov.ph/lisdata/3163229242!.pdf.

Couldry, Nick, and Ulises Ali Mejias. 2021. "The Decolonial Turn in Data and Technology Research: What Is at Stake and Where Is It Heading?" *Information, Communication & Society*, November (online). https://doi.org/10.1080/1369118X.2021.1986102.

Crenshaw, Kimberle. 1989. "Demarginalizing the Intersection of Race and Sex: A Black Feminist Critique of Antidiscrimination Doctrine, Feminist Theory and Antiracist Politics." *University of Chicago Legal Forum* 1: Article 8.

Department for Digital, Culture, Media and Sport. 2021. "Draft Online Safety Bill." UK Government, May 29. https://assets.publishing.service.gov.uk/government/uploads/system/uploads/attachment_data/file/985033/Draft_Online_Safety_Bill_Bookmarked.pdf.

European Commission. 2020.*Proposal for a Regulation of the European Parliament and of the Council on a Single Market for Digital Services (Digital Services Act) and Amending Directive 2000/31/EC*. December 15. https://digital-strategy.ec.europa.eu/en/library/proposal-regulation-european-parliament-and-council-single-market-digital-services-digital-services.

European Union. 2020. "For How Long Can Data Be Kept and Is It Necessary to Update It?" https://ec.europa.eu/info/law/law-topic/data-protection/reform/rules-business-and-organisations/principles-gdpr/how-long-can-data-be-kept-and-it-necessary-update-it_en.

Federal Democratic Republic of Ethiopia. 2020. "Hate Speech and Disinformation Prevention and Suppression Proclamation/ Proclamation No. 1185 /2020." Access Now, March 23. https://www.accessnow.org/cms/assets/uploads/2020/05/Hate-Speech-and-Disinformation-Prevention-and-Suppression-Proclamation.pdf.

Federal Senate of Brazil. 2020. "Law PL 2630/2020." https://www25.senado.leg.br/web/atividade/materias/-/materia/141944.

German Government. 2017. "Act to Improve Enforcement of the Law in Social Networks (Network Enforcement Act)." Gesetzgebungsverfahren (Federal Ministry of Justice), July 12. https://www.bmj.de/SharedDocs/Gesetzgebungsverfahren/Dokumente/NetzDG_engl.pdf?__blob=publicationFile&v=2.

Government of Canada. 2021. "The Government's Proposed Approach to Address Harmful Content Online." July 29. https://www.canada.ca/en/canadian-heritage/campaigns/harmful-online-content/technical-paper.html.

Government of Pakistan. 2020. "e Citizens Protection (Against Online Harm) Rules, 2020." Ministry of Information Technology, January 21. https://moitt.gov.pk/SiteImage/Misc/files/CP%20(Against%20Online%20Harm)%20Rules%2c%202020.pdf.

Government of Zimbabwe. 2019. "63246-W Cyber Security & Data Bill." Veritaszim. https://t3n9sm.c2.acecdn.net/wp-content/uploads/2020/05/Cyber-Security-and-Data-Protection-Bill.pdf.

Horwitz, Jeff, and Newly Purnell. 2021. "India Threatens Jail for Facebook, WhatsApp and Twitter Employees." *Wall Street Journal*, March 5. https://www.wsj.com/articles/india-threatens-jail-for-facebook-whatsapp-and-twitter-employees-11614964542.

Indian Ministry of Information and Broadcasting. 2021. "Digital Media Guidelines and Policies: I.T. (Intermediary Guidelines and Digital Media Ethics Code), Rules, 2021." March 2. https://mib.gov.in/digital-media-guidelines-and-policies.

Karadeglija, Anja. 2021. "Privacy Commissioner Not Consulted over Controversial Online Harms Bill." *National Post*, October 25. https://nationalpost.com/news/politics/privacy-commissioner-not-consulted-over-controversial-online-harms-bill.

Karanicolas, Michael. 2020. "Newly Published Citizens Protection (Against Online Harm) Rules Are a Disaster for Freedom of Expression in Pakistan." Yale Law School, February 29. https://law.yale.edu/isp/initiatives/wikimedia-initiative-intermediaries-and-information/wiii-blog/newly-published-citizens-protection-against-online-harm-rules-are-disaster-freedom-expression.

Keller, Daphne. 2019. "Who Do You Sue? State and Platform Hybrid Power over Online Speech." Aegis Series Paper No. 1902, Hoover Institution. https://www.hoover.org/sites/default/files/research/docs/who-do-you-sue-state-and-platform-hybrid-power-over-online-speech_0.pdf.

Khamlichi, Yasmine El. 2020. "Projet de loi 22.20: Quid des droits du consommateur marocain?" *Maroc Diplomatique*, April 29. https://maroc-diplomatique.net/projet-de-loi-22-20-quid-des-droits-du-consommateur-marocain/.

Komaitis, Konstantinos. 2017. "The 'Wicked Problem' of Data Localisation." *Journal of Cyber Policy* 2, no. 3: 355–365. https://doi.org/10.1080/23738871.2017.1402942.

Parashar, Swati. 2016. "Feminism and Postcolonialism: (En)gendering Encounters" *Feminism Meets Postcolonialism: Rethinking Gender, State and Political Violence* 19, no. 4: 371–377.

Kwet, Michael. 2021. "Digital Colonialism: The Evolution of American Empire." *ROAR Magazine*, 3 March 3. https://roarmag.org/essays/digital-colonialism-the-evolution-of-american-empire/.

Liberties EU. 2021. "Free Speech Advocates Urge EU Legislators to Vote 'No' to Automated Censorship Online." Civil Liberties Union for Europe, March 25. https://www.liberties.eu/en/stories/terrorist-content-regulation-open-letter-to-meps/43410.

MacKinnon, Catharine A. 1987. *Feminism Unmodified: Discourses on Life and Law*. Cambridge, MA: Harvard University Press.

Manurung, Rahel O., et al. 2021. "New Regulation on Electronic System Organizers in the Private Sector." Makarim & Taira S Advisory: Counsellors at Law, January 7. https://www.makarim.com/storage/uploads/7b6937fc-15ba-41ab-a8ba-96f29d9c746c/583428_Jan-2021---New-Regulation-on-Electronic-System-Organizers-in-the-Private-Sector-(final).pdf.

National Assembly of the Federal Republic of Nigeria. 2019a. "An Act to Make Provisions for the Protection from Internet Falsehoods and Manipulation and other Related Offences Bill." Policy and Legal Advocacy Centre. https://placbillstrack.org/upload/SB132.pdf.

National Assembly of the Federal Republic of Nigeria. 2019b. "National Commission for the Prohibition of Hate Speeches (Est, etc) Bill, 2019 (SB. 154)." *Premium Times Nigeria*. https://media.premiumtimesng.com/wp-content/files/2019/11/ational-Commission-of-Prohibition-of-Hate-Speeches-Bill-2019-1.pdf.

New Zealand Parliamentary Counsel Office. 2021. "Films, Videos, and Publications Classification (Urgent Interim Classification of Publications and Prevention of Online Harm) Amendment Bill 268-3 (2020), Government Bill—New Zealand Legislation." https://www.legislation.govt.nz/bill/government/2020/0268/latest/whole.html#LMS294551.

Nojeim, Greg. 2020. "Update on Brazil's Fake News Bill: The Draft Approved by the Senate Continues to Jeopardize Users' Rights." *Center for Democracy and Technology*, July 24. https://cdt.org/insights/update-on-brazils-fake-news-bill-the-draft-approved-by-the-senate-continues-to-jeopardize-users-rights/.

OECD. 2021. "Transparency Reporting on Terrorist and Violent Extremist Content Online: An Update on the Global Top 50 Content Sharing Services." *OECD Digital Economy Papers* N313, no. N313: 5.https://www.oecd-ilibrary.org/, https://www.

oecd-ilibrary.org/https://www.oecd-ilibrary.org/, https://www.oecd-ilibrary.org/science-and-technology/transparency-reporting-on-terrorist-and-violent-extremist-content-online_8af4ab29-en.

Official Gazette of the Republic of Turkey. 2007. "Organization of Publications Made on the Internet and This Fighting Crimes Committed Through Publications About the Law." *Resmi Gazete*, May 23. https://www.resmigazete.gov.tr/eskiler/2007/05/20070523-1.htm.

Official Journal of the European Union. "L172." *Official Journal of the European Union* 64 (online, EUR-Lex). https://eur-lex.europa.eu/legal-content/EN/TXT/PDF/?uri=OJ:L:2021:172:FULL&from=EN.

Parliament of Australia. 2021. "Online Safety Bill 2021—Parliament of Australia." https://www.aph.gov.au/Parliamentary_Business/Bills_LEGislation/Bills_Search_Results/Result?bId=r6680.

Polish Ministry of Justice. 2021. "Zachęcamy do zapoznania się z projektem ustawy o ochronie wolności użytkowników serwisów społecznościowych—Ministerstwo Sprawiedliwości." February 1. https://www.gov.pl/web/sprawiedliwosc/zachecamy-do-zapoznania-sie-z-projektem-ustawy-o-ochronie-wolnosci-uzytkownikow-serwisow-spolecznosciowych.

Republic of Kenya. "National Assembly Bills 2019." *Kenya Gazette Supplement*, 125, no. National Assembly Bills No. 61, 2019, p. 941. *Bowmans Law,* https://www.bowmanslaw.com/wp-content/uploads/2019/10/Kenya-Information-and-Communication-Amendment-Bill-2019-No.2_compressed.pdf.

Republic of Singapore. "Protection from Online Falsehoods and Manipulation Act 2019—Singapore Statutes Online." Government Gazette Acts Supplement, June 3. https://sso.agc.gov.sg/Acts-Supp/18-2019/Published/20190625.

Russian Federation. 2019. "Федеральный закон от 02.12.2019 № 405-ФЗ · Официальное опубликование правовых актов · Официальный интернет-портал правовой информации (Federal Law No. 405-FZ of December 2, 2019 "On Amendments to Certain Legislative Acts of the Russian Federation."). *Официальное опубликование*, December 2. http://publication.pravo.gov.ru/Document/View/0001201912020045.

Spelman, Elizabeth V. 1988. *Inessential Woman: Problems of Exclusion in Feminist Thought*. Boston: Beacon Press.

Tech Against Terrorism. 2021. "The Online Regulation Series: The Handbook." July. https://www.techagainstterrorism.org/wp-content/uploads/2021/07/Tech-Against-Terrorism-%E2%80%93-The-Online-Regulation-Series-%E2%80%93-The-Handbook-2021.pdf.

Thatcher, Jim, et al. 2016. "Data Colonialism Through Accumulation by Dispossession: New Metaphors for Daily Data." *Environment and Planning D: Society and Space* 34, no. 6 (December): 990–1006. https://doi.org/10.1177/0263775816633195.

UN Human Rights Council. 2011. "Report of the Special Rapporteur on the Promotion and Protection of the Right to Freedom of Opinion and Expression, Frank La Rue." May 16. https://www2.ohchr.org/english/bodies/hrcouncil/docs/17session/A.HRC.17.27_en.pdf.

US Government Publishing Office. 1996. "Page 80 Title 47—Telegraphs, Telephone, and Radiotelegraphs § 230 (3)." Govinfo.gov, February 8. https://www.govinfo.gov/content/pkg/USCODE-2011-title47/pdf/USCODE-2011-title47-chap5-subchapII-partI-sec230.pdf.

Yackley, Jean. "Turkey's Social Media Law: A Cautionary Tale." POLITICO, March 29. https://www.politico.eu/article/turkeys-social-media-law-a-cautionary-tale/.

PART II
CYBERSECURITY AND SOCIETY IN THE GLOBAL SOUTH

3
Gendered and Postcolonial Perspectives on Data Weaponization in Armed Conflict

The Case of Afghanistan

Julia-Silvana Hofstetter

Introduction

After the Taliban seized control over significant parts of Afghanistan in August 2021, concerns were raised regarding the masses of personal data collected and shared over 20 years by various international actors that could put hundreds of thousands of Afghans at risk. Confirming these fears, the Taliban communicated early on that they had gained access to biometric data and started using it to identify and hunt down Afghans who had worked with international actors and the former Afghan government. Thousands of Afghans also rushed to delete their online identities and digital histories and remained in hiding over a year after the takeover, still fearing death by data. In the aftermath of the seizure, technology companies, such as Facebook and Twitter, and international and regional civil society organizations quickly came to help Afghans, providing support and guidance on how to erase their online identities and evade surveillance.

The case of Afghanistan has forced the international community to reassess how data collection and digital communication tools become risk factors for vulnerable populations in times of crisis. Yet, while a growing body of research and policy debate addresses how digital technologies increasingly impact conflict dynamics and provide authoritarian regimes and conflict parties with new instruments to perpetrate violence and persecute adversaries, the risks of data weaponization in armed conflict are still underexplored, particularly regarding gender-specific vulnerabilities.

Based on an empirical analysis of Afghanistan, the chapter explores how conflict actors weaponize personal data to prosecute adversaries and how this affects women and other marginalized groups. It discusses the role of data collected by international actors—from foreign militaries to international humanitarian organizations and national government agencies—and personal information, available online and accessed through surveillance technology. The chapter also discusses the limitations of the international community's emergency response strategies. Finally, analyzing the case of Afghanistan through a postcolonial and feminist perspective, the chapter further builds theory on how gendered and colonial discriminatory structures and ideologies enable and shape data weaponization in conflict contexts and also outlines how deconstructing these underlying factors serves to improve data management and crisis response mechanisms addressed at mitigating the risks of data weaponization in conflict contexts, emphasizing citizens' digital agency and the need to address gender-specific vulnerabilities.

Literature Review and Research Gaps

The chapter speaks to three main areas of policy debate and scholarly literature that approach data weaponization through different angles: digital authoritarianism, humanitarian data governance, and gender-based cyber violence. Especially the discussion on technocolonialism in the humanitarian sector and feminist approaches to cybersecurity hold valuable insights for a deeper discussion of a postcolonial and gender-sensitive analysis of data weaponization, as discussed in more detail later in the chapter.

Under the term "digital authoritarianism," a growing body of literature analyzes how authoritarian regimes increasingly use digital technologies for political repression, including strategies ranging from censoring online content to spreading online propaganda and disinformation, online harassment, or digital surveillance (e.g., Dragu and Lupu 2021). Digital repression strategies aim to not only assert control by prosecuting political opponents directly but also limit civic spaces for political mobilization. In extreme cases, states establish an all-encompassing and society-wide surveillance ecosystem, instrumentalizing vast amounts of digital data ranging from social media activities to online consumption behavior, travel bookings, medical records, and cell phone location data to identify possible threats to their authority. In this context, "data weaponization" can be defined as a digital repression strategy in which data gathering and digital surveillance are used to identify and locate political opponents or specific demographic groups to control and, in severe cases, physically harm them. Digital data and modern technologies allow repressive governments to assess or identify who is a political opponent or part of the target group as well as to locate already identified targets with greater efficiency and precision. Current discussions in the field also address the critical role of private companies cooperating with authoritarian regimes, providing invasive surveillance technologies or sharing user data from apps and social media platforms. While feminist scholars have long pointed to the dangers of authoritarian regimes using gender politics and prosecuting women human rights defenders to secure their power (e.g., Lorch and Bunk 2016), less research exists on how technology facilitates these tactics. In the literature on digital authoritarianism, the weaponization of data aimed at discriminating against women as well as other gender and sexual minorities has not been systematically studied yet. The few scholars that analyze digital repression strategies by state actors through a gendered lens primarily focus on online harassment and disinformation against women in politics (Bardall 2023) and LGBTQ groups (Acconcia et al. 2022), and some authors have also looked at the gendered impacts of internet shutdowns (Shoker 2022). Recent examples of data sharing between reproductive health apps providers and anti-abortion politicians in the US or reports of government agencies infiltrating dating apps to identify and arrest LGBTQ individuals in Egypt, Iran, and Lebanon also indicate the need for further analysis of the gender-specific vulnerabilities of seemingly non-weaponizable data in light of state surveillance.

Human rights organizations are also increasingly documenting cases where governments use surveillance and other strategies of digital repression in the context of armed conflict. For example, well documented is the Syrian regime's systematic expansion of a mass surveillance system resulting in arrests, torture, and deaths of opponents (Dávila et al. 2021). Also, recent examples from Myanmar, where online harassment against women drastically increased in the aftermath of the military's seizure of power in February 2021, Al Jazeera Staff (2023) raise questions on how fragile contexts and armed conflict settings alter and increase certain gendered risks associated with digital authoritarianism.

While systematic research on the specificities of digital repression in armed conflict is still lacking, the literature on humanitarian data governance can provide some insight into the difficulties of data protection and privacy in fragile contexts (see, e.g., Jacobsen and Fast 2019). Humanitarian organizations have considerable experience with collecting and managing highly sensitive data in conflict-affected contexts and how the potential abuse of sensitive data puts vulnerable populations at risk—not only in cases where sensitive information falls into the hands of warring factions due to data leakages or data breaches, but also where humanitarian organizations voluntarily share data with third-party actors such as host governments, multilateral organizations, and private service providers likewise opening up opportunities for the weaponization of sensitive data. Under the terms of "surveillance humanitarianism" (Latonero 2019) and "technocolonialism" (Madianou 2019), humanitarian organizations have been criticized for their extensive use of biometric technology, which reproduces colonial forms of exploitation, extraction, and control. By theorizing colonial mechanisms that shape data collection in armed-conflict contexts, this literature also helps better understand the enabling factors of data weaponization in fragile contexts. However, while the literature on humanitarian data governance offers essential insights into the dangers of digital data in armed-conflict contexts, especially biometric data, other data sources and types, such as public data collected by national governments or social media and other online data, are not being addressed. Also, a gender perspective is still largely missing. Although data governance guidelines from the humanitarian sector acknowledge women and other gender and sexual minorities as especially vulnerable groups, an in-depth discussion on the gendered risks associated with humanitarian data does not exist.

The growing field of policy and academic literature on gender-based cyberviolence helps address this gap to a certain extent. "Cyberviolence" refers to a wide range of technology-facilitated violence, from cyberstalking to online hate speech and harassment, the nonconsensual sharing of private information, and attacks on communication channels. This literature offers insights into the gendered risks associated with cyberviolence on an not only at the individual level, for example, women and other gender and sexual minorities are at a higher risk from privacy breaches that lead to physical violence (Yao 2019; Brown and Pytlak 2020), but also at the societal level, for instance, when limited access to technology or verified online information further limits these groups access to economic opportunities or education or when online violence leads to the (self-)silencing of these voices in public discourse. Beyond gendered cyberviolence, current discussions in the broader field of cybersecurity policy also consider gender-specific risks associated with cybersecurity threats that are not gendered, for example, when cyberattacks on critical infrastructure have different consequences for different population groups. However, much of the literature on gender-based cyberviolence focuses on the citizen-to-citizen level. It is based on a traditional understanding of cybersecurity where the state is seen as the primary security provider and is generally not considered a cyber-threat actor for its citizens. Acknowledging that the state can be a perpetrator of gender-based cyberviolence as well would be crucial to capture gendered cybersecurity risks in their entirety while allowing one to make a connection to the digital authoritarianism literature. Critical cybersecurity studies have long advocated for such a shift in the conceptualization of cybersecurity toward a human-centric approach (see, e.g., Deibert 2018). While conventional definitions of cybersecurity focus on businesses and state infrastructure as targets of cyberattacks and nonstate-threat actors with criminal objectives as perpetrators, human-centric cybersecurity focuses on threats to citizens. It allows for conceptualizing the co-production of cybersecurity (on citizen co-production of cybersecurity, see Chang Zhong and Grabosky 2018), where citizens and civil society are contributors to the security infrastructure. The traditional focus of cybersecurity scholars and practitioners on state institutions as targets of cyberattacks is also reflected in the emerging field of cyberwar research, which focuses on interstate cyber conflict and critical infrastructure and military data as targets of cyberattacks (e.g., Shires 2020; Smeets 2018; Thomas and Zhang 2020).

This chapter adds to the literature discussed above by analyzing data weaponization in armed conflict, relying on a human-centric definition of cybersecurity and adding a feminist and postcolonial lens. It connects different research strains and fills a gap in the discussions on the nexus between digital repression, gender, and armed conflict.

Postcolonial and Feminist Theory

For the empirical analysis of data weaponization in the context of the 2021 Taliban takeover in Afghanistan, the chapter applies concepts from feminist and postcolonial studies as a theoretical framework. Theoretical notions of technocolonialism help explain the formation of the digital infrastructure in fragile contexts that enables data weaponization, while feminist theory allows informing the discussion on how patriarchal ideology shapes data weaponization opportunities and gender-specific vulnerabilities.

Technocolonialism

Two main logics help describe how the use of technology in the context of humanitarian operations reflects and reconstructs colonial relationships and power hierarchies between international actors and local populations (broadly based on Madianou 2019): Colonial rationality places primacy in the governing potentials of external actors and inferiorizes local populations, which strips their agency and rights and reproduces relationships of dependency; the discriminatory structures of colonial legacies enable the extraction of value from humanitarian data through public and private actors, especially when humanitarian crises are treated as testing sites for new technological applications.

The colonial logic legitimizes international actors to prioritize the collection of vast amounts of data and the deployment of invasive surveillance technologies to assert control in crisis situations over local populations' rights to data privacy and agency. This de-prioritization of the local population's digital rights creates a "digital underclass" forced to share data in exchange for basic needs without the dignity of choice (Latonero 2019).

The technocolonialist critique also sheds light on how this colonial logic enables various stakeholders, from humanitarian organizations to donor countries and private companies, to use humanitarian crises for value extraction. Moreover, this extractive dynamic is reinforced by technology as it introduces a "capitalist logic" to the humanitarian sector that merges humanitarian aid with business interests (Madianou 2019, 5), where humanitarian settings are seen as investment opportunities (see, e.g., Aglionby 2018) or used as testing sites for new technologies (such as the iris-scan devices deployed by EyeHood in UNHCR refugee camps; see Leurs et al. 2019, 94–96). Technocolonialism's critique, however, also expands to the colonial behavior of global technology companies and social media platforms in the Global South in general, where these actors pay less attention to data security standards of their devices and services, are often reluctant to invest resources in online content moderation that would make online spaces safer (Takhshid 2021), or provide free services to extract personal data (Vaidhyanathan 2018; Bhatia 2016).

Data Privacy and Surveillance in the Patriarchy

A gender analysis of data weaponization in armed conflict involves examining how gender roles influence individuals' needs, opportunities, activities, and rights. A few key concepts from feminist research on patriarchy (Hunnicutt 2009; Runyan and Peterson 2013.) can help guide such an analysis. First, patriarchal ideology retains gender as a central organizing feature of society. Patriarchal societies are based on systems of male domination and female subordination. Men are positioned at the head of households, communities, and states, which incentivize heterosexual family structures and the repatriation of women to the private sphere. Thus, gender discrimination in patriarchal societies also has implications for defining what constitutes sensitive data. Whether data puts individuals at risk for political prosecution or discrimination depends on preexisting discriminatory structures reflected in society and in government institutions. Suppose the government is based on a patriarchal ideology that discriminates against women. In that case, specific categories of information that are not sensitive for men can put women and other gender and sexual minorities at risk. Moreover, patriarchal control is not only asserted with state violence. The social control mechanisms are also based on women's victimization and emphasis on threats to their security in public spheres, which places them in a constant state of fear and makes them compliant with the system by incentivizing self-censoring (Stanko 1985).

The Case of Afghanistan

Afghanistan and the recent Taliban takeover are crucial to address the research gap between the literature discussed earlier and build a theory on gender-specific vulnerabilities of data weaponization in armed conflict. While most of the literature on digital authoritarianism has looked at how authoritarian regimes gradually turned to technology to repress citizens—based on the same discriminatory structures but using new, digital means—Afghanistan constitutes a case of a relatively sudden regime change, where the technological infrastructure for surveillance and data weaponization was already in place, but where the regime change brought about a shift toward an extremist ideology of governing institutions. This shift in terms of who controls the data weaponization enabling infrastructure also has consequences for the types and sources of public and online data that potentially put people at risk and should be considered "sensitive" data. Thus, looking at the Taliban takeover allows us to think further about how data privacy considerations should consider shifts in the political environment. Afghanistan also allows adding to the literature that discusses specific risks associated with digital repression in contexts of armed conflict. The strong presence of international actors, the vast amount of data gathered, and the biometric technology left behind when these actors left the country make Afghanistan a relevant case and allow us to analyze data weaponization from a postcolonial perspective. Moreover, analyzing the crisis response of various stakeholders in the context of the Taliban takeover also holds lessons for the improvement of data management and crisis preparedness of governments, multilateral actors, and foreign militaries, as well as regarding multistakeholder emergency response mechanisms that involve civil society organizations, technology platforms, and affected citizens. Lastly, since the Taliban's governance system is based on a highly patriarchal, misogynist ideology, this also allows analyzing how digital instruments of repression mainly affect women and other gender and sexual minorities.

The Who, What, and Why of Data Collection in Afghanistan

Started in the context of the global war on terror and the rising availability of new technological possibilities, the US and its allies built a vast infrastructure of data collection and surveillance in Afghanistan over the last two decades— in the name of security, government accountability, and modernization (Jacobsen 2021a). With as many actors involved in the funding, deployment, and management of data collection programs as in Afghanistan—from international institutions such as the World Bank and the United Nations that funded or helped build extensive databases of biometric and other personal data for the former Afghan government, with the support of foreign and national technology companies such as Grand Technology Resources, Leidos, and Netlinks, while foreign governments and militaries such as the US also collected data for their operations on the ground—it is difficult to trace who precisely collected which data, where the data is stored, who it was shared with, and if there might have been data breaches. However, several databases have faced criticism regarding the risks they pose if they fall into the wrong hands long before the Taliban takeover in 2021. Most concerns were raised regarding the possible abuse of the US Defense Department Automated Biometric Identification System (ABIS) and the Afghan Automated Biometric Identification System (AABIS) (Toft Djanegara 2021; Access Now 2021). While the biometric data collected in Afghanistan constitutes only a small part of the data-gathering practices of a much larger digital and nondigital information infrastructure, these databases received the most attention. Biometric data is particularly sensitive since it is almost impossible for data subjects to deceive these information systems. Moreover, digitized, searchable databases make it much easier for malicious actors to use personal data to identify and surveil targets.

To analyze data collection processes in Afghanistan through a gendered and postcolonial lens, it is helpful to categorize three actor groups that somewhat differ in the rationales they had for data collection, the data security standards they implemented, and the segments of the Afghan population they collected data on: foreign militaries, especially the US military; the former Afghan government; and international humanitarian organizations, such as United Nations High Commissioner for Refugees (UNHCR) and the World Food Program (WFP).

The ABIS, which the US military operates with NATO and local forces, holds biometric data from over 2.5 million Afghans (Voeltz 2016, 187). The US military collected the data to identify individuals it believed might pose a security risk but also contained information on Afghans working for the US government. The data was reportedly used to identify persons on the battlefield thousands of times and was supposed to be a key innovation in the United States' counterinsurgency strategy, allowing the military to separate insurgents from the civilian population with great precision (Gershgorn 2019). Likely based on the assumption that combatants are usually men, the data gathered by the US military had a specific focus on males of fighting age (Shanker 2011). Notable about the system is that the US military also deployed portable scanning devices for iris, fingerprint, and face pattern recognition, the Handheld Interagency Identity Detection Equipment (HIID), that were widely distributed across security forces on the ground, and which allowed them to scan through millions of digital files in a matter of seconds, even at remote checkpoints.

Also, the former Afghan government collected vast amounts of (biometric) data with the help of international actors and technology corporations. Most notably: The AABIS, which was developed by the US and NATO and administered by the Ministry of Interior in Kabul, collected biometric data from criminals as well as army and police applicants, to keep Taliban infiltrators out of the Afghan army; the Ministry of Interior and Defense Afghan Personnel and Pay Systems (APPS) used to administer payments for the national army and police, and into which the AABIS was subsequently integrated in early 2021; and the Afghan National Biometric System, on of the Afghan national identity card system, called e-Tazkira, was based. Notable about the APPS, which holds data on more than 700,000 security forces, is the range of information it contains for each profile. Its more than 40 data fields include sensitive relational data, such as employees' grandparents' names and ties to community members, and seemingly random details, such as recruits' favorite fruits and vegetables (Guo and Noori 2021).

While the ABIS, AABIS, and APPS contained security-sector-related data, the Afghan National Biometric System held data on diverse population segments and a wide range of public institutions used it. The database includes fingerprints and iris scans of about 9 million Afghans, which Afghanistan's National Statistics and Information Authority collected with the support of the International Organization for Migration (IOM). Moreover, the e-Tazkira system holds a wealth of personal and biometric data, including a person's name, ID number, place and date of birth, gender, marital status, religion, ethnicity, language, profession, iris scans, fingerprints, and photographs. The ID was needed to access a vast range of public services. For example, it was required to obtain passports; driver's licenses; birth, death, and marriage certificates; to register land and property; to take civil service and university entrance exams; for employment with the public sector and much of the private sector; to register mobile SIM cards (which were needed for mobile banking); obtain bank loans; and to vote. It was praised for empowering women, especially in registering land ownership and securing bank loans.

Two other databases that received much less international attention but which hold equally sensitive personal data are the payroll system of the Afghan Supreme Court, which has extensive personal data on all judges as well as their family members, including biometrics, current addresses, and license plate numbers; and the payroll system of the National Directorate of Security, the former Afghan state intelligence agency that was established by the US Central Intelligence Agency after 2001 and entirely funded by the US government, and which contains the same sensitive information on their staff.

Similarly, humanitarian actors have collected data linked to millions of Afghans, including biometric data, to improve the efficiency of aid delivery and prevent fraud. The WFP, for example, has registered more than 6 million Afghans in its biometric beneficiary management system for food and cash transfers (WFP 2020). Also, UNHCR introduced mandatory iris recognition as early as 2002 to collect data on millions of former Afghan refugees who returned from Pakistan over the past 20 years (UNHCR 2021).

While databases containing personal information on government and especially security-sector employees received much more attention after the takeover in 2021—regarding the risk of this data being used by the Taliban to prosecute adversaries—the abuse of databases such as the e-Tazkira ID system might impact Afghans daily lives on a much broader scale. Also, from a gender perspective, databases such as e-Tazkira and the payroll system of the Supreme Court and humanitarian data and databases that contain information on citizens that received government aid might have just as sensitive information as security-sector-related and biometric data.

A colonial perspective explains how the invasive data collection structure developed by foreign militaries (based on a securitization rationale) together with the striving for a comprehensive digitization of the Afghan administration and the extensive data gathering on government employees (which can be attributed to the need to meet donors' accountability expectations and ideas of good governance) ultimately led to prioritizing the fight against corruption and terrorism over Afghans' right to data privacy. It also highlights how the US military and humanitarian actors used Afghanistan as a testing ground for new technologies. The US military, for example, deployed biometric devices in Afghanistan to test their performance in different climates (Shanker 2011). But also humanitarian actors, such as the UNHCR and the WFP, ran pilot programs to test new technological applications despite the risks such experimental technologies carry, regarding not only data privacy but also the dangers of being denied access to humanitarian support in light of their high failure rates (Hosein and Nyst 2013).

How the Taliban Accessed and Weaponized Data

Following the withdrawal of foreign militaries from Afghanistan in August 2021, many feared the Taliban would gain access to the vast amounts of data that a variety of international and national actors had been collecting over two decades and use this data to identify Afghans that had worked for or collaborated with international actors and the former Afghan government. Early reports by human rights organizations and UN agencies documented hundreds of enforced disappearances and killings of individuals with ties to the former government, particularly members of the Afghan National Security Forces, from military personnel to police, intelligence service members, judges and prosecutors, and civil servants (Amnesty International

2022a). However, not only representatives from the security and justice sector became a target, but also regime critics, journalists, human rights activists, the LGBTQ community, and women working in any profession the Taliban deemed unsuitable for them were prosecuted. This forced hundreds of thousands of Afghans into hiding, frequently moving between safe houses or attempting to flee the country altogether.

While most concerns on the potential dangers of sensitive data falling into the hands of the Taliban focused on data collected by international actors and the former Afghan government discussed above, concerns have also been raised regarding the risks associated with two additional data sources: online data that might be used to get access to personal information to identify and prosecute political opponents and vulnerable groups (from social media platforms such as Facebook; to email and messaging apps; to websites of governments, businesses, civil society organizations, and media outlets) and surveillance technologies (e.g., by gaining control over the state-owned Afghan Telecom, which enables access to phone records and geolocation data). While it is difficult to determine which data the Taliban have access to, rumors and fear of such possibilities alone already had a decisive impact on the life of ordinary citizens in Afghanistan and even jeopardize their security, for example, in cases where the fear of having to undergo biometric screening prevented citizens from accessing public services such as healthcare facilities (Nader and Amini 2022).

However, evidence gathered by human rights organizations and the Taliban's official statements suggest that they are likely to have gotten at least partial access to biometric data on Afghan police and army members; former collaborators with foreign governments and aid agencies; payroll data of the national security agency and the Supreme Court (Watkins 2021; Human Rights Watch 2021; Gall 2021); US military biometric devices (Klippenstein and Sirota 2021); and data from the e-Tazkira ID system. Already in August 2021, the Taliban publicly stated that they had access to biometric data and scanning devices and that they had mobilized a special unit, the Al Isha, to use this data to identify and hunt down Afghans who had worked with US and allied forces (Roy and Miniter 2021). Moreover, concerns have been raised regarding the Taliban possibly gaining access to government databases only accessible by authorized users, by forcing former government employees or by hacking these systems, possibly with technical assistance from foreign governments, such as Pakistan's ISI intelligence service, a long-time ally of the Taliban, likely also interested in these data bases for its national security agenda. But also Chinese, Russian, and Iranian intelligence are expected to offer such services. Equally concerning is the possibility that the Taliban could use biometric technology not only to access existing biometric databases but also to expand them by registering citizens on their own (Bajak 2021). The Taliban have reportedly approached former Afghan government employees in charge of the national data systems to extend national data sets.[1]

Fewer concerns were raised regarding the Taliban accessing the information on employees of international humanitarian actors and data collected on beneficiaries of humanitarian aid because international humanitarian organizations stored their data on servers outside of Afghanistan. However, despite the sector's decades of experience in managing sensitive data and high-security standards, risks remain that humanitarian data is not entirely out of reach for malicious actors in conflict regions. A cautionary example of this is a reported incident from early 2022, where the International Committee of the Red Cross (ICRC), a role model when it comes to data security standards in the humanitarian sectors, was the victim of a cyberattack in which hackers seized data from servers located in Switzerland and thereby gained access to personal data from over 515,000 extremely vulnerable individuals worldwide (ICRC 2022). Moreover, data is routinely shared among humanitarian actors and often with local governments and military actors on the ground that is administered by private security providers. UNICEF Afghanistan, for example, provided cash transfers to vulnerable families with adolescent girls as part of a program to support girls' education and prevent child marriage (Awad and Nezami 2020). Often administered through commercial service providers, cash transfer programs are hazardous regarding exposing sensitive data and making their recipients targets for the Taliban's prosecution.

Besides gaining control over biometric databases and technology, the Taliban quickly turned to social media platforms and other online data to identify and persecute opponents. Reportedly, they used information from social media platforms, like Facebook or LinkedIn and websites of governments, businesses, and civil society organizations, to identify people who have worked for the former Afghan government, foreign security forces, or international NGOs. They evaluated photos available online, for example, with facial-recognition software, and searched people's mobile phones for contacts in email and messaging apps at checkpoints and during home visits (Welchering 2021). Worried about retribution, many Afghans rushed to delete their online identity and digital history, erasing social media profiles, deleting foreign contacts on their phones, and resetting devices to their factory settings (Stokel-Walker 2021). The Taliban's presence on social media platforms has also silenced regime critiques on social media.[2]

Concerns have also been raised regarding the Taliban's control over the state-owned telecommunication company Afghan Telecom, from which the Taliban regime could order phone records and geolocation data, for example, to trace calls to international actors or visits to military bases. While Afghan Telecom initially also managed the country's internet service, in the mid-2010s, the country started to open up to private telecommunication operators, such as the United Arab Emirates' Etisalat Group and South Africa's MTM Group (Cerulus 2021). Concerns have been raised that the Taliban might try to pressure these companies for access to data records and messaging logs to gather information on exit visa applications, for instance. Afghans also fear for their access to the internet and other telecommunication services, as these companies could eventually be forced or simply incentivized to discontinue their services in Afghanistan for good.

The Prosecution of Women Since the Taliban Takeover in 2021

Since the Taliban takeover in 2021, the Ministry for the Propagation of Virtue and Prevention of Vice has issued a series of policies and guidelines that increasingly restrict women's most basic rights and exclude them from public life, barring them from their workplaces, from higher education, and from moving freely (Davidian 2022). Human rights organizations also reported increased repressive measures against female human rights defenders and women who went to the streets to protest the new oppressive rules, from threats to arrests, detentions, torture, and forced disappearances. Most measures have made women invisible, pushed them back into private spaces, and silenced them in public debates. However, women's situation in Afghanistan not only worsened due to direct repressive measures by Taliban members but the new rules established by the regime have also been reported to be enforced by family and community members on their own accord or upon receiving instructions from the Taliban (Stancati 2021). In addition, outsourcing surveillance and repression to community and family members has allowed the Taliban to control women in physical or online spaces that the Taliban government itself does not have direct access to. While many

Afghan women have been faced with social control by their communities long before the Taliban takeover in 2021, the control that male community members can, and feel obligated to, exercise over women's daily lives was decisively and structurally increased due to new government decrees that made male family members responsible for women's and girls' adherence to the new rules and put them at risk for detention if female family members fail to comply (Amnesty International 2022b, 37).

While most of the new restrictions target Afghan women in general and put them at risk for prosecution and detention if they don't comply, there are also specifically vulnerable groups whose chances of becoming a target for prosecution is facilitated by the Taliban's ability to weaponize digital and online data. For example, the Taliban have been reported to take tough actions against women who protested and spoke out against the newly imposed restrictive rules. This also included women voicing their criticism on social media, even when using private profiles.

Moreover, survivors of domestic and sexual violence have faced a particularly dire situation since the Taliban took over in 2021. They closed down women's shelters and released domestic violence perpetrators from prison. Many survivors reported that their newly released perpetrators are now hunting them down, often husbands and family members, and by the Taliban, who have been reported to imprison former shelter residents. Survivors and divorced women or women who live separated from their husbands in general also fear being forcibly separated from their children. However, not only survivors of domestic and sexual violence are at risk, looalos many women who worked within the system of protective services for gender-based violence survivors—including shelter staff, psychologists, doctors, lawyers, prosecutors, judges, employees of the Ministry of Women's Affairs, and others—are hiding in secret locations, fearing revenge from the Taliban, as well as convicted perpetrators and family members of survivors (Amnesty International 2022b, 47). Service providers reported being forced to flee their houses and change their phone numbers, receiving daily threats. Especially former judges fear arrests by the Taliban due to their reported access to the Afghan Supreme Court payroll database, which holds extensive personal information. A judge known for her work on domestic violence cases reported that not only her own home but also her mother's house was searched by Taliban fighters the first night they had taken control of her city, with both addresses only maintained in the payroll database (Human Rights Watch 2022). But also other vulnerable groups that received support from international actors were put at risk by the personal data they shared with support organizations. The Taliban have, for instance, been reported to have compiled "hit lists" for the Afghan LGBTQ community based on information that international organizations such as Rainbow Railroad, an international LGBTQ organization based in Afghanistan, voluntarily shared with the Taliban in the context of evacuation requests and through data leakages and phishing attacks (Nordstrom 2021).

Gender-Specific Vulnerabilities of Data Weaponization

Based on the empirical analysis of Afghanistan, this chapter identified gendered risks of data weaponization in patriarchal societies on three levels:

1. Preexisting discriminatory beliefs and structures in government and society define what type of information can be weaponized, which extends the range of data that can be risky for women and other marginalized groups and the range of weaponization strategies and implementing actors.
2. Discriminated, already vulnerable, groups are more likely to be captured as data subjects in humanitarian and government databases due to their higher dependence on support and protection services and restricted data privacy rights and provisions.
3. Women's and other marginalized groups' limited access to public spheres in patriarchy make them more dependent on ICTs in their daily lives and thus more vulnerable to digital surveillance and the repercussions from other digital repression strategies such as internet shutdowns.

Concerns regarding biometric and other digitized personal data gathered by international actors and the former Afghan government focused on the risks of personally identifiable data of former employees in the security sector and collaborators with international organizations. Likewise, efforts to erase this data before leaving the country focused on security-sector data that was considered especially sensitive. While women worked in these sectors, more men are affected by the risks this data poses. However, looking at the conceptualization of "sensitive" data through a gendered lens, it becomes evident that data from other sectors and government programs also pose severe risks to individuals facing discrimination under the new Taliban regime. Information categories that would not be considered sensitive for men can be weaponized against women and other vulnerable groups. In the context of Afghanistan, evidence of any aspect of daily life that is restricted by the Taliban's gender roles and which could be considered immoral behavior for women—from women exercising fundamental rights such as working in a specific sector, owning a business or land, being enrolled at a university, exercising political rights, participating in sports, or simply being outspoken in public—has to be considered sensitive information that could put women at risk. This has consequences for considering what kinds of public databases and what types of online platforms hold sensitive information that can be weaponized. In Afghanistan, this included anything containing information that could be linked to activities considered immoral behavior for women, which ranges from registers of land ownership to data on bank loans, driver's licenses, and voter registries, as well as online data and identities, such as businesses websites, online journalism, political activism online, social media behavior, and messaging. Especially women involved in public life, from human rights defenders (PBS 2021), journalists (Banville 2021), politicians (Faheid 2021), business owners (Bhalla 2021), and activists (Smith and Mengli 2021), rushed to delete their online identities for fear of becoming a target of the Taliban's reprisals.

Preexisting discriminatory beliefs in the broader society also allow governing actors to outsource the surveillance and prosecution of women they want to target to community members, thus expanding the range of implementing actors and creating additional opportunities to weaponize the information they extract. The patriarchal system implemented by the Taliban can rely not only on those community members who already share their ideology as accomplices for data weaponization against women but also creates new accomplices by holding male family members responsible for women's behavior. This is facilitated through technology, as reaching out and mobilizing a large number of accomplices via social media platforms has become more manageable in the digital age, and the increased accessibility of spy- and stalker-ware enable the surveillance and tracking of family members through something as simple as a mobile app purchase.

Additionally, the impact data weaponization has on its targets is also gendered. For women living in patriarchal societies, publishing intimate photos or private conversations online can lead to alienation, harassment, and physical attacks within their communities. In contexts like Afghanistan, where patriarchal ideology condemns the public display of any behavior that the Taliban confines to private spaces, the destruction of the inviolability of women's private spaces (physically in their homes and their digital devices or also virtually in private online communication spaces), due to the proliferation of invasive surveillance technology, creates an atmosphere of constant fear that their personal information could be used against them at any point, which means that women self-censor their behavior even in the private spaces they have been pushed back into. For example, beyond the context of Afghanistan, women rights activists have been reported to fear the repercussions of state surveillance in countries such as Jordan and Bahrain, with some women whose devices were hacked feeling forced to wear a veil even when home alone, afraid of being watched (Fatafta 2022).

Looking through a feminist and postcolonial lens also explains why women and other marginalized groups might be more likely to appear as data subjects in humanitarian and government databases. This is due to their vulnerable position in society, which makes them more likely to depend on government support and protection services in general and on humanitarian aid in fragile contexts in particular. In patriarchal societies, women might rely on state services and humanitarian assistance more often as they are more affected by gender-based violence, live in economically more precarious situations due to limited access to income and independent housing, and rely more on public shelters. In addition, they might carry more significant financial burdens due to childcare, to name just a few examples. Marginalized groups are also more often dependent on the support of civil society organizations and humanitarian actors as they might have to hide or flee from political repression. Afghan women and children, for example, made up the majority of refugees who fled to Pakistan and Iran after the armed conflict broke out in Afghanistan in 1979 (Khan 2002).

Moreover, patriarchal societies often assign women the role of victims, treating them as a vulnerable group in need of protection or equating them with legal minors who have no agency over their lives. A similar process of victimization and incapacitation can be observed in the humanitarian sector, where international actors treat local populations in fragile contexts as incapable and needing external protection. Both cases legitimize prioritizing protective measures over the individual's right to data privacy and agency, creating a power imbalance between the data subject and the controller. The greater the power imbalance between the data controller and the subject, the more invasive or extractive the data collection process. Vulnerable groups are more likely to suffer from lower data privacy and protection provisions since they are in a weaker position to stand up for privacy rights or to give meaningful consent to sharing their data. In Afghanistan, databases that reflect such gender-based vulnerabilities and could be used to target women and other marginalized groups include databases containing information on support structures for victims of domestic and sexual violence (from hospital records to court files and shelter registries). These civil society support systems were in contact with or collected data on the LGBTQ community, government assistance programs for single mothers, refugee registries, financial aid programs for women's rights organizations, and many more. The extent to which databases contain sensitive information and who could become targets is not always straightforward. For instance, child protection databases could also hold sensitive information on single mothers and victims of sexual violence.

Lastly, women are particularly vulnerable to data weaponization due to their greater dependence on information and communications technologies when navigating their everyday life in patriarchal societies, where women's roles in and access to the public sphere are limited.

Following the withdrawal of US troops from Afghanistan, social media has been crucial for Afghans in sharing information, organizing to find support, and escaping the new regime. But the dependence on internet access and ICTs have disproportionally increased for women. With the Taliban restricting women's right to free movement and access to employment, education, healthcare, and other public services, many Afghan women have resorted to online use (Scollon 2021). In addition, patriarchy's banishment of women to the private sphere increases their dependence on ICTs in their private as well as political life to stay connected with family members and friends, to mobilize and advocate for their rights, or to access news or information, and, particular to crises, to reach out to the international community to share their stories or ask for help.

While the private space can also be a powerful site for advocacy, and technology might facilitate agency and provide an alternative platform to stay connected, women's resulting use and dependence on ICTs also make them more vulnerable to the risks of digital surveillance and cause more significant harm to them if their access to ICTs is restricted, due to internet shutdowns for example.

International Responses to Data Weaponization in Crisis Situations

This section discusses the international community's response to the risk of data being weaponized by the Taliban after their takeover in 2021. It examines how different actor groups can help vulnerable populations protect and delete sensitive data in crises. It also highlights the downsides and challenges of erasing sensitive data in these contexts. The section subsequently argues that international actors need to develop a comprehensive strategy for dealing with sensitive data in conflict contexts and crises, emphasizing the role of a multistakeholder approach. It also discusses how these strategies can be improved by applying a gendered and postcolonial lens, from data governance practices and data privacy considerations in fragile contexts to emergency response mechanisms addressing the risks of online data weaponization.

How Different International Actors Supported the Erasure of Sensitive Data After the Taliban Takeover

In the run-up and aftermath of the Taliban takeover in 2021, foreign governments and international organizations rushed to delete data they had collected, and technology companies, such as Google, Facebook, and Twitter, as well as civil society organizations, supported Afghans in erasing their online identities and evading surveillance.

Aware of the danger that sensitive data might fall into the hands of the Taliban after coalition troops left the country, foreign militaries, humanitarian actors, and diplomats destroyed equipment, scrubbed databases, and removed evidence of Afghan employees and collaborators from government websites before they evacuated (Jacobs et al. 2021). Social media platforms reacted quickly to the Taliban takeover in August 2021 by helping Afghans safely remove their social media profile content or temporarily suspend their accounts, making it more challenging to search others' social media profiles (Culliford 2021). Facebook, for example, created a "one-click tool" that allowed citizens to delete their accounts and temporarily removed the ability for people to view or search the friends lists of accounts in Afghanistan. Twitter closely monitored and suspended suspicious accounts and contacted the NGO Internet Archive to delete sensitive tweets archived on the platform. Similarly, LinkedIn temporarily hid the connections of its users in Afghanistan so the Taliban could not see individuals' network contacts.

However, the efforts by international actors who operated the vast data infrastructure in Afghanistan have been criticized for their shortcomings in a comprehensive emergency data erasure strategy, leading to rushed and insufficient measures. Human rights organizations also called out international actors for missing to inform data subjects in Afghanistan about the use of their data, which should have included revisiting data risk assessments and communication with data subjects regularly but also calling on them to improve transparency regarding data breaches as the crisis unfolded in 2021 (Human Rights Watch 2022).

Social media companies have been criticized for reacting too slowly to help Afghan people safely remove their profile content and for not translating help pages into local languages (Glaser and Smith 2021). Calls were also raised for search engines, such as Google, to accelerate the delisting of sensitive information and for technology companies to pledge to deny governments backdoors to private data and to invest in encryption and prevention of data leakages.

Stepping in for governments' and private actors' shortcomings, regional and international civil society networks played a crucial role in supporting Afghans with information on deleting their digital history and evading biometrics. Organizations such as Access Now, the Digital Rights Foundation, and Human Rights First ran helplines for Afghans seeking advice on erasing their digital traces. In addition, they quickly translated guidelines on evading biometrics and deleting digital histories in local Afghan languages.

Challenges with Data Protection and Trade-Offs of Deleting Online Information

While the case of Afghanistan has proven that the erasure of online identities and sensitive data collected by public actors is crucial to protect vulnerable populations in crises, there remains challenges and considerable downsides associated with the removal of online information and the deletion of official data in such contexts.

Practical challenges of deleting sensitive data include, for example, the possibility that data can be forensically reconstructed and delistings circumvented with virtual private networks (VPNs). Some humanitarian organizations even abstain from having clauses on data deletion in data collection consent forms, seeing themselves unable to guarantee this in light of complex data-sharing processes and fragile contexts (Jacobsen 2021b). Moreover, there might be more time to erase online data only once a crisis arises. For example, in Afghanistan, the Taliban had already kept records on journalists, government employees, and women's rights activists before the takeover of Kabul.

Even if data deletion is successful, erasing personal data in crises comes with considerable trade-offs. Many Afghans, especially the ones who collaborated with foreign militaries and the former Afghan government but also other groups that were outspoken critics of the Taliban, such as journalists, found themselves faced with a dilemma: the exact data that put them at risk for being targeted by the Taliban was also a crucial proof of their status as refugees when applying for emergency evacuation and asylum. Also, dependence on social media and mobile phone contacts to stay in touch with allies within Afghanistan and abroad to exchange information and seek support made deleting profiles and contacts difficult. Similarly, taking down social media profiles and online content produced by female journalists and activists also meant silencing women's voices in the public sphere. Moreover, data sets and online articles documenting international crimes and other human rights abuses in Afghanistan, while holding significantly compromising information for victims and witnesses, constitute essential evidence for international prosecution of war crimes (Milaninia 2021).

Lastly, trade-offs are associated with erasing online information that raises critical questions from a democratic perspective. There is an inherent trade-off between people's right to privacy and free access to information. Especially in fragile contexts, concerns regarding the proliferation of sensitive information online could be abused by authoritarian regimes as a pretext to cover-up human rights abuses or censor regime critics—thereby serving rather than preventing digital repression. There is also a common concern regarding the discretion given to corporations, such as Google, in weighing personal safety risks versus public interest when deciding what information is delisted in search results for instance.

Coming up with a comprehensive response to the risks associated with data weaponization in the context of armed conflict will thus have to balance these trade-offs, which might include extending strategies of digitally archiving information securely or temporarily limiting access to online content, as well as in-depth discussions on how decision-making processes in the context of removing sensitive online information can be democratized. Moreover, given the time sensitivity of crises, the difficulty will be in speeding up these processes as part of a comprehensive multistakeholder emergency response mechanism.

Rethinking Data Governance and Cybersecurity Emergency Support Through a Gendered and Postcolonial Lens

The analysis of Afghanistan has demonstrated the need for better emergency support mechanisms involving multiple stakeholders—from multilateral actors, technology companies, and civil society organizations—and for improved data management practices to prevent data weaponization in crisis and regime change situations.

Regarding the emerging threat of the weaponization of online identities, the international community will need to develop best practices and emergency response mechanisms for the erasure of sensitive data while mitigating potential trade-offs. A more in-depth discussion must be held on how to prevent the establishment of data infrastructures that enable the weaponization of data when it comes to data collected and managed by public actors, from national governments, multilateral organizations, and foreign militaries. Next to more transparent communication regarding data breaches and emergency support for affected individuals once a crisis has unfolded, these efforts will have to address the root causes of extractive data collection in conflict contexts. Once collected, securing and erasing sensitive data in a crisis is almost impossible to guarantee, especially in light of an extensive data infrastructure that involves as many actors as in Afghanistan. Accordingly, discussions on data management in the aftermath of the Taliban takeover centered on lessons learned and preventative strategies and urged international and humanitarian actors to commit to storage time and purpose limitations (Human Rights Watch 2022).

While the humanitarian sector's decades of experience with the collection and management of highly sensitive data in fragile contexts has produced valuable best practices and guidelines (see, e.g., ICRC 2020; Inter-Agency Standing Committee 2021) on data protection and ethical data governance in fragile contexts, including critical concepts such as "do no digital harm" and "data minimization," as well as remedy mechanisms for victims of data protection violations, the analysis of Afghanistan sheds light on how these discussions need to be elaborated by filling blind spots on gender-specific vulnerabilities and by further deconstructing colonial logics.

Analyzing Afghanistan through a gender lens has pointed out three levels on which such blind spots need to be addressed in the current discussion on data weaponization after the Taliban takeover: Gender impacts (1) what has to be considered "sensitive" information, expanding the scope of relevant databases and online information beyond the security sector; (2) the means and mechanisms of data weaponization, shedding light on the role of community members as accomplices and shifting the focus on the surveillance of private homes, mobile devices, and private online spaces; and (3) the security threats resulting from digital repression, which urges one to consider not only direct physical violence and prosecution but also indirect and structural consequences of data weaponization such as creating an atmosphere of constant fear and the self-silencing of women.

The first blind spot implies the need to improve data management practices and emergency response mechanisms to be informed by gender-specific risk analyses. The second blind spot highlights that international efforts to mitigate the risks of data weaponization also need to address and condemn the proliferation of surveillance technology and hold technology platforms accountable for securing online spaces, including guaranteeing data privacy standards and withholding from sharing sensitive data with third actors. Also, women's specific vulnerabilities regarding the risk of silencing them completely in public (online) spaces within Afghanistan and abroad must be considered in this context. Finally, it also makes the case that the international community needs to assess risks associated with surveillance technologies and online security beyond the immediate crisis and regime transition period, as the consequences of data weaponization under the newly established extremist patriarchal regime hold not only direct threats to women's physical safety but also has society-wide, long-term consequences.

The field of feminist data governance and internet principles (see, e.g., APC's "Feminist Principles of the Internet") hold valuable insights for addressing the challenges discussed above. Next to emphasizing a human rights perspective on internet governance, relevant feminist concepts on which this field is based include consent, anonymity, and control over one's online memory. This includes, for example, the critique of guaranteeing meaningful consent in light of lacking transparency on privacy breaches and deceptive terms of services. Using allegories of victim blaming, this literature also discusses the problem that digital hygiene solutions put the burden of cybersecurity on the user rather than addressing structural risks in digital infrastructure directly, for example, holding technology companies and telecommunication service providers accountable.

Colonial logics underpinning the establishment of data infrastructures in contexts of armed conflict also have implications for the improvement of data weaponization mitigation strategies, as they not only establish the vast amount of data that is being collected in these contexts but also restrict local populations' ability for digital self-protection due to lack of inclusion and transparency.

Armed-conflict contexts have a high surveillance potential and vast amounts of data collected. These extractive data collection practices are based on the deprioritization of local populations' digital rights, combined with the presence of numerous international actors employing different kinds of technological innovations for various reasons (securitization, efficiency, donor accountability, or market logic). Additionally, the reproduction of colonial power hierarchies also increases the local population's dependence on international actors regarding data protection and cybersecurity in crisis situations. Local people's lack of agency regarding the data collected on them also expands to a need for more agency regarding data handling in crisis response mechanisms. Missing to involve affected citizens in data management mechanisms has especially dire consequences if, like in Afghanistan, international actors in charge of data management flee the site of the conflict and leave citizens behind to bear the risks associated with the collected data but not with the agency to mitigate them.

The disinterest of ICT providers and technology platforms to invest in data protection standards of digital devices, online content moderation, and local language capacities in the Global South opens up opportunities for the weaponization of online identities and restricts local citizens' ability to mitigate these threats on their own accords.

Current discussions in humanitarian data management and decolonial approaches to technology use and proliferation more broadly offer insight into providing citizens with greater agency regarding their data. Human rights–based approaches to humanitarian data management advocate the concept of "data agency," which includes the concepts of informed consent, participation, and notification of data collection and uses (Greenwood et al. 2017). Broader discussion from decolonial data and technology research (see, for example, Couldry and Mejias 2023) expand on these notions calling to boycott extractivist technologies and use alternative tools to reappropriate data and the products of data on behalf of the data subjects to hold technology companies accountable for the damage done by their products and to educate the public on digital literacy, cybersecurity, and digital rights. Discussion in the context of digital self-determination further calls for digital infrastructures that promote individuals' self-determination, including equal and free access, better privacy protections, and control over their online identities, emphasizing the role of digital literacy on how to protect oneself from government and corporate surveillance and exploitation online, sometimes also referred to as "digital self-defense" (on the concept of digital self-defense, see Kwet 2020).

While civil society organizations have made efforts to restore the agency of local populations in the context of Afghanistan by strengthening their digital literacy—including awareness raising regarding digital hygiene and surveillance protection strategies and translating social media protection protocols to local languages—postcolonial approaches to data management, data agency, and digital self-determination could help the international community to come up with more comprehensive crisis response strategies to mitigate data weaponization risks. Emphasizing the need for a multistakeholder approach and cybersecurity co-production should include the following:

- Holding technology companies accountable.
- Relying on local civil society organizations' expertise regarding affected populations' needs.
- Empowering citizens by strengthening their digital agency and the ability for digital self-defense.

Conclusion

Building on theoretical concepts from feminist and postcolonial studies and insights from an empirical analysis of data weaponization in the aftermath of the Taliban takeover in 2021, the chapter built theory on how gendered and colonial discriminatory structures and ideologies shape data weaponization strategies in the context of armed conflict and regime change, and it discussed how deconstructing these underlying factors should inform data management and crisis response mechanisms to mitigate the risks of data weaponization.

The chapter argued that colonial logics adopted by international actors—from international humanitarian organizations to multilateral donor organizations, foreign militaries, and technology companies—create a digital infrastructure that is based on invasive technology use and extractive data collection practices and that deprioritizes local populations' data protection and digital rights, leading to the collection of vast amounts of data containing highly sensitive personal information, which lays the groundwork for data weaponization enabling digital infrastructure. It further finds that in contexts where the ruling regime holds a patriarchal ideology, especially in contexts of sudden regime change toward this ideology, women and other marginalized groups face additional risks. In patriarchal societies, gender defines what has to be considered sensitive information, how data weaponization is implemented, and its consequences on the individual and societal levels. Patriarchal ideology extends the scope of information that can be weaponized. It allows outsourcing the implementation of digital repression strategies to citizens who hold the same doctrine. It makes women and other marginalized groups more likely to become data subjects due to their higher dependence on government support and protection services and limited ability to assert their data privacy rights. Additionally, women and other marginalized groups limited access to public spheres in patriarchy makes them more dependent on ICTs, increasing their susceptibility and vulnerability to digital repression.

The chapter also discussed how international and regional actors helped Afghans to protect and delete sensitive data in the aftermath of the Taliban takeover, and it pointed out the challenges and trade-offs associated with the erasure of sensitive data in crisis situations, referring to practical difficulties with data deletion (insufficient or too late), to the trade-off of crucial information getting lost (in the light of Afghans' dependence on online identities when trying to flee the country; their reliance on social media and digital contact databases to stay in contact with allies within the country and abroad; the silencing of women and other vulnerable groups voices in the national and international public sphere; the documentation of human rights violations that is crucial evidence for the international prosecution of war crimes); and broader anti-democratic implications (if data protection is used by authoritarian governments as a pretense to cover up human rights abuses; risks giving decision power to technology companies on what online information gets removed). Analyzing these dynamics through a postcolonial and gendered lens also helped identify blind spots in international actors' emergency response. The gender lens helped identify additional relevant data sources beyond the security sector and made the case to expand considerations to the complicity of implementing data weaponization strategies by community members but also technology companies proliferating surveillance capabilities, and it made the case why these response strategies also need to consider long-term structural consequences of gendered vulnerabilities of data weaponization in terms of creating an atmosphere of fearing constant surveillance and censorship of women. The postcolonial lens emphasizes the need to strengthen affected populations' digital rights and agency in conflict contexts, holding not only international actors accountable that collect and manage sensitive data but also technology companies gatekeeping people's safety online, drawing from local civil societies' knowledge of the situation on the ground and strengthening citizens' ability for digital self-defense.

Building theory on gendered vulnerabilities of data weaponization in armed conflict, the chapter helped fill gaps in several bodies of literature dealing with data weaponization: The literature on digital authoritarianism, which lacks a gender perspective and does not account for the specific vulnerabilities in the context of armed conflict and regime change; discussions in the context of humanitarian data governance and technocolonialism, which miss emphasizing local populations' right to data agency beyond data protection and neglect the risks and responsibilities associated with online identities; and research on gender-based cyberviolence, which mainly focuses on the citizen-to-citizen level and dangers posed to the individual, failing to make bridges to structural consequences on a societal level. Moreover, adding a new perspective to discussions on the cyberdimension of armed conflict, the chapter makes a case for bringing together critical cybersecurity studies notions on human-centric cybersecurity—which emphasizes that the state can be a perpetrator of cyberviolence toward its citizens and that cybersecurity should be co-produced by multiple stakeholders including individual citizens—with discussions around international cyberwar and multilateral cybersecurity efforts, the latter of which usually center on responsible state behavior in the context of interstate conflicts and threats posed by external cybersecurity threat actors.

The critical cybersecurity perspective and the emphasis on cybersecurity co-production are especially relevant in fragile contexts, where the state cannot guarantee citizens' data privacy and safety online, or in authoritarian regimes where the state is a threat actor. Multilateral cybersecurity discussions should address the international community's role and responsibilities in contexts where state actors cannot provide their citizens with cybersecurity. Especially regarding the provision of an emergency response to data weaponization risks in armed conflict, the international community should consider its responsibilities as a cybersecurity provider. Following human-centric conceptualizations of cybersecurity co-production, such efforts should be conceptualized as multistakeholder processes, acknowledging the crucial role that national and regional civil society organizations play in providing local expertise and the need to emphasize strengthening citizens' ability for digital self-defense and data agency.

Notes

1. Interview with a representative of an international human rights organization, January 2023.
2. "Their intelligence is monitoring everything. . . . Whatever I do, there will be a reaction from the Taliban," reported a participant of the street protests that followed the Taliban's invasion of Kabul in August 2021 about her social media postings, when interviewed by Amnesty International (Amnesty International 2022).

References

Access Now. 2021. "Civil Society Calls on International Actors in Afghanistan to Secure Digital Identity and Biometric Data Immediately." https://www.accessnow.org/cms/assets/uploads/2021/08/Civil_Society_Afghanistan_Biometrics_Letter.pdf.
Acconcia, G., A. Perego, and L. Perini. 2022. "LGBTQ Activism in Repressive Contexts: The Struggle for in Visibility in Egypt, Tunisia and Turkey." *Social Movement Studies*, 1–19. DOI: 10.1080/14742837.2022.2070739.
Aglionby, J. 2018. "World Bank Urges Private Sector Interest in Refugee Camps." *Financial Times*, May 5. https://www.ft.com/content/e2d6588a-5042-11e8-b3ee-41e0209208ec.
Al Jazeera. 2023. "Myanmar Women Target of Online Abuse by Pro-Military Social Media." Al Jazeera, January 26. https://www.aljazeera.com/news/2023/1/26/myanmar-women-target-of-online-abuse-by-pro-military-social-media?utm_source=substack&utm_medium=email
Amnesty International. 2022a. "Afghanistan" In *Amnesty International Report 2021/22*, 64–68.
Amnesty International. 2022b. *Death in Slow Motion: Women and Girls Under Taliban Rule*. https://www.amnesty.org/en/documents/asa11/5685/2022/en/.
APC. 2016. "Feminist Principles of the Internet." https://www.apc.org/en/pubs/feminist-principles-internet-version-20.
Awad, M., and S. Nezami. 2020. "Cash Transfer Supports Girls' Education in Afghanistan." UNICEF. loombergn

Bajakt, F. 2021. "U.S.-Built Databases, Biometric Data a Potential Tool of the Taliban." PBS, September 7. https://www.pbs.org/newshour/world/u-s-built-databases-biometric-data-a-potential-tool-of-the-taliban.

Banville, K. 2021. "'We see silence filled with fear'": Female Afghan Journalists Plead for Help." *The Guardian*, August 16. https://www.theguardian.com/world/2021/aug/16/we-see-silence-filled-with-fear-female-afghan-journalists-plead-for-help.

Bardall, G. 2023. "Nasty, Fake and Online: Distinguishing Gendered Disinformation and Violence Against Women in Politics." In *Gender and Security in Digital Space*, ed. Gulizar Haciyakupoglu and Yasmine Wong, 109–123. Routledge.

Bhalla, N. 2021. "'Now, we are back to zero': Afghan Businesswomen on the Run." Reuters, August 26. https://www.reuters.com/article/us-afghanistan-women-business/now-we-are-back-to-zero-afghan-businesswomen-on-the-run-idUSKBN2FR1SJ.

Bhatia, R. 2016. "The Inside Story of Facebook's Biggest Setback." *The Guardian*, May 12. https://www.theguardian.com/technology/2016/may/12/facebook-free-basics-india-zuckerberg.

Brown, D., and A. Pytlak. 2020. *Why Gender Matters in International Cyber Security*. Women's International League for Peace and Freedom.

Cerulus, R. 2021. "Fears Loom over Afghanistan's Internet." POLITICO, August 25. https://www.politico.eu/arti cle/Afghanistan-braces-for-fight-over-taliban-internet-information-control/.

Chang, L. Y., L. Y. Zhong, and P. N Grabosky. 2018. "Citizen Co-Production of Cybersecurity: Self-Help, Vigilantes, and Cybercrime." *Regulation & Governance* 12, no. 1: 101–114.

Couldry, N., and U. A. Mejias. 2023. "The Decolonial Turn in Data and Technology Research: What Is at Stake and Where Is It Heading?" *Information, Communication & Society* 26, no. 4, 1–17.

Culliford, E. 2021. "Facebook, Twitter and LinkedIn Secure Afghan Users' Accounts Amid Taliban Takeover." Reuters, August 20. https://www.reuters.com/article/us-afghanistan-conflict-social-media-idCAKBN2FK2D7.

Davidian, A. 2022. "The Situation of Women and Girls in Afghanistan." Press Briefing, UNWOMEN. https://www.unwomen.org/en/news-stories/speech/2022/07/press-briefing-the-situation-of-women-and-girls-in-afghanistan.

Dávila A, S., N. Guruli, and D. Samaro. 2021. "DIGITAL DOMINION: How the Syrian Regime's Mass Digital Surveillance Violates Human Rights." UIC Law White Papers, March 2021. https://repository.law.uic.edu/whitepapers/20

Deibert, R. J. 2018. "Toward a Human-Centric Approach to Cybersecurity." *Ethics & International Affairs* 32, no. 4: 411–424.

Dragu, T., and Y. Lupu. 2021. "Digital Authoritarianism and the Future of Human Rights." *International Organization* 75, no. 4: 991–1017.

Faheid, D. 2021. "These Female Afghan Politicians Are Risking Everything for Their Homeland." NPR, August 18. https://www.npr.org/2021/08/18/1029014825/afghan-women-politicians-taliban-resistance.

Fatafta, M. 2022. "Unsafe Anywhere: Women Human Rights Defenders Speak Out About Pegasus Attacks." Access Now. https://www.accessnow.org/women-human-rights-defenders-pegasus-attacks-bahrain-jordan/.

Gall, C. 2021. "As the Taliban Tighten Their Grip, Fears of Retribution Grow." *New York Times*, August 29. https://www.nytimes.com/2021/08/29/world/asia/afghanistan-taliban-revenge.html.

Gershgorn, D. 2019. "Exclusive: This Is How the U.S. Military's Massive Facial Recognition System Works." *OneZero Medium,* November 6. https://onezero.medium.com/exclusive-this-is-how-the-u-s-militarys-massive-facial-recognition-system-works-bb764291b96d.

Glaser, A., and S. Smith. 2021. "As Taliban Search Phones, Experts Fear Security Features Aren't Enough to Keep Afghans Safe." NBC News, August 20. https://news.yahoo.loo mbeiban-violence-drives-afghans-wipe-154040354.html.

Greenwood, F., C. Howarth, D. E. Poole, N. A., Raymond, and D. P. Scarnecchia. 2017. "The Signal Code: A Human Rights Approach to Information During Crisis." Harvard Humanitarian Initiative. https://hhi.harvard.edu/publications/signal-code-human-rig htsapproach-information-during-crisis

Guo, E., and H. Noori. 2021. "This Is the Real Story of the Afghan Biometric Databases Abandoned to the Taliban." *MIT Technology Review,* August 30. https://www.techn ologyreview.com/2021/08/30/1033loombergnstan-biometric-databases-us-military-40-data-points/.

Hosein, G., and C. Nyst. 2013. "Aiding Surveillance: An Exploration of How Development and Humanitarian Aid Initiatives Are Enabling Surveillance in Developing Countries." https://papers.ssrn.com/sol3/papers.cfm?abstract_id=2326229.

Human Rights Watch. 2021. *"No Forgiveness for People Like You": Executions and Enforced Disappearances in Afghanistan Under the Taliban.*

Human Rights Watch. 2022. "New Evidence That Biometric Data Systems Imperil Afghans." Human Rights Watch, March 30. https://www.hrw.org/news/2022/03/30/new-evidence-biometric-data-systems-imperil-afghans.

Hunnicutt, G. 2009. "Varieties of Patriarchy and Violence Against Women: Resurrecting 'Patriarchy' as a Theoretical Tool." *Violence Against Women* 15, no. 5: 553–573.

Inter-Agency Standing Committee. 2021. *IASC Operational Guidance on Data Responsibility in Humanitarian Action.* https://interagencystandingcommittee.org/oper ational-response/iasc-operational-guidance-data-responsibility-humanitarian-action.

International Committee of the Red Cross. (ICRC). 2020. *Handbook on Data Protection in Humanitarian Action.* 2nd ed. https://www.icrc.org/en/publication/430501-handb ook-data-protection-humanitarian-action-second-edition.

International Committee of the Red Cross. (ICRC). 2022. *Cyber Attack on ICRC: What We Know.* https://www.icrc.org/en/document/cyber-attack-icrc-what-we-know#:~:text= Update%3A%2024%20June%202022.,in%20a%20sophisticated%20cyber%20attack.

Jacobs, J., N. Wadhams, and J. Wingrove. 2021. "U.S. Embassy in Kabul Told to Destroy Files in Case Taliban Wins." Bloomberg, August 13. https://www.bloomberg.com/news/articles/2021-08-13/u-s-embassy-shredding-burning-documents-in-case-tali ban-wins.

Jacobsen, A. 2021a. *First Platoon: A Story of Modern War in the Age of Identity Dominance.* New York: Dutton.

Jacobsen, K. L. (2021b). "Biometric Data Flows and Unintended Consequences of Counterterrorism." *International Review of the Red Cross* 103, no. 916–917, 619–652.

Jacobsen, K. L., and L. Fast. 2019. "Rethinking Access: How Humanitarian Technology Governance Blurs Control and Care." *Disasters* 43: S151–S168.

Khan, A. 2002. "Afghan Refugee Women's Experience of Conflict and Disintegration." *Meridians: Feminism, Race, Transnationalism* 3, no. 1: 89–121.

Klippenstein, K., and S. Sirota. 2021. "The Taliban Have Seized US Military Biometrics Devices." *The Intercept,* August 17. https://theintercept.com/2021/08/17/afghanistan-taliban-military-biometrics/.

Kwet, M. 2020. *People's Tech for People's Power: A Guide to Digital Self-Defense & Empowerment*, September 1. https://ssrn.com/abstract=3748901 or http://dx.doi.org/10.2139/ssrn.3748901.

Latonero, M. 2019, "Stop Surveillance Humanitarianism." *New York Times*, July 11. https://www.nytimes.com/2019/07/11/opinion/data-humanitarian-aid.html.

Leurs, K. 2019. Migration Infrastructures. In *The Sage Handbook of Migration and Media*, ed. K. Leurs, K. Smets, M. Georgiou, S. Witterborn, and R. Gajjala, 91–102. London: Sage.

Lorch, J., and B. Bunk. 2016. "Gender Politics, Authoritarian Regime Resilience, and the Role of Civil Society in Algeria and Mozambique." GIGA-German Institute of Global and Area Studies Working Paper 292.

Madianou, M. 2019. "Technocolonialism: Digital Innovation and Data Practices in the Humanitarian Response to Refugee Crises." *Social Media + Society* 5, no. 3, 1–13.

Milaninia, N. 2021. "Evidence Destruction and the Crisis in Afghanistan." Just Security, August 20. https://www.justsecurity.org/77831/evidence-destruction-and-the-crisis-in-afghanistan/.

Nader, Z., and N. Amini. 2022. "The Taliban Are Harming Afghan Women's Health." *Foreign Policy*, March 2. https://foreignpolicy.com/2022/03/02/the-taliban-are-harming-afghan-womens-health/.

Nordstrom, L. 2021. "The Taliban Has a Hit List for the Afghan LGBT Community, NGO Says." *France24*, November 2. https://www.france24.com/en/asia-pacific/20211102-the-taliban-has-a-kill-list-for-the-afghan-lgbt-community-ngo-says.

PBS. 2021. "Taliban Interrogating Women Activists, Creating a 'Climate of Fear and Intimidation.'" August 18. https://www.pbs.org/newshour/show/taliban-interrogating-women-activists-creating-a-climate-of-fear-and-intimidation.

Roy, S., and R. Miniter. 2021. "Exclusive: First-Ever Interview with Terror Leader Who's Hunting Americans and Allies in Afghanistan." *Zenger News*, August 28. https://www.zenger.news/2021/08/28/taliban-team-is-using-us-made-biometric-database-and-scanners-to-hunt-american-and-afghan-enemies/.

Runyan, Anne Sisson, and V. Spike Peterson. 2013. *Global Gender Issues in the New Millennium*. 4th ed. Boulder, CO: Westview Press.

Scollon, M. 2021. "Armed With Online Option, Afghan Girls Say 'Bring It On' When It Comes to Taliban Education Ban." RFERL, November 5. https://www.rferl.org/a/afghan-girls-online-education/31547925.html.

Shanker, T. 2011. "To Track Militants, U.S. Has System That Never Forgets a Face." *New York Times*, July 13. https://www.nytimes.com/2011/07/14/world/asia/14identity.html.

Shires, James. 2020. "The Simulation of Scandal: Hack-and-Leak Operations, the Gulf States, and U.S. Politics." *Texas National Security Review* 3, no. 4: 10–28.

Shoker, S. 2022 "What Can Internet Shutdowns Tell Us About Gender and International Security?" In *Gender and Security in Digital Space*, ed. Gulizar Haciyakupoglu and Yasmine Wong, 33–48. London: Routledge.

Smeets, Max. 2018. "The Strategic Promise of Offensive Cyber Operations." *Strategic Studies Quarterly* 12, no. 3: 90–113.

Smith, S., and A. Mengli. 2021. "Wave of Killings Targets Afghan Female Judges, Journalists, Intellectuals." NBC News, January 24. https://www.nbcnews.com/news/world/wave-killings-targets-afghan-female-judges-journalists-intellectuals-n1255302.

Stancati, M. 2021. "After Taliban Return, Afghan Women Face Old Pressures from Fathers, Brothers." *Wall Street Journal*, December 15. https://www.wsj.com/articles/after-taliban-return-afghan-women-face-old-pressures-from-fathers-brothers-11639564204.

Stanko, E. 1985. *Intimate Intrusions: Women's Experiences of Male Violence*. London: Routledge.

Stokel-Walker, C. 2021. "Afghans Are Racing to Erase Their Online Lives." *Wired*, August 17. https://www.wired.co.uk/article/afghanistan-social-media-delete.

Takhshid, Z. 2021. "Regulating Social Media in the Global South." *Vanderbilt Journal of Entertainment and Technology Law* 24: 1.

Thomas, Elise, and Albert Zhang. 2020. "Snapshot of a Shadow War in the Azerbaijan-Armenia Conflict." *The Strategist*, October 9. aspistrategist.org.au/snapshot-of-a-shadow-war-in-the-azerbaijan-armenia-conflict.

Toft Djanegara, N. 2021. *Biometrics for Counter-Terrorism: Case Study of the US Military in Iraq and Afghanistan*. Privacy International.

UN High Commissioner for Refugees (UNHCR). 2021. "Government Delivered First New Proof of Registration Smartcards to Afghan Refugees." May 25. https://www.unhcr.org/pk/12999-government-to-deliver-first-new-por-smartcards-to-afghan-refugees.html.

Vaidhyanathan, S. 2018. *Anti-Social Media*. Oxford: Oxford University Press.

Voelz, G. 2016. "Catalysts of Military Innovation: A Case Study of Defense Biometrics." *Defense AR Journal* 23, no. 2: 178.

Watkins, A. 2021. "An Assessment of Taliban Rule at Three Months." *CTC Sentinel*, 14, no. 9, 1–14.

Welchering, P. 2021. "Taliban jagen ihre Gegner auch via Netz." *Golem*, August 20. https://www.golem.de/news./afghanistantaliban-jagen-ihre-gegner-auch-via-netz-2108-158996.html.

World Food Program. (WFP). 2020. *Annual Country Report 2020: Afghanistan*. https://www.wfp.org/operations/annual-country-report/?operation_id=AF01&year=2020#/20257.

Yao, S. 2019. "Gender Violence Online." In *Handbook on Gender and Violence*, ed. L. Shepherd, 217–230. Cheltenham, UK: Edward Elgar.

4
Gendered Transnational Authoritarianism in Cyberspace

A Case Study of Uyghurs

Murat Yılmaz

Introduction

This chapter explores gendered transnational authoritarianism in the context of the global Uyghur emigrant and diaspora communities, focusing on digital information and communication technology (ICT). The chapter does so to highlight what I term "digital transnational authoritarianism," particularly its gendered impacts, which is done by building on the burgeoning area of transnational authoritarianism. By digital transnational authoritarianism, I mean the cyber-based aspects of transnational authoritarianism. Transnational authoritarianism refers to "any effort to prevent acts of political dissent against an authoritarian state by targeting one or more existing or potential members of its emigrant or diaspora communities" (Tsourapas 2021, 618). While the term has only recently been coined to describe the oppressive reach of the state to its citizens and diaspora communities living beyond its borders, such repressive strategies have a long history. However, given the increased rates of migration in recent decades—linked to the trifecta of globalization, human rights–abusing governments, and climate change, all of which drive emigration abroad—the spread of ICTs, particularly within the cybersphere and increasing autocratization globally, transnational authoritarianism is rising in occurrence. This is because it is more efficient for states to engage in transnational authoritarian practices digitally to ensure that emigrant and diaspora communities do not go against the state's wishes. ICTs are defined in various ways in scholarship, but the term generally refers to technologies that drive communication, including the internet (UN n.d.). For this reason, studying the growing role of the cybersphere in transnational authoritarianism is needed. Further, thus far, there has been a dearth of work examining the gendered implications of transnational authoritarian tactics.

In this chapter, I build on the growing scholarly interest in transnational authoritarianism (Moss 2016; Baser and Ozturk 2020; Tsourapas 2021) and increasing attention to the problem by the transnational human rights community (Gorokhovskaia and Linzer 2022) by highlighting China's Uyghur emigrant and diaspora communities—who have received global attention in recent years due to the Chinese Communist Party's (CCP) use of detention centers and other discriminatory and violent tactics within the Uyghur homeland of China's Xinjiang region, as well as thanks to the increased attention to decades of lobbying by diaspora Uyghur organizations and individuals working to end these human rights abuses. Further, this chapter brings this work into conversation with the literature on the role of the cybersphere in facilitating transnational (beyond borders) repression and manipulation, primarily surveillance (Sanders 2018; Pomerantsev 2019) and feminist security studies (Amar 2011; Sjoberg 2016) to expose the profoundly gendered nature of transnational authoritarian repression and persecution. This chapter argues that while Uyghurs abroad are at significant risk when they challenge the Chinese state's denial of Uyghur human rights abuses at home—which many scholars have argued is outright, or is tantamount to, genocide ("The Uyghur Genocide" 2021), women and men face differently gendered state attacks with women facing more significant personal attacks compared to men.

Uyghurs in China: Increasingly Oppressed, Yet Even Outside of China, Not Free from the Digital Grasp of the State

Before continuing to the methodology of the chapter, this subsection first provides a brief background on China's Uyghurs. China's current policies have resulted in a growing emigrant and diaspora Uyghur community outside of China as people flee state oppression. The next section will outline the digital reach of gendered transnational authoritarianism through cyber technologies that have meant that even upon leaving China, Uyghurs are not free from the state. Here I first account for changes in China's approach to the Uyghur community within Xinjiang, which traces back to 2014.

The conflict between Uyghurs and various Han-dominated kingdoms and regimes has been ongoing for centuries, although with periods of nonconflict as well (Millward 2007). However, since 2014, Chinese state policy toward the Uyghur community has grown increasingly hostile and oppressive. Uyghurs have collectively been portrayed as a severe security threat to the state and (Han) citizens, partially justified through US-driven post-9/11 discourses that conflate Islam with terrorism and continuous terrorist threat (Roberts 2020). To combat the supposed security threat presented by Uyghurs, the Chinese state has adopted massive digital technologies of state surveillance and data collection to keep a close watch over Uyghurs. These practices have led some to characterize the Uyghur homeland as an "open prison" given the unrelenting (digital) eye of the state (Haas 2019).

China launched its "People's War on Terror" as part of its "strike hard campaign" in 2014, which follows a US-styled post-9/11 counterterrorism strategy. New laws were introduced in China, including 2015's Counter-Terrorism Law and Xinjiang Uighur Autonomous Region Religious Affairs Regulations (2015) and later, 2017's Xinjiang Uighur Autonomous Region Regulation on De-extremification Ordinance, as part of the "People's War on Terror." Further, as part of this strategy, in 2016, Chen Quanguo, former party secretary of the Tibet Autonomous Region, was named the Xinjiang party secretary (Zenz and Leibold 2017). Following the same playbook in Xinjiang as in Tibet, Chen introduced a dense policing network that included "convenience police stations" to harass and harm Uyghurs while also adopting new ICTs to engage in intense state surveillance of and data collection in the Uyghur community (Wong 2019). These digital technologies were deployed as part of the Integrated Joint Operations Platform (IJOP) (also known as China's big brother system of mass surveillance). IJOP uses an application to monitor and collect data on people (HRW 2019). Whenever any human activity in Xinjiang is deemed "suspicious," an alert message is sent to local police, who launch an investigation to ensure "security" is maintained (Millward and Peterson 2020).

The data collection for IJOP derives from ubiquitous closed-circuit television cameras (loaded with facial-recognition software) that are placed throughout the Xinjiang region and by spying on Uyghurs' cell phone usage. ICTs form a core part of IJOP, but biometric data is also collected by forcing Uyghurs to undergo regular medical exams. Yet even ICTs are used to engage in biometric state surveillance, including making digital copies of Uyghurs' voice prints and gait prints to track better and confirm their identities (Millward and Peterson 2020). Such massive state surveillance and data collection on such a minutia level ensure almost total control by the state of the

Uyghur community. IJOP and the "People's War on Terror" are rooted in justifications that such extreme measures are necessary to prevent religious extremism from this Muslim-majority population and to uphold state security (Yılmaz 2021).

The results on Uyghurs of the "People's War on Terror" include a massive jump in arrests and prosecutions of security threats and the removal of Uyghurs from their homes into forced re-education camps to counter violent extremism, supposedly. Another occurrence has been the widespread removal of children from their parents, with children placed in orphanages where it is suspected that the children will be socialized to comply with the state's view of security. The steep drop in the Uyghur birthrate has been most troubling, likely tied to forced sterilization and abortion ("China Cuts Uighur Births" 2020). To outline just how extreme these combined security, re-education, and enforced sterilization policies have been, in 2017, the courts in Xinjiang sentenced 10 times the number of people compared to 2016, and arrests jumped eight times as high that year compared to 2016 (Buckley 2019). These individuals are deemed clear security threats. Those not seen as risky enough to warrant arrest are sent to "re-education" camps where they are supposedly cleansed of their extremist views. A suspected 3 million individuals have been impacted by this policy (Stewart 2019). Many Uyghurs who are sent to re-education camps have young children who are then placed in orphanages to be raised by non-Uyghurs ("Orphaned by the State" 2020). By the end of 2019, an estimated 880,500 children were put into state boarding schools because their parents were sent to re-education camps. Finally, from 2015 to 2018, Uyghur birthrates have dropped by an astonishing 60%, suggesting that the population is experiencing extreme repression linked to forced sterilization ("Orphaned by the State" 2020).

The factors identified by the Chinese state as flags for "extremism" among Uyghurs can only be called mild. This could include having a Western-based social media account or having a relative living abroad (Rajagopalan 2017; Shih 2018). Another factor that could land Uyghurs in a re-education camp is having contact with a journalist or foreign researcher. Finally, something as simple as having a beard or wearing long clothes (such as robes) or asking an imam to bless a child are deemed examples of "extremist" behavior (Finley 2019). Given the ubiquity of state surveillance, engaging in any of these practices without being spied upon is nearly impossible.

This brief introduction to Uyghurs' recent experiences under the Chinese state is intended to explain why Uyghurs are increasingly fleeing the state. Yet as will become clear, even far from the physical borders of China, Uyghurs are entangled in the digital transnational authoritarianism of the state.

Methodology and Roadmap for the Chapter

The chapter takes a qualitative approach using the Uyghur diaspora as a theoretically important case study in the growing work on transnational authoritarianism. Gerasimos Tsorapas (2021) provides an excellent framework for understanding the general process of transnational authoritarianism. However, both Tsorapas and the burgeoning literature that examines the roles of autocratic states enacting their power across borders concentrates mainly on developing countries in the Global South, such as Turkey (Baser and Ozturk 2020), Middle Eastern and North African countries (Brand 2006; Moss 2016), and Central Asia (Cooley 2018). China's position as a global power—albeit an increasingly troubled one given the ongoing economic impacts the country is experiencing related to its continued COVID-19 lockdowns—marks the Uyghurs as a theoretically significant and analytically different case given the greater international influence of China compared to the likes of countries such as Syria, Kazakhstan, and Tunisia. To flesh out the case, I expand upon my previous research (Yılmaz 2021) by performing a theoretically driven review of secondary resources, including non-governmental organization (NGO) reports and Uyghur lobbies' social media platforms that describe the repression faced by Uyghurs in the diaspora by the Chinese state. I argue that the cybersphere plays an integral role in the CCP's efforts to silence and harm Uyghurs living outside of China and that this cyberviolence of the CCP in its transnational authoritarianism holds concerning implications for democracy and human security. While Uyghurs use the cybersphere to resist the Chinese state, the state's cyber tentacles' far reach threatens the security of individuals outside of China who are mobilizing against the regime. This chapter calls attention to the need for protecting diaspora populations and promoting human rights in the cybersphere.

This chapter proceeds as follows. First, I overview my theoretical framework that combines transnational authoritarianism, surveillance studies in the cybersphere, and feminist security studies' emphasis on gender and intersectionality. Second, I present accounts of Uyghurs in the emigrant and diaspora communities who have spoken out against the Chinese state and emphasize how the CCP has engaged in gendered transnational authoritarian repression to harm these individuals. Both Uyghurs and state officials engage digital ICTs in their respective actions. In the discussion and conclusion, I emphasize how the cybersphere refracts the same inequalities that exist in the physical world, meaning that women in emigrant and diaspora communities generally face far more personal and misogynistic threats in the context of gendered transnational authoritarianism, which thus far has not been emphasized in the literature on transnational authoritarianism.

Digital Transnational Authoritarianism and Its Gendered Effects

I begin with Tsorapas's (2021, 618) comprehensive framework of transnational authoritarianism that includes "repression, legitimation, and co-optation." To enact transnational repression that attempts to suppress state criticism by emigrant and diaspora members, authoritarian states (1) surveil emigrant and diaspora communities; (2) make threats against individuals abroad; (3) rely on "coercion-by-proxy," which refers to threats made by the state against a member of the emigrant/diaspora's family still within the state's borders; (4) forcibly disappear individuals; (5) coerce individuals' return home, including the use of intergovernmental organizations, such as the International Criminal Police Organization (INTERPOL), as well as embassies where people are coerced inside on the pretext of required government paperwork; and (6) lethal retribution, which includes assassination or attempted assassination (p. 622).

Saudi-born Jamal Khashoggi's murder by the Saudi state in the Saudi Arabian embassy in Istanbul in 2018 is one of the most well-known uses of the pretext of apparent routine paperwork to marry his fiancée. This ruse was used to lure Khashoggi into the embassy, where he was murdered (Tsorapas 2021, 636). Likewise, there have been a recent spate of apparent murders linked to the Russian Federation against Russians who have fled abroad and spoken out against Putin or advocated opposition to Russia's 2022 invasion of Ukraine (Brezar and Mac Dougall 2022). However, the former Soviet Union has a long history of transnational authoritarianism, most infamously Leon Trotsky's assassination in Ciudad de México (Tsorapas 2021, 629).

Tsorapas's (2021) framework also acknowledges non-repressive means that authoritarian states seek to control emigrant and diaspora populations through legitimation and cooptation. A major form of influence exists through the cultivation of patriotism, which the authoritarian state insinuates is the civic duty of its "citizens" living abroad. China, in particular, has long used this strategy among its ethnic Han diaspora and emigrants, who are known as "Overseas Chinese," demanding what James To (2014) terms "transnational loyalty" to China through "persuasion, influence, and manipulation" of these Han communities beyond China's borders (p. 4). China offers tours of the country to Overseas Chinese to induce commitments by these individuals to promote China abroad (p. 144). Authoritarian states also seek to induce compliance from diaspora communities through the threat of exile—that challenging the state would result in their never being permitted to return to their ancestral homelands. Regarding cooptation, transnational authoritarian tactics also include patronage—the offer of perks—to guarantee support from diaspora communities (Tsorapas 2021). China, for example, offers scholarships (To 2014, 144) or, as part of its "Thousand Grains of Sand" concept, offers perks (not all necessarily direct monetary payments) to those who share information and technology knowledge with the state—or the CCP threatens those who refuse to comply (To 2014, 44–45).

Finally, returning to Tsorapas's (2021) framework, transnational authoritarian states also "blacklist" individuals whom they deem noncompliant, which could include preventing these persons' ability to access promised scholarships. It may also involve labeling these individuals as "untrustworthy," which could lead to their social isolation, a concerning threat to many living abroad in spaces where they may face discrimination for being a minority (Tsorapas 2021, 633).

An Increasingly Fraught Cyber Surveillance Climate

Tsorapas's (2021) framework is a comprehensive starting point for this chapter, although I will zoom in on one key area, the role of digital surveillance in transnational authoritarian practices. Surveillance generally is an increasingly normalized and routine practice undertaken by authoritarian states not only within their borders but also among overseas populations (Tsorapas 2021, 623). According to Freedom House, China has "one of the most prolific" and "advanced" government programs to monitor the social media of not only its citizens within its borders but also emigrants abroad and diaspora communities. CCP surveillance has impacted not only those who identify as activists but also many everyday people who use social media, including those with private social media accounts. Regardless of private social media and living outside China's borders, the CCP threatens individuals living abroad who make critical social media posts by intimidating their relatives who remain in China (Gorokhovskaia and Linzer 2022, 27). This has been an ongoing issue for many Uyghurs living outside of China.

To flesh out digital transnational authoritarianism, I draw upon the expanding interdisciplinary area of surveillance studies and related international relations literature. Mark Andrejevic (2015, xv) suggests that the world has entered a "surveillance climate" that features both "dramatic developments in information collection, storage, and processing" and burgeoning "techniques of watching" that rely on "automated, multidimensional forms of surveillance." Several essential works have documented the surveillance by the state (Sanders 2018; Doss 2020) as well as private companies (notably, Google, Apple, Facebook, and Amazon) (Zuboff 2019; Doss 2020), particularly emphasizing the dangers to people's right to privacy by these new surveillance measures. Intimately linked to these privacy concerns is the rise in propaganda, which is easily transmitted via the cybersphere and is increasingly easy to do so, thanks to increased surveillance measures. Russia employs journalists and others to operate social media platforms that misrepresent their identities to both surveille and promote state propaganda (Pomerantsev 2019). Ronald Glassman (2021) questions whether democracy can survive this onslaught of cyber-based propaganda (see chapter 25 especially) but emphasizes that the risks to civil liberties and civil rights for authoritarian states such as China are far graver, which is a direct result of increased cyber-based surveillance (vii).

The implications of cyber and technological surveillance developments have been recognized as particularly risky for minority populations within states (democratic and authoritarian alike), including ethnic, racial, and religious minority communities (Smith 2015; Sanders 2018)—notably such as Uyghurs in China—(Daly 2019), as well as other vulnerable groups including trans communities (Moore and Currah 2015), as well as populations engaged in stigmatized activities such as sex work (Kang 2015). Further, women often experience specific forms of surveillance, not just by the state and commercial companies (Mason and Magnet 2012; Roberts 2015) but also by their families—often their romantic partners—as well as by other nonstate actors who target them online through surveillance techniques that constitute hate crimes and gender-based cyber harassment (Mason and Magnet 2012; Citron

2014; Vickery and Everback 2018; Slupska 2019). Notably, violence against women by family members as well as by others in society is exacerbated by other systems of oppression, including racism, ableism, and neocolonialism (Mason and Magnet 2012, 106). These insights are particularly relevant in thinking about Uyghur women in emigrant and diaspora communities and their experiences of digital transnational authoritarianism.

These studies have performed an excellent analysis of state and nonstate surveillance on populations primarily within state boundaries and have emphasized the importance of protecting data and ensuring greater rights to data privacy (Sanders 2018; Zuboff 2019; Slupska 2019). However, with Sanders (2018) and Pomerantsev (2019) being the exceptions, most of these studies have ignored the issue of state surveillance beyond borders. Emphasizing the role of digital or cyber transnational authoritarianism helps correct this overlook. Further, with feminist and gender studies surveillance studies the exception, much of this work overlooks the gendered implications of surveillance. With this, the chapter turns to feminist security studies to highlight the role of gender in cyber transnational authoritarianism.

Gendering Transnational Authoritarianism Practices in the Cybersphere

Feminist security studies is a diverse area of international relations and security studies, which seeks to (among other things) unpack the role of gender in concerns of security (Amar 2011; Sjoberg 2016). Additionally, much of the feminist security studies literature de-emphasizes a focus on national security to consider the security of people and communities (Sylvester 2012; True and Tanyag 2019). For example, within research on war and armed conflicts, feminist security scholars emphasize that the end of war does not typically result in peace or a lack of violence, but rather much of the violence that took place among armed combatants now moves into the domestic sphere. There is often an uptick in violence against women in postconflict societies. For this reason, feminist security scholars draw attention to the need for individuals' security both during conflicts and in their aftermath to better promote peace (Alexander 2019). Further, feminist security studies as a whole emphasizes the variance among differently situated people in society, such as the interacting role of class and gender in Global South states such as Egypt, where working-class Arab men are constructed as inherently threatening to societal order (Amar 2011). Such insights come through the adoption of intersectional lenses.

Intersectionality is a crucial insight from feminist scholarly traditions with a long history that recognizes the diversity of women and, therefore, the different needs and interests of differently situated women (Crenshaw 1989; Ackerly and True 2010, 30). In seeking to better women's position within the gender hierarchy, women of color, women from the Global South, and women living with disabilities (among others) have emphasized that their challenges are not limited strictly by gender hierarchies but intersect with other systems of oppression, including racism, neocolonialism, and ableism, among other structurally embedded forms of discrimination (Dhamoon 2013). Further, this study also takes into account postcolonial IR and postcolonial feminist security studies, work that sheds light on "multiple sites of oppression and to reject universalisms around gendered experiences of both men and women" (Parashar 2016, 371). Postcolonialism is interested in those who experience marginalization and injustice (Agathangelou and Ling 2004; Parashar 2016).

Building on the work of feminist security studies, which complicates traditional notions of security beyond the state and taking differences among men, women, and those who identify outside the gender identity binary, I follow an intersectional lens to emphasize that although Uyghurs in the diaspora are all at risk of experiencing repression and other disciplinary measures by the CCP, gender plays a significant role in how Uyghurs experience digital transnational authoritarianism. As noted, women in the cybersphere not only experience misogyny at the hands of other users (both affiliated and not with the state), but minority women are likely to experience a double-edged sword that combines misogyny with other forms of oppression, such as racism (Vickery and Everback 2018). Uyghur women experience personal attacks related to their gender and identification as Muslim and Turkic women. Islamophobia is a well-known phenomenon in online spaces within China (Miao 2020), and as I demonstrate in the following sections, while Uyghurs living outside of China experience this almost across the board when speaking out against the CCP, women face attacks related to their gender identity as well.

I conclude this section by emphasizing that all digital transnational authoritarianism is inherently gendered. With digital transnational authoritarianism a relatively new concept in scholarship, its gendered aspects have not been addressed. As feminist international relations scholars emphasize, gender is inherent to global politics whether gender and gendering are recognized or not. One aim of this chapter is to emphasize that men, women, and others (including trans men, trans women as well as the gender nonbinary, gender queer, gender fluid, intersex, and others) experience differently gendered effects in undergoing digital transnational authoritarianism. However, given my intersectional approach, gender is not the only factor that matters in understanding digital transnational authoritarianism. Han Chinese women and Uyghur women who experience digital transnational authoritarianism undergo different gendered experiences (and so would Han Chinese men and Uyghur men) from one another since Han Chinese women are viewed differently by the CCP (as part of the hegemonic group), while Uyghur women are highly stigmatized by the state as backward minorities. With this, I now turn to the next section, which is composed of case studies.

Gendered Digital Transnational Authoritarianism

This section houses the core of this chapter. The following examples exemplify gendered digital transnational authoritarianism, specifically arising from the ongoing resistance by Uyghurs against the Chinese state, both within China and globally. I do not claim that these examples are wholly representative of a "typical" woman's experiences when speaking against the Chinese state (even by explaining their own experiences) by those in the Uyghur homeland, emigrant, and diaspora communities. Instead, I claim that these examples qualitatively contextualize the treatment of Uyghur women when they undergo gendered transnational authoritarianism and highlight the cybersphere's role in this process.

Uyghur Resistance to China's Repression

Before 2018, not many voices outside of China spoke about the now infamous internment camps in Xinjiang, where Uyghurs are sent on the bases of either gainful employment or re-education to deter them from violent extremism. Such an absence allowed the CCP to deny Uyghur claims about forced labor and forced detainment in the camps. However, by the fall of 2018, reports by Human Rights Watch (HRW 2018) and the Australian Strategic Policy Institute (Ryan et al. 2018) attested to the veracity of the internment camps.

Not long after, Reuters (Wen and Auyezov 2018) released a widely read story about the detention camps that included satellite imagery of the camps. These high-profile organizations brought credibility to growing Uyghur voices speaking up about the internment camps' existence, particularly the irrefutable evidence of satellite images of the camps released by Reuters. By the end of 2018, the Uyghurs' plight became known globally. Notably, Uyghur women were prominent in speaking out against the camps. For example, Mihrigul Tursun spoke about her experiences at an internment camp at the end of November at the National Press Club in Washington (Connell 2018). This would lead to a pattern of women prominently taking on the CCP.

Tursun spoke in Washington, DC, far outside China's borders, where Uyghurs have a more remarkable ability to share their stories than within China, given the state's surveillance and crackdowns on media. Uyghur emigrant and diaspora communities globally have become critical spaces for the Uyghur resistance against the CCP to take shape. In these spaces, women have spoken before the US Congress and other parliaments globally and at the Uyghur Tribunal, providing testimony of their experiences in China. Given the sensitivity of the issues discussed and the harm that may come to not only those who speak out but also their families who reside in China, the willingness of the women to give their full names and bear their faces to the media is powerful. Such willingness likely speaks to just how unbearable the situation has become.

While women like Tursun speak to international human rights organizations and major media platforms, others who lack such access turn to social media. The cybersphere has provided new avenues for Uyghur resistance to the CCP and empowered a greater number of people to resist more publicly against the Chinese state. Uyghurs have increasingly opted to speak to both human rights and journalism organizations and use social media platforms to share their stories. What has been notable since 2018 is that people are more willing to attach their personal information to these stories. Previously, Uyghurs shared their experiences online (such as in Uyghur lobby newsletters) but did so anonymously. Typically, these stories were shared by relatives of those impacted outside of China. Since these testimonies were shared anonymously, journalists hesitated to publish them since fact-checking was difficult under such circumstances.

The global attention to the plight of Uyghurs has altered this situation, with many now seeking to share their stories themselves on traditional and social media and to publicize their names and share their faces unconcealed.

This change is significant given that the Chinese state does not hesitate to harm those who share these stories. Tursun and Gulbahar Jelilov have been two such women at the forefront of this movement, sharing their stories despite the risks.

China's Gendered Transnational Authoritarianism Against Uyghurs

China's Transnational Repression of Uyghurs data set has documented 5,530 cases of transnational repression of Uyghurs by the CCP over 19 years, most of which have been cyber based (Hall and Jardin 2021). This repression has impacted Uyghurs living in 22 countries. However, according to a report by the Uyghur Human Rights Project and the Oxus Society for Central Asian Affairs, most instances of transnational repression are unreported, meaning that the actual number of cases is likely to be far higher than the documented 5,530. In a report by the Uyghur Human Rights Project and the Oxus Society for Central Asian Affairs, 72 diaspora Uyghurs who had relocated to democratic states in North America, Europe, and Asia were interviewed to document specifics about transnational authoritarian oppression (Hall and Jardin 2021). In this report, an incredible 95.8% of these individuals attested to feeling threatened by the CCP while living abroad, and 73.5% of these individuals had endured cyber-based repression, including threats and harassment online (Hall and Jardin 2021). Of the 5,530 cases of transnational authoritarian repression documented in China's Transnational Repression of Uyghurs data set, 50.2% of these examples are cyberattacks and the use of malware against Uyghurs, while 36.3% of these include intelligence and data gathering done via the cybersphere (Hall and Jardin 2021). Other cyber-based repression included intimidation and sending out demands to return home. The ease and cheapness of communication with digital ICTs make it much easier for the Chinese state to harass Uyghurs outside its borders.

The other component of the CCP's gendered cyber transnational authoritarianism includes propaganda sent out virtually as part of smear campaigns against Uyghur women. Such repression also constitutes cyberbullying. The women who speak up against the Chinese state are regularly disparaged, discredited, and humiliated by the CCP in a gender-specific manner. For example, several Uyghur women recently testified that they experienced sexual violence while being forced to live in internment camps, which led to their infertility. Another woman claimed that she underwent enforced birth control with an IUD implanted against her will (Gunter 2021). Wang Wenbin—a spokesperson for China's Foreign Ministry—and Xu Guixiang—an official from Xinjiang—held several press conferences to denounce these women's accusations. During the press conferences, photos of these women were shown to the press conference attendees (including the media present) while the state officials worked to discredit the women. The women were derided as being "morally depraved" and accused of having "inferior character" (Gunter 2021). The officials shared a state media video in which the former husband of one of the women called her "a bitch of bad moral quality." The video appears to have been staged. The state officials called another woman "a scumbag and child abuser." Wang and Xu decried the women's statements as outright lies, claiming that the women were "actresses" and explained away one woman's IUD and the other women's infertility problems (Gunter 2021). Wang stated that he had the woman's medical records that showed she had sought out the IUD and stated that the other women had sexually transmitted infections that caused their fertility problems.

The staging of videos by the Chinese state is often how such accusations are handled. After two Uyghur women spoke about their abuses in China to the BBC, Chinese state media released a series of what appeared to be staged videos in which the women's family members and friends hurled abuses at them. The women were accused by their family and friends of "stealing money" and "telling lies" (Gunter 2021). In March 2021, the Uyghur Human Rights Project documented over 20 videos of Uyghurs in China forced to proclaim their loved ones as liars and thieves to discredit them. The videos are released online, causing great fear in the women for having spoken out (Gunter 2021).

Discussion and Conclusion

In this section, I offer a brief discussion and conclusion that overviews an intersectional analysis of Uyghur women's targeting by the Chinese state, China's two-pronged approach to cyber-based transnational authoritarianism, and end by highlighting the positive side of the cybersphere that has empowered many Uyghur women to speak out against the CCP. I emphasize that the cybersphere refracts the same inequalities in the physical world. This renders Uyghur women in emigrant and diaspora communities especially vulnerable, generally facing personal and misogynistic threats in the context of gendered transnational authoritarianism.

The intersectional analysis brings attention to the different power relations embedded in structural systems based on people's positionality. Uyghur women are part of an ethnic and religious minority in China who are under intense repression that constitutes (minimally) a cultural genocide and potentially meets the requirements for a legal genocide. Further, the Uyghur community suffers economic injustice (among other injustices), which places them in a subordinated class position. Uyghur women are even more disadvantaged by their gender, given hierarchal gender relations. As part of a conservative society where women are expected to conform to wifely and maternal ideals emphasizing their sexual purity, the Chinese state actively attacks Uyghur women's womanhood. State officials disparage women as sexually impure by smearing them as having sexually transmitted infections, implying that they are unfaithful to their husbands, or the state portrays them as being bad mothers. Intersectionality highlights the extreme vulnerability of Uyghur women who are disadvantaged by ethnicity, religious identity, class, and gender, putting them in a fundamentally different category compared even to Uyghur men. Attacks on Uyghur women's "womanhood" are understood by the state to be especially devastating, and this is a track often pursued.

The CCP takes a two-pronged approach to gendered cyber transnational authoritarian repression of Uyghurs, seeking to both engage in cyberattacks on Uyghurs and use the cybersphere to spread propaganda that discredits Uyghurs. While Uyghurs at home and abroad endure cyberattacks (such as through malware) and face threats to return home (where they will likely endure state torture), the cyber realm has eased the state's ability to engage in this harassment against Uyghurs abroad. ICTs make digital communications both cheap and inescapable. For example, an Uyghur woman who had relocated to the Netherlands recounted a story to the BBC that she was preparing breakfast one morning when she had an incoming video call from her sister (Gunter 2021). The woman was immediately nervous since she had recently spoken about being interned in a detention camp in Xinjiang, where she described the rape and torture that she had undergone at the hands of state officials. Instead of her sister, a police officer appeared on the screen when she answered the call, demanding to know where she was (Gunter 2021). While Uyghurs, regardless of gender, must endure this cyberbullying, women Uyghurs have explicitly been targeted by the Chinese state to endure attacks on their womanhood. These attacks are propagated through traditional means (such as press conferences) and online. Such propaganda intends to humiliate the women so they will remain silent and silence other women who might consider speaking out.

Despite the harm brought through the cybersphere against Uyghurs, the digital sphere also promotes digital activism. Online spaces allow Uyghurs to share their stories more easily and provide a platform for those lacking access to traditional media and human rights organizations. The cybersphere is a double-edged sword in this sense. I seek to end this chapter by emphasizing that regardless of the Chinese state's ongoing transnational authoritarian repression and repression at home in China against Uyghurs, Uyghurs—especially women—are standing up against the state. However, given that the cybersphere mirrors the same injustices found in the real world, Uyghur women endure misogynistic attacks against them by the Chinese state. This particular issue has not been emphasized in the literature on transnational authoritarianism, which has largely neglected to examine how transnational authoritarianism is highly gendered.

In summary, the cyber realm is increasingly salient to the Chinese state as a means to enact transnational authoritarian repression against Uyghurs outside China. Such cyber violence holds important implications for democracy and human security, demonstrating both the negative side of the cybersphere. Although Uyghurs—increasingly women—can use the cybersphere to share their experiences and denounce the CCP, the Chinese state's cyber tentacles' far reach threatens these individuals' security. This chapter calls attention to the need for protecting diaspora populations and promoting human rights in the cyber sphere.

References

Ackerly, B. and True J. 2010. *Doing Feminist Research in Political and Social Science*. New York: Palgrave Macmillan.

Agathangelou, Anna M., and Lily HM Ling. "Power, Borders, Security, Wealth: Lessons of Violence and Desire from September 11." *International Studies Quarterly* 48, no. 3 (2004): 517–538.

Alexander, R. 2019. "Gender, Structural Violence and Peace." In *The Routledge Handbook of Gender and Security*, ed. C. Gentry, S. Laura, and L. Sjoberg, 27–36. New York: Routledge.

Amar, P. 2011. "Turning the Gendered Politics of the Security State Inside Out? Charging the Police with Sexual Harassment in Egypt." *International Feminist Journal of Politics* 13, no. 3: 299–328.

Andrejevic, M. 2015. "Foreword." In *Feminist Surveillance Studies*, ed. R. E. Dubrofsky and S. A. Magnet, ix–xviii. Durham, NC: Duke University Press.

Baser, B., and Ozturk, A. E. 2020. "Positive and Negative Diaspora Governance in Context: From Public Diplomacy to Transnational Authoritarianism." *Middle East Critique* 2, no. 9: 319–334.

Brand, L. 2006. *Citizens Abroad: Emigration and the State in the Middle East and North Africa*. Cambridge: Cambridge University Press.

Brezar, A., and D. Mac Dougall. 2022. "Updated: A List of Oligarchs and Putin Critics Found Dead Since Ukraine War." EuroNews, September 22. https://www.euronews.com/2022/09/12/accidental-defenestration-and-murder-suicides-too-common-among-russian-oligarchs-and-putin.

Buckley, C. 2019. "China's Prisons Swell After Deluge of Arrests Engulfs Muslims." *New York Times*, August 31. https://www.nytimes.com/2019/08/31/world/asia/xinjiang-china-uighurs-prisons.html.

"China Cuts Uighur Births with IUDs, Abortion, Sterilization." 2020. Associated Press, June 29. https://apnews.com/article/ap-top-news-international-news-weekend-reads-china-health-269b3de1af34e17c1941a514f78d764c.

Citron, D. K. 2014. *Hate Crimes in Cyberspace*. Cambridge, MA: Harvard University Press.

Connell, C. 2018. "A Tale of Torture in a Chinese Internment Camp for Uyghurs." *Share America*, December 4. https://share.america.gov/tale-of-torture-in-chinese-internment-camp-for-uyghurs/.

Cooley, A. 2018. *Dictators Without Borders: Power and Money in Central Asia*. New Haven: Yale University Press.

Crenshaw, K. 1989. "Demarginalizing the Intersection of Race and Sex: A Black Feminist Critique of Antidiscrimination Doctrine, Feminist Theory and Antiracist Politics." *The University of Chicago Legal Forum*, 139–167.

Daly, A. 2019. *Global Information Society Watch 2019: Artificial Intelligence: Human Rights, Social Justice and Development: Algorithmic Oppression with Chinese Characteristics: AI Against Xinjiang's Uyghurs*. Association for Progressive Communications (APC), Article 19 and the Swedish International Development Cooperation Agency (SIDA). https://strathprints.strath.ac.uk/71586/1/Daly_GISW2019_Algorithmic_oppression_Chinese_characteristics_AI_against_Xinjiang_Uyghurs.pdf.

Dhamoon, R. K. 2013. "Feminisms." In *The Oxford Handbook of Gender and Politics*, ed. G. Waylen, K. Celis, J. Kantola, and S. L. Weldon, 88–110. Oxford: Oxford University Press.

Doss, A. F. 2020. *Cyber Privacy: Who Has Your Data and Why You Should Care*. Dallas: BenBella Books.

Finley, J. S. 2019. "Securitization, Insecurity and Conflict in Contemporary Xinjiang: Has PRC Counter-Terrorism Evolved into State Terror?" *Central Asian Survey* 38, no. 1: 1–26.

Glassman, R. M. 2021. *Can Democracy Survive in the 21st Century? Oligarchy, Tyranny, and Ochlocracy in the Age of Global Capitalism*. Cham, Switzerland: Springer.

Gorokhovskaia, Y., and I. Linzer. 2022. *Defending Democracy in Exile: Policy Responses to Transnational Repression*. Freedom House. https://freedomhouse.org/report/transnational-repression.

Gunter, J. 2021. "The Cost of Speaking Up Against China." BBC, March 31. https://www.bbc.com/news/world-asia-china-56563449.
Haas, B. 2019. "European Companies Get Rich in China's 'Open Air Prison.'" *New York Times*, August 21. https://www.nytimes.com/2019/08/21/opinion/xinjiang-business.html.
Hall, N., and B. Jardine. 2021. "'Your family will suffer': How China Is Hacking, Surveilling, and Intimidating Uyghurs in Liberal Democracies." Uyghurs Human Rights Project and Oxus Society for Central Asia Affairs. https://oxussociety.org/wp-content/uploads/2021/11/Your-Family-Will-Suffer-Report.pdf.
Human Rights Watch (HRW). 2018. "'Eradicating Ideological Viruses' China's Campaign of Repression Against Xinjiang's Muslims." September 9. https://www.hrw.org/report/2018/09/09/eradicating-ideological-viruses/chinas-campaign-repression-against-xinjiangs.
Human Rights Watch (HRW). 2019. "Interview: China's 'Big Brother' App." May 1. https://www.hrw.org/news/2019/05/01/interview-chinas-big-brother-app.
Kang, L. H. Y. 2015. "Surveillance and the Work of Antitrafficking: From Compulsory Examination to International Coordination." In *Feminist Surveillance Studies*, ed. R. E. Dubrofsky and S. A. Magnet, 39–57. Durham, NC: Duke University Press.
Mason, C. L., and S. Magnet. 2012. "Surveillance Studies and Violence Against Women." *Surveillance and Society* 10, no. 2: 105–118.
Miao, Y. 2020. "Sinicisation vs. Arabisation: Online Narratives of Islamophobia in China." *Journal of Contemporary China* 29, no. 125: 748–762.
Millward, J. A. 2007. *Eurasian Crossroads: A History of Xinjiang*. New York: Columbia University Press.
Millward, J. A., and D. Peterson. 2020. *China's System of Oppression in Xinjiang: How It Developed and How to Curb It*. Brookings Institution. https://www.brookings.edu/research/chinas-system-of-oppression-in-xinjiang-how-it-developed-and-how-to-curb-it/.
Moore, L. J., and P. Currah. 2015. "Legally Sexed: Birth Certificates and Transgender Citizens." In *Feminist Surveillance Studies*, ed. R. E. Dubrofsky and S. A. Magnet, 58–76. Durham, NC: Duke University Press.
Moss, D.M. 2016. Transnational Repression, Diaspora Mobilization, and the Case of the Arab Spring. *Social Problems* 63, no. 4: 480–498.
"Orphaned by the State: How Xinjiang's Gulag Tears Families Apart." 2020. *The Economist*, October 17. https://www.economist.com/china/2020/10/17/how-xinjiangs-gulag-tears-families-apart.
Parashar, Swati. 2016. "Feminism and Postcolonialism:(En)Gendering Encounters." *Postcolonial Studies* 19, no. 4: 371–377.
Pomerantsev, P. 2019. *This Is Not Propaganda: Adventures in the War Against Reality*. London: Faber and Faber.
Rajagopalan, M. 2017. "This Is What A 21st-Century Police State Really Looks Like." BuzzFeed, October 17. https://www.buzzfeednews.com/article/meghara/the-police-state-of-the-future-is-already-here#.td4om9yG2.
Roberts, D. E. 2015. "Race, Gender and Genetic Technologies: A New Reproductive Dystopia?" In *Feminist Surveillance Studies*, ed. R. E. Dubrofsky and S. A. Magnet, 169–186. Durham, NC: Duke University Press.

Roberts, S. R. 2020. *The War on the Uyghurs: China's Internal Campaign Against a Muslim Minority.* Princeton, NJ: Princeton University Press.
Ryan, Fergus, Danielle Cave, and Nathan Ruser. 2018. "Mapping Xinjiang's 'Re-education' Camps." Australian Strategic Policy Institute (ASPI), November 1. 2018. https://www.aspi.org.au/report/mapping-xinjiangs-re-education-camps.
Sanders, R. 2018. *Plausible Legality: Legal Culture and Political Imperative in the Global War on Terror.* Oxford University Press. https://global.oup.com/academic/product/plausible-legality-9780190870553?cc=tr&lang=en&.
Shih, G. 2018. "China's Mass Indoctrination Camps Evoke Cultural Revolution." Reuters, May 17. https://apnews.com/article/kazakhstan-ap-top-news-international-news-china-china-clamps-down-6e151296fb194f85ba69a8babd972e4b.
Sjoberg, L. 2016. "Centering Security Studies Around Felt, Gendered Insecurities." *Journal of Global Security Studies* 1, no. 1: 51–63.
Smith, A. 2015. "Not Seeing: State Surveillance, Settler Colonialism and Gender Violence." In *Feminist Surveillance Studies,* ed. R. E Dubrofsky and S.A. Magnet, 21–38. Durham, NC: Duke University Press.
Slupska, J. 2019. "Safe at Home: Towards a Feminist Critique of Cybersecurity." *St Antony's International Review* 15, no. 1: 83–100.
Stewart, P. 2019. "China Putting Minority Muslims in 'Concentration Camps,' U.S. Says." Reuters, May 3. https://www.reuters.com/article/us-usa-china-concentrationcamps/china-putting-minority-muslims-in-concentration-camps-us-says-idUSKCN1S925K.
Sylvester, C. 2012. *War as Experience: Contributions from International Relations and Feminist Analysis.* New York: Routledge.
"The Uyghur Genocide: An Examination of China's Breaches of the 1948 Genocide Convention." 2021. Newlines Institute, March. https://newlinesinstitute.org/wp-content/uploads/Chinas-Breaches-of-the-GC3.pdf.
To, J. J. H. 2014. *Qiaowu: Extra-Territorial Policies for the Overseas Chinese.* Leiden: Brill.
True, J., and Tanyag, M. 2019. "Toward A Feminist Conceptualization of Global Violence." In *The Routledge Handbook on Gender and Security,* ed. C. Gentry, S. Laura, and L. Sjoberg, 15–26. New York: Routledge.
Tsourapas, G. 2021. "Global Autocracies: Strategies of Transnational Repression, Legitimation, and Co-Optation in World Politics." *International Studies Review* 23, no. 3: 616–644.
UN. n.d. *Information and Communication Technologies.* https://www.un.org/development/desa/socialperspectiveondevelopment/issues/information-and-communication-technologies-icts.html.
Vickery, J. R., and Everback, T. 2018. "The Persistence of Misogyny: From the Streets, to Our Screens, to the White House." In *Mediating Misogyny: Gender, Technology, and Harassment,* ed. J. R. Vickery and T. Everback, 1–27. Palgrave Macmillan.
Wen, P., and O. Auyezov. 2018. "Tracking China's Muslim Gulag." Reuters, November 29. https://www.reuters.com/investigates/special-report/muslims-camps-china/.
Wong, C. H. 2019. "China's Hard Edge: The Leader of Beijing's Muslim Crackdown Gains Influence." *Wall Street Journal,* April 7. https://www.wsj.com/articles/chinas-hard-edge-the-leader-of-beijings-muslim-crackdown-gains-influence-11554655886.
Yılmaz, M. 2021. "China's Development Model as Internal Colonialism: The Case of the Uyghurs" (PhD diss., University of Cincinnati).

Zenz, A., and J. Leibold. 2017. "Chen Quanguo: The Strongman Behind Beijing's Securitization Strategy in Tibet and Xinjiang." *China Brief* 17, no. 12. https://jamestown.org/program/chen-quanguo-the-strongman-behind-beijings-securitization-strategy-in-tibet-and-xinjiang/.

Zuboff, S. 2019. *The Age of Surveillance Capitalism: The Fight for a Human Future at the New Frontier of Power*. New York: Public Affairs.

5

Disciplinary Power and Feminism

Nudity as Resistance to Cyberspace Bullying in Kenya

Margaret Monyani and Allan Wefwafwa

Introduction

The chapter explores cyberbullying resistance among Kenyan women. It focuses on the rise of nude-photo sharing on social media platforms in Kenya and the resulting cyberbullying. Kenya is experiencing an increase in social media usage. The accessibility and dependability of the internet in Kenya are the pillars upon which social media thrive. During media liberalization in the 1990s, internet infrastructure was established nationwide (Kenya Information and Communication Act 2012). Consequently, 2G, 3G, 4G, and 5G internet coverage is available throughout Kenya to facilitate people's economic activities, which has unlocked economic potential in rural areas (Communication Authority of Kenya [CA] 2020; Standard 2016). According to Article 23 of the Kenya Information and Communication (KIC) Act (2012), the government is responsible for providing and regulating mass media.

In addition, the failure of private media to provide the audience with the type of information they require—defying established norms, criticizing the government, and involving the audience as content co-producers—contributed to the rise in social media usage (Media Council of Kenya 2020; Oriare et al. 2010). The chapter defines private media as media institutions whose ownership and/or editorial decisions are not under the current government's control. It is assumed that these media can criticize the current government without fear of revenue loss if the government decides to reduce advertising with these media. This contradicts the claim that the government is the largest advertiser in every country where media exist. The government may also restrict media freedom by tightening media laws. Consequently, in the case of social media, the government frequently interprets the resistance portrayed by users as defamatory (see Kenya Law 2018). However, this has not prevented the emergence of a form of citizen journalism in Kenya, where individuals with a strong online presence, such as Robert Alai, Denis Itumbi, Boniface Mwangi, Cyprian Nyakundi, and Akothee, among others, have amassed a huge following, larger than some media outlets (Ogola 2015).

User Interface, Real-Time Experience, and Nudity

The concept of social media is based on the World Wide Web (WWW) technology with a web 2.0-enabled user interface (Curran et al. 2016). User interface refers to the platform's capacity to facilitate a real-time exchange of data. For instance, in contrast to email, social media allows users to respond to specific posts with comments. This has significantly enhanced online experiences and piqued the interest of citizen users. It has also increased awareness of the power and influence of social media. People may hold influential individuals accountable for their actions if they are able to respond to specific posts made by those members of society by commenting directly below them. The user interface also makes influential individuals, such as those elected to public office, feel as though they are being observed by the populace, who can recall them if they disapprove of their conduct while in office. Thus, individuals effectively use social media to curb the abuses of power in society. Castells (2008) argues that the digital public sphere, which emerged from the well-known Habermas public sphere, enlarges the public space, allowing for greater inclusivity and participation by the people in electoral debates, as well as debates on security. Although criticized by Afrocentric scholars for being too Westernized (Ekeh 1975; Osaghae 2006), the concept of the public sphere was introduced in the early 1970s to describe the rational public space in which citizens deliberate on matters of public interest (Habermas 1989). The advent of the internet gave rise to the digital public sphere, where individuals use internet-enabled cell phones and computers to discuss public issues. Some African nations, such as Kenya, have invested in internet infrastructure to facilitate citizen participation in public interest issues such as electoral and public morality debates and the provision of government services (Wamuyu 2020). The average global social media usage increased from 40% in 2015/2016 to 53% in 2020, with Nigeria, Egypt, Kenya, and South Africa leading the continent (Wamuyu 2020, 20; World Internet Stats, 2020, 2). To exert their influence on matters of public interest, Kenyan internet users, such as social activists, "wrestle" with the government and societal norms for a fair share of social media use. In response, digital activism has emerged to curb the excesses of governments, combat institutionalized oppression, and liberate the people. Thus, social media has become a new site for ideological struggles between citizenry and governments seeking to shape public perception (see Althusser 1971, 7).

Kenyan Statistics

In the Kenyan context, social media is being used in the fight to expand social and economic freedom. According to Social Media Lab Africa (SIMElab 2019), an African center for research in big data and social media analytics, WhatsApp is the most used social media in Kenya (see table 5.1).

Kenyans use social media primarily for online citizenship, political debates, news acquisition, resource mobilization, entertainment, and maintaining relationships with others. Most urban users access social media via mobile phones and laptops, whereas the majority of rural users use mobile phones and cyber cafés. Out of a population of over 53 million, Kenya had over 46.9 million internet subscribers by the end of 2020. (CA 2021; Internet World Stats 2020). The majority of users are between the ages of 21 and 35 and spend an average of three hours per day on the platform (Wamuyu 2020). More than 66% of this age group participates in public debates through these platforms, frequently through WhatsApp groups (Wamuyu 2020, 20). People

Table 5.1 Social Media Usage in Kenya, by Platform

Social media platform	Percentage
WhatsApp	88.6
Facebook	88.5
YouTube	51.2
Instagram	39.0
Twitter	27.9
Yahoo	18.6
LinkedIn	9.3
Snapchat	9.0

Source: Adapted from Social Media Lab Africa, 2019, 3.

over the age of 46 are the least likely to use social media, visiting the platform only for "interesting" and "viral" news (SIMElab 2019, 13). Viral news refers to the "spreadability" of news that becomes popular through rapid sharing among individuals via the internet, based on the perception that the news is interesting (Papacharissi 2016, 28). Influencers on social media are regarded as credible public figures (Budzinski and Gaenssle 2018). Users of social media believe that public figures keep the government in check, challenge societal norms, and set trends.

Nevertheless, according to the Bloggers Association of Kenya (BAKE 2021), Internet freedom in Kenya continues to diminish rapidly. Despite the robust protections for freedom of expression in Articles 33 and 34 of the Kenyan Constitution of 2010, the country's Parliament passed some of the most restrictive media laws in 2013. According to Ifree (2021), a platform that promotes online freedom, Twitter removed 100 Kenyan accounts due to false information in the recent past. However, the notion of disinformation is subjective and ideologically biased (Wasserman 2017). Citizens of the internet, including social media users, are therefore at a crossroads. Evidently, the Twitter management team poses a greater threat to free speech than governments. This is because, unlike government leaders who can be voted out of office for stifling free speech, the Twitter management team cannot be recalled by the people. However, in many instances in Kenya, Twitter was responsible for removing the above 100 accounts in response to complaints. Due to the ease with which the Twitter management team can remove citizenry accounts in response to complaints, individuals who dislike other people's posts report them for removal. The government also reports individuals who criticize its public programs online. This is how the government uses Twitter's management team to silence government critics by removing their accounts.

Overall, the Kenyan government has been progressive about digital migration, arguing it would unlock the great potential in local content production and create job opportunities. However, the state and social media ownership control the online space through the use of repressive legislation to muzzle government critics or those ideologically opposed to ownership rules (BAKE 2021; Wasserman 2017). For instance, the Communication and Multimedia Appeals Tribunal was established by the KIC Act 2013/19, which falls under the state-controlled Communication Authority of Kenya (as mentioned, CA). There was no representation of online communities at the time of creation. This violates Article 10 of the Kenyan Constitution, which permits public participation in the formation of tribunals. The KIC Act 2013/19 created a tribunal with the authority to impose hefty fines on media/social media users, recommend the de-registration of journalists, and issue any order pertaining to freedom of expression (Ifree 2021).

According to the Kenya National Commission on Human Rights (2017), there are persistent threats to suspend the social media accounts of influential Kenyans who criticize the status quo. According to Article 19 (2018), dominant social actors in Kenya are attempting to restrict the freedom of social media. Large-scale social media activists, including prominent bloggers, are subject to arbitrary government arrests, detentions, and suspensions of their social media accounts (CIPESA 2019, 36). Boniface Mwangi, a social media activist, went public a few years ago about the threats he and his family face, including harassment (Standard 2019). Despite the vibrancy of social media on the African continent and in Kenya, dominant social actors frequently attempt to impose draconian legislation and shut down infrastructures that support it. The Kenyan government contends that the spread of inciting messages on social media threatens the peaceful coexistence of its citizens.

Other dominant actors, including religious leaders and conservative individuals/moralists, are more concerned with societal moral values than the government is. Depending on their attire, women in Kenya and Africa as a whole are commonly viewed as the root cause of sexual immorality in society. For instance, the discussions surrounding the adoption of Kenya's Constitution in 2010 centered primarily on women's access to sexual and reproductive rights, particularly abortion. A segment of society, led by the clergy, argued that the Constitution granted too many sexual rights to women, which would lead to moral decline. Article 34 of the Constitution grants the people the right to expression, which includes dress code, whereas Article 36 grants the people the right to belong/associate. The two articles, when read together, grant women the right to dress as they please and to associate/perform at/attend functions of their choosing. According to conservatives and moralists, this is nakedness. Since there is no standard for nudity, some women have stretched their imaginations, regarding the dress code, to the point where they appear naked. They post images of their naked bodies on social media to attract attention. Although the nudity culture among Kenyan women became more explicit after the 2010 Constitution was ratified, this is primarily due to the development of social media technology. The women feel safer posting their nude photographs from the security of their homes and other nudity-friendly locations, such as concerts.

This is because moralists may find it embarrassing if women appeared nude in public places such as malls and parks. We could argue that women are safer online than in the real world. Although emotional and psychological bullying occurs in cyberspace, women do not experience physical bullying. Since then, they have embraced nudity online, from which they resist emotional and psychological attacks.

Considering these considerations, this study employs Foucault's (1979) concept of discipline and power to explain women's resistance to the shrinking freedom caused by the Kenyan government and traditional societal norms. In addition, we employ Foucault's (1977) concept of "dynamic normalization," also known as the panopticon (26f). He argues that governments use surveillance technology such as observatory towers to make citizens "think and act" in fear of the watching government, which would punish them if they broke the law; this creates conformity even when the government is not observing. If read inversely, this concept would reveal that the women use their nude photographs on social media to resist the forms of moral policing by dominant social actors; creating a new conformity that makes the actors "think and act" in fear of condemning the women nudes, thereby regarding them as the new normal. The dominant actors are concerned that the women and their followers will punish them if they resist their dominance and challenge their authority.

Theoretical Framework

This chapter about feminist resistance and cyberbullying leverages technological determinism theory (McLuhan 1994) and qualitative content analysis (Maxwell 2013). The framework describes how Kenyan activists, particularly women, have utilized social media for resistance despite government and other dominant social actors' censorship efforts. The technology of social media provides a platform for activists to reach the masses—to articulate issues of public interest that force the government to provide services. The women use social media to repackage and sell their self-images for financial gain, in ways that certain segments of society disapprove of. The success rate of activists and women using cyberspace for resistance, despite government and dominant social actor disapproval, is based on the space's capacity to reach the masses rapidly and at low operational cost. Social media is also designed to be sensational. Thus, the government censorship of activists and the moralist harassment of women are made alarming to attract the attention of the masses, thereby generating publicity. Consequently, the government and moralists are thrust into the spotlight, causing them to fear attacking activists and women when the public is watching.

The technological determinism theory explains why activists and women persist in their actions despite threats of censorship and bullying. Since the chapter is about women and nude photographs, the remainder of the explanation will exclude activists. The theory contends that social media has heightened women's self-awareness and resistance to oppressive societal norms in a way that traditional media could not. McLuhan (1994) argues that people adapt to their environment through a particular balance of the senses and that a primary medium of age brings out a specific sense of proportion, thereby influencing perception. In other words, the awakening of the senses indicates that women embrace nudity because it meets their specific needs. To better comprehend this, we can paraphrase McLuhan's (1994) infamous phrase "the medium is the message" to argue that social media is the message. This indicates that social media can awaken women's senses (McLuhan, 1994, 64), allowing them to post nude photographs that they would not otherwise post on television or in the newspaper. This is because features such as filters on social media make women's images appear more attractive than they are. In contrast to television, where they must visit TV studios or invite outside broadcasting (OB) equipment into their homes, women can post their naked photographs on social media from the comfort of their homes. Thus, it is possible to argue that women's messages are determined by social media and that social media itself is the message. The McLuhan theory idealizes channels as a dominant force that must be comprehended to understand how the media influence society and culture. If there were no smartphones in society, for instance, women would not share their nude photographs in the public sphere as they do. Without the filters, they may not have appreciated their photographs as much. In addition, the logistical difficulties of accessing TV studios to share their nude photographs may have prevented them from posting as many as they do. This means we can focus on the characteristics of social media rather than what it conveys to comprehend why and how women in Kenya share nude photos with the public. In this instance, it is possible to argue that social media is not merely a medium. Rather, it is the symbolic context of any act of communication. Consequently, social media provides a sense of proportion that enables women to view the sharing of nude photographs as a fashionable form of feminine resistance that enables them to defy societal norms. Through the Kenya Films and Classification Board (KFCB), the government condemns indecent depictions of women. Section 5(ii) of the board's statute (2012) grants it the authority to prohibit nudity, which it terms indecent exposure. In accordance with Karina's (2014) discussion of nudity protest and transnational feminist body politics, the Kenyan government is hesitant to ban online women's nudity because it would only increase the demand for the content. This was the case with *Shackles of Doom*, a play that was deemed too critical of the government. It was prohibited, but it received more attention after being prohibited than when it was performed. Also, in social media terms, the act of banning content can be loosely equated to closing one's social media account. The board is hesitant to do so for two reasons: first, it would spark controversy among followers, and second, the ease with which another account can be created renders the ban/closure ineffective. Consequently, society remains divided regarding women who post nude photos on social media to gain followers. Observably, there is a growing acceptance of nude photography, with some women who participate in the practice being appointed brand ambassadors.

We can illustrate how the "sense of proportion" affects perception by examining how social media posts and cell phone cameras arouse varying senses in women. For instance, some women's senses may be heightened by their hair, others by their legs, and still others by their nakedness. It all depends on what they wish to exhibit, or their communicative requirements. Those with an awakened nudity sense would post more nude photos than those with a less awakened nudity sense. Therefore, each woman who posts nude photographs does so based on the extent to which social media and cell phone cameras stimulate her senses. In McLuhan's view, these modern communication devices can stimulate women's awareness of their nakedness more than traditional media could. Smartphone applications such as filters, for instance, make women's images appear more appealing to followers than they would on live television. Observably, Kenya's commercial environment, technological infrastructure, and legal frameworks motivate women to package their nudities for public consumption due to the economic benefits (Mendelson 2007). As we will see in the following sections of this chapter, some women are approached by commercial advertisers to market their products on their social media timelines due to their enormous following. Others are approached privately by men willing to take them out on dates, among other economic favors, in a practice known in Kenya as "sliding to one's inbox." Ironically, the social media provision for private chats awakens the women's sense of privacy, from which they feel safer conducting their business, away from the public moral police who would despise their nude photos but still follow them. There are instances, however, in which private chats are made public when men and women develop differences and attempt to humiliate one another by releasing screenshots of their private conversations. Any aggrieved person who believes sharing the screenshots will embarrass and/or benefit them would do so. In such situations, public figures are harmed more than anonymous individuals. The implicated female public figures come forward to accept responsibility, claiming they are as human as anyone else in their pursuit of love, belonging, and sex. One woman said: "I'm simply attempting to live my life. Unfriend me if you don't like what I do."

The public's reaction to such a bold statement was a mixture of sympathy and condemnation. In many instances, the number of followers would increase, contrary to expectations. This is due to people's inherent desire to learn more about public figures. If their authorized screenshots are shared, some public figures may choose not to comment and continue with business as usual. Others develop depression and seek medical treatment. Still, the trend of women sharing naked photographs with the public is on the rise. The women interact culturally with social media technology to create a space for self-expression, economic freedom, and resistance to conventional thought.

Methodology

During data collection, the researchers combined traditional and digital ethnography. The researchers recognized that the main challenges with the method would be the difficulties inherent in mapping out a field site that effectively captures the complexity of online/offline connections; developing a sufficient degree of immersion and co-presence for a rich understanding to be attained; and appreciating the challenges offered by the emergence of mobile internet, algorithmic filtering of information, and unpredictable flows of information (Hine 2017). As internet ethnographers, the researchers effectively framed their study of women's resistance to cyberbullying as an investigation into a socially constructed yet technologically mediated phenomenon. They immersed themselves in the cyberbullying phenomenon, investigating how women experience and resist it. They mapped how the bullying became relevant to the research while navigating the complexities involved. First, the researchers joined five popular social media groups in Kenya. They included Facebook, Twitter, WhatsApp, Instagram, and Telegram, where they observed and participated in the women's online lives/resistance. The groups were made up of men and women, but the researchers were more interested in the women and nude photographs because society views women's nudity as a major cause of societal moral decadence. In addition, the sharing of women's naked photographs is rising, which needs to be investigated. While on the groups, the researchers used nonprobability sampling techniques known as purposive/judgmental sampling to identify six respondents for face-to-face interviews. After identifying the six, the researchers began following them on their social media platforms such as Twitter, Instagram, and Facebook. The researchers were interested in the participants' experiences using nude photographs for feminist resistance, as well as how they dealt with the associated cyberbullying from the moral policing society. The selection was also informed through the observations of the group members participating in the discussions; thus, the selection was based on the respondents'/participants' ability to communicate their lived experiences in an articulate, expressive, and reflective manner; about how and why they use their controlled and sanctioned nude photographs for feminist resistance. The participants/respondents were sampled, and face-to-face interviews were conducted. They also observed what the social media group members said about the respondents/participants chosen. This informed the researchers about the participant's ability to participate in the interviews and whether they possessed the lived experiences. The availability of the respondents for the interviews was also taken into consideration. The researchers were careful not to choose participants solely based on their "loudness" or domineering nature in groups.

While joining the groups, the researchers introduced themselves to the group administrators and informed them of the research objective. The researchers avoided directly introducing themselves to the group members because they wanted to maintain "covertness" even after the members were informed about the study (see Takyi 2015, 865). For the three months that the researchers were conducting the digital ethnography, the administrators also informed the group members about the research objective every morning by reposting the same chat. The researchers were aware that digital ethnographic approaches could infringe on privacy, consent issues, and anonymity, among other things (Langer and Beckman, 2005; Sugiura et al. 2017). The members were notified three months later that the digital ethnography had come to an end. After three months, the researchers followed up with the information-rich participants who had been selected for face-to-face in-depth interviews.

The researchers also accessed viral nude photographs of women while in the groups and observed the group members' reactions to the photographs. The researchers were able to understand how and why the women used social media platforms for resistance by employing a covert participant observation method. The emphasis was on how women use social media for performative feminist resistance, the corresponding economic gain, and how they deal with the associated bullying, particularly from societal norm custodians. The researchers were interested in observing the availability of meaningful space for nude performance, the forms of resistance used in the performances, the types of cyberbullying the women face during their performances, and how they resist it.

The researchers identified observable forms of performative actions and the associated cyber purchasing and attempted to understand how the women resisted and/or negotiated the bullying. The researchers also learned how to interpret unusual behavior among the women and group members in the study's social media groups (see Scott 1990). These involved subtle but decisive gestures/actions informed by the cultural practices of the participants, expressed through emojis, GIFs, and textual symbols such as exclamation marks and dots, among others. The researchers filled the observation schedules on a continuous basis and took standardized notes about the nude performative posts and the reactions of the groups, which were later transcribed into meaningful information and used to invalidate/validate the responses from the in-depth interviews.

Discussion of Findings

Foucauldian View of Kenyan Women's Performative Resistance

This section employs Foucault (1979) to analyze the women's performative lives by discussing their use of feminine resistance against Kenyan laws and societal norms. This subsection examines six cases of middle-aged black Kenyan women who live "deviant" performative lifestyles and resistances on social media. The ladies picked for in-person interviews are unquestionably influential, with tens of thousands of followers on their social media platforms. We utilized Foucault's (1979) idea of "discipline and power" to examine the relationship between power/government/societal norms and feminist opposition in Kenya. We can view disciplinary power/laws/norms as the respondents' comparable point of reference for feminist resistance techniques, particularly nudity, but also obscene speech. Using their cases, we argue that disciplinary power/government/societal norms train and control women through institutions and scientific discourses while simultaneously punishing them pedagogically in proportion to the violations they commit; as a result, we established that disciplinary power primarily constructs, educates, and shapes. In contrast, women's modes of resistance challenge the status quo and counteract the power of discipline. For example, in one of her Facebook photo posts, Atieno Otieno (not her true social media account name) poses naked in a white towel with the message, "I know 60% of women who shower once per day, lady, how do you do it? Is it morning, evening, or whenever you recall?"

As the description implies, the debate surrounding such a picture is about her physique, not feminine hygiene. The followers are divided as to whether Atieno's decision to expose her breasts was appropriate or inappropriate. More men than women are opposed to women uploading naked photos online. However, men and women who are opposed to the posting do not unfollow women who upload nude images. This suggests two potential outcomes: First, the men and women who oppose the posting want to reverse the trend from within. Second, they appreciate the postings but claim to be against it because society expects them to. The examination of the respondents' debates reveals that women circumvent the norm through rearticulating discourses, and they may strive to undermine the institutional regulation of behavior in the long run. The women's resistance has been made feasible by the widespread ownership of information communication technology (ICT) devices, especially smartphones, which they utilize to further the feminist resistance agenda in many forms. According to the women's comments, it is straightforward for women to bundle their self-body images in order to assert their feminist opposition in the internet arena. According to McLuhanian (1994), ICT devices decrease women's reluctance to use nudity. The opposition is bolstered by women's employment of their own controlled and sanctioned nudities for economic advantage, which can be viewed as the emergence of a consciousness of this phenomenon. In the past, men owned, controlled, and sanctioned the bodies of women for economic and physiological gain.

Using Foucault's (1977) theory of dynamic normalization, we can link the respondents' feminine resistance to the advancement in ICT, which has enabled massive outreach to the people, either as group members or as followers, due to the ease of sharing images and video clips through the social media's networked memberships. Additionally, the women may readily monitor their nude posts, which are also observed by interested parties. As previously stated, we can identify the women's opposition philosophically by reading the dynamic normalization backward (Foucault 1977). Aware that people in power/moralists are observing them via social media, they chose to flout the power's expectation in ways that excite the women's followers, depriving those in power of the courage/power to prevent the women from fulfilling their want—publishing the nudes. The ladies lead their followers and group members in establishing a new norm that diminishes the moralists' influence. This makes it less effective for the powerful to intimidate or impose their "moral" desires.

Consequently, some powerful people/moralists, such as advertisers, join the bandwagon because of the economic benefits associated with the new kind of feminine resistance. In opposition to the current order, the ladies pool audiences by shocking them with nudity and obscenities. To reach their following, advertisers ask women to promote on their social media platforms. In Foucauldian terms, there is monitoring and countersurveillance between the powerful and the women hawking nudity as a kind of resistance, with a portion of the powerful learning to accept the women's new standard while others, such as advertising, join them. There is an additional group of powerful people/moralists who refuse to back down; they continue to bully women. These are the topics covered in this chapter. In the following section, the chapter examines how women cope with cyberbullying. By inverting the concept of dynamic normalization, we are able to see how women have transformed the long-standing, institutionalized moral policing and objectification of their bodies into resistance and, accordingly, economic advantage. Despite the fact that differing cultural perceptions on women's rights violations have hampered efforts to establish an internationally acceptable legal framework, ICT devices are facilitating the formation of a worldwide consciousness of women's self-awareness in the Global South. More women are finding the courage to resist repressive societal norms, which are expressed in numerous ways, bullying being the most prominent. As a kind of feminist resistance, women have acquired conspicuous online nudity via daring. In addition, right-wing organizations have strengthened their efforts to educate women about their potential, fortitude, and capacity to unite against long-standing institutional oppression.

How Do Women in Kenya Resist Institutionalized Bullying?

Long-standing systematic moral policing of women in Kenyan society is the primary cause of cyberbullying against women. Based on dynamic normalization, portions of Kenyan society police women's online activity, which underpins the bullying. The major type of resistance to cyberbullying is, essentially, the women's inversion of the principle described above. Due to their minority status, the bullies are now compelled to remain silent because of the inverted surveillance on social media. Moreover, ICT devices enable women to avoid those who make them uncomfortable. The followers who are not interested in the women's posts have the option to unfollow them, allowing bullies to leave whenever they choose. Unlike in the past, when audiences lacked authority over their public environment, this is not the case. The researchers were cognizant of the particular group of bullies who would troll women, even though they could unfollow them if they did not like their message.

For example, Nasombi (not her real name) hails from a chicken-farming region, where chicken is a popular holiday food. During a discussion regarding the sustainability of the recently created chicken slaughterhouse in the region, Nasombi shared a photo of herself wearing a revealing outfit while holding a rooster. She captioned the photo as follows: "Christmas offer has arrived, who wants an early Christmas present? *Mapema ndio best.*" In response to her post, a member replied, "I'll start taking you seriously when your posterior becomes larger than the hen you're holding." She responded by stating that she does not reply to infantile comments and admonishing the member not to comment on her future articles. Observably, some group members applauded while others disapproved. The researchers observed that many women, like Nasombi, erase bullies' comments in addition to publicly reprimanding them. The women view bullying as negative energy and dismiss it openly, stating that they do not wish to engage such energies. However, the tens of thousands of comments the women receive may aid in addressing bullying more effectively. The remarks of many bullies go nearly overlooked since they are buried among the numerous favorable and neutral responses to the women's nude posts. Although the government is the most powerful actor ostensibly regulating bullying, it is also perhaps one of the most formidable bullies on social media platforms. For instance, the KFCB frequently disapproves categorically of naked women's posts on the grounds that it corrupts public morality. Frequently, the board questions sarcastically why a mature lady would upload nude images of herself. The director of the board previously advised, "As you publish these nude images, consider how you will feel when you realize that your children have access to nude images of other women."

It is arguable that the board is tolerant of women who upload nude images, mostly because prohibiting the practice may simply encourage it. In some instances, however, the board has prohibited the screening of certain films, particularly ones featuring gay relationships, on the grounds that they violate nature and God's will.

Conclusion

In conclusion, disciplinary power attempts to train and control women through institutions and scientific discourses, while pedagogically punishing them in proportion to their violations. To keep women's nudity in check, the disciplinary power body shames, condemns certain women's practices, threatens, intimidates, and restricts freedom of expression. By daring to defy the laws and norms, rearticulating the control and sanctions on their bodies, and generally destabilizing the institutional control of behavior, women have utilized social media to resist disciplinary power. They openly call out the bullies, delete the bullying comments, unfollow the bullies, ignore them, and occasionally engage them in online fights. As evidenced by the inverted dynamic normalization, the women have inverted the disciplinary power, whereby they defy and punish the perceived moral powers. The reversal of roles has been made possible by ICT, which has awakened women's senses and created a perceived and/or actual majority online presence that enables them to resist disciplinary power psychologically and virtually. The women primarily assert feminist resistance by repackaging their self-body images, which enables them to command a massive online following that ultimately attracts advertisers and brand sellers who pay them to access their followers. This trend of women posting nude photographs on social media for financial gain is new. However, this is the primary reason why the women refuse to stop despite the bullying of the disciplinary authority. The development of ICT and the adoption of a relatively rights-based constitution in Kenya are additional factors. The ICT has enabled women to access and become familiar with the practices of other women around the world. This has increased awareness of women's self-consciousness in general. It has also affirmed to women the possibility of gaining economically from rearticulated resistance to discipline, as practiced in other parts of the world. As a result, women have shattered the legal and social constraints that bind their body images and what they can do with them.

References

Althusser, Louis. 1971. "Ideology and Ideological State Apparatuses." In *Lenin and Philosophy and Other Essays*. Translated by Ben Brewster. 121–176. New York: Monthly View Press.

Bloggers Association of Kenya (BAKE). 2021. "The State of Blogging & Social Media in Kenya." https://www.ifree.co.ke/.

Budzinski, Oliver, and Sophia Gaenssle. 2018. "The Economics of Social Media (Super-)Stars: An Empirical Investigation of Stardom and Success on YouTube." *Journal of Media Economics* 31, no. 3–4: 75–95.

Castells, Manuel. 2008. "The New Public Sphere: Global Civil Society, Communication Networks, and Global Governance." *Annals of American Academy* 616: 78–93.

Collaboration on International ICT Policy for East and Southern Africa (CIPESA). 2019. *State of Internet Freedom in Africa 2019*. Kampala, September.

Communication Authority of Kenya (CA). 2020. *Report of the Public Consultation of USF Phase 2 of Cellular Mobile Infrastructure and Service Project*. October. https://ca.go.ke/consumers/public-consultations/published-findings/.

Communication Authority of Kenya (CA). 2021. *A Fourth Quarter Sector Statistics Report for the Financial Year 2020/21*. April–June. https://www.ca.go.ke/sites/default/files/2023-06/Sector%20Statistics%20Report%20Q4%202020-2021.pdf

Constitution of Kenya. 2010. https://www.museums.or.ke/wp-content/uploads/2020/04/ConstitutionofKenya-2010.pdf.

Curran, James, Natalie Fenton, and Des Freedman. 2016. "Misunderstanding the Internet." *Pedagogies* 11, no. 3: 270–273.

Ekeh, Peter. 1975. "Colonialism and the Two Publics in Africa: A Theoretical Statement." *Comparative Studies in Society and History* 17, no. 1: 91–112.

Foucault, Michael. 1979. *Discipline and Punish: The Birth of the Prison*. New York: Random House.

Foucault, Michael. 1977. *The History of Sexuality: An Introduction*. Hammonsworth, UK: Penguin.

Habermas, Jurgen. 1989. "The Public Sphere: An Encyclopedia Article." In *Critical Theory and Society: A Reader*, ed. Eric Stephen and Douglas Kellner, 136–142. New York: Routledge.

Hine, Christine. 2017. "Ethnography and the Internet: Taking Account of Emerging Technological Landscapes." *Fudan Journal of the Humanities and Social Sciences* 10: 315–329.
Ifree. 2021."Twitter Removes 100 Kenyan Accounts After Gross Misinformation Violations." September. https://www.ifree.co.ke/2021/09/twitter-removes-100-kenyan-accounts-after-gross-misinformation-violations-report/.
Internet World Stats. 2020. *Number of Internet Users in African Countries.* https://www.statista.com/statistics/505883/number-of-internet-users-in-african-countries/.
Karina, Eileraas. 2014. "Sex(t)ing Revolution, Femen-izing the Public Square: Aliaa Magda Elmahdy, Nude Protest, and Transnational Feminist Body Politics." *Journal of Women in Culture and Society* 40, no. 1: 40–52.
Kenya Film and Classification Board. 2012. "KFCB, Regulations and Guidelines." https://kfcb.go.ke/sites/default/files/2021-01/Film_Classification_Guidelines.pdf.
Kenya Information and Communication Act. 2012. "KIC Act." https://eregulations.invest.go.ke/media/Kenya%20Information%20and%20Communications%20Act%201998.pdf.
Kenya Law. 2018. "Civil Appeal 156 of 2017, February." http://kenyalaw.org/caselaw/cases/view/148468/.
Kenya National Commission on Human Rights. 2017. *A Human Rights Monitoring Report on the 2017 Repeat Presidential Elections.* Nairobi: KNCHR.
Langer, Roy, and Suzanne Beckman. 2005. "Sensitive Research Topics: Netnography Revisited." *Qualitative Market Research, An International Journal* 8, no. 2: 189–203.
Maxwell, Joseph. 2013. *Qualitative Research Design: An Interactive Approach.* Los Angeles: SAGE.
McLuhan, Marshall. 1994. *Understanding Media: The Extensions of Man.* Cambridge, MA: MIT Press.
Media Council of Kenya. 2020. "The State of the Media in Kenya." https://mediacouncil.or.ke/node/387.
Mendelson, Andrew. 2007. "On the Function of the United States Paparazzi: Mosquito Swarm or Watchdogs of Celebrity Image Control and Power." *Visual Studies* 22, no. 2: 169–183.
Ogola, George. 2015. "Social Media as a Heloroglossic Discursive Space and Kenya's Emergent Alternative/Citizen Experiment." *African Journalism Studies* 36, no. 4: 66–81.
Oriare, Peter, Rosemary Okello-Orlale, and Wilson Ugangu. 2010. *The Media We Want: The Kenya Media Vulnerability Study.* Nairobi: Friedrich Ebert Stiftung (FES).
Osaghae, Eghosa. 2006. "Colonialism and Civil Society in Africa: The Perspective of Ekeh's Two Publics." *Voluntas* 17, no. 3: 233–245.
Papacharissi, Zizi. 2016. *Affective Publics Sentiment, Technology, and Politics.* New York: Oxford University Press, 2016.
Scott, James. 1990. *Domination and the Arts of Resistance: Hidden Transcripts.* New Haven and London: Yale University Press.
Social Media Lab Africa (SIMElab). 2019. *Social Media Consumption in Kenya.* Nairobi: USIU. https://www.usiu.ac.ke/1346/simelab-launches-social-media-consumption-in-kenya-report/-.
Standard. 2014. "Njeri Mwangi: My Life with an Activist." March. https://www.standardmedia.co.ke/sunday-magazine/article/2000106376/njeri-mwangi-my-life-with-an-activis.

Standard. 2016. "Bungoma County Tops in 2G and 3G Use." November. https://www.standardmedia.co.ke/ureport/article/2000224894/n-a.

Standard. 2019. "Activist Boniface Mwangi Arrested. " May. https://www.standardmedia.co.ke/nairobi/article/2001324230/n-a.

Sugiura, Lisa, Rosemary Wiles, and Catherine Pope. 2017. "Ethical Challenges in Online Research: Public/Private Perceptions." *Research Ethics* 13, nos. –43: 184–199.

Takyi, Emmanuel. 2015. "The Challenge of Involvement and Detachment in Participant Observation." *The Qualitative Report* 20, no. 6: 864–872.

Wamuyu, Patrick. 2020. *The Kenyan Social Media Landscape: Trends and Emerging Narratives*. Nairobi: SIMElab.

Wasserman, Herman. 2017. "Fake News from Africa: Panics, Politics and Paradigms." *Journalism* 21, no. 1: 3–16.

6
The Application of IHL on Israeli's Cyber Strategies Against the Palestinians

A Feminist Perspective

Anwar Mhajne

Cyberattacks' increased frequency and sophistication make cyberwarfare and espionage critical for policymakers and military leaders globally. Weaponizing a heavily populated civilian space has enormous implications for the human rights of the civilian population. Existing international humanitarian law (IHL) treaties and customary law, also known as the law of armed conflict, offer guidelines for states' behavior on several armed conflict issues (Gisel and Rodenhäuser 2019). IHL regulates the rights and obligations of fighting parties and provides certain protections for noncombatants. According to the International Committee of the Red Cross (ICRC), "International humanitarian law is a set of rules which seek, for humanitarian reasons, to limit the effects of armed conflict. It protects persons who are not or are no longer participating in the hostilities and restricts the means and methods of warfare" (2004). The four Geneva Conventions of 1949 constitute a significant part of IHL. Additional Protocols of 1977 protecting armed conflict victims supplement the Conventions (ICRC 2004). Other agreements, such as the 1954 Convention for the Protection of Cultural Property in the Event of Armed Conflict and the 2000 Optional Protocol to the Convention on the Rights of the Child, ban specific weapons and military tactics and protect some categories of people (ICRC 2004).

These laws are relevant in cyberspace, especially concerning the rules on the conduct of hostilities. IHL applies to cyberattacks as part of a war or an armed conflict, where the parties concerned must respect the rules of permissible means and methods of warfare and the principles of proportionality, the distinction between civilians and fighters, and military necessity (Kittichaisaree 2017). In addition, the laws include the principle precautions to "the prohibition to render useless objects indispensable to the survival of the population, the obligation to respect and protect medical services, and many others" (Gisel and Rodenhäuser 2019). For instance, the law of armed conflict bans cyberattacks that could damage critical infrastructures such as dams and power stations. It also prohibits targeting nuclear and other facilities because they could cause excessively devastating consequences (Kittichaisaree 2017).

Some feminist legal scholars have critiqued IHL for being inherently discriminatory for prioritizing men, specifically male combatants, and usually perceive women as victims or give them legitimacy only in their role as mothers (See Gardam and Jarvis 2001). Gardam and Jarvis (2001) highlight that about half of the 42 provisions addressing women within the Geneva Conventions and their 1977 Supplementary Protocols focus on women's roles as mothers. They also contend that the protections for women from sexual violence are framed using patriarchal language such as chastity and modesty (Gardam and Jarvis 2001). For example, Article 27 of Geneva Convention IV states that women in international armed conflict should be protected "against any attack on their honour, in particular against rape, enforced prostitution, or any form of indecent assault." The provision is problematic because the focus on women's honor reinforces "the notion of women as men's property, rather than because they constitute violence. This proprietary image is underlined by the use of the language of protection rather than prohibition of the violence" (Charlesworth 1999, 386). Protocol I was endorsed to address this issue and change the reference to a woman's honor with the notion that women should "be the object of special respect." Charlesworth (1999) also critiqued this modification for denoting that women's role in childbirth is the basis of special status. In addition she argues that "the provisions on rape are not specifically included in the category of grave breaches of international humanitarian law" (Charlesworth 1999, 386). IHL, Charlesworth (1999) argues, "treats rape and sexual assault as an attack on (the warrior's) honor or the sanctity of motherhood and not explicitly as of the same order as grave breaches such as compelling a prisoner of war to serve in enemy forces" (387). However, the statutes of the two ad hoc tribunals and the ICC offer more comprehensive responses to sexual violence by considering it as a possible crime of genocide, crime against humanity, or a war crime, depending on the context (Charlesworth 1999). This chapter argues that feminist scholars should extend their critique of the limitation of IHL to protecting data and guaranteeing civilians the right to data privacy in conflict settings. In examining the use of cyberspace in the Israeli-Palestinian conflict, I argue that there is a need to include data protection and safe civilian access to information technology under IHL protections. The lack of regulation is alarming due to the potential dangers that gross abuses of the rights to privacy and data protection may introduce in conflict zones.

Why Should Feminists Care About Data Privacy and Protection?

Questioning power and pushing for justice, equity, and equality are central to feminist thought (Floreani 2021). Data privacy and protection are infused in systems of inequality and colonialism. Data is arguably becoming the most crucial assistance we have as individuals. States and companies utilize their access to data to accumulate power and attempt to control and suppress oppositional and non-normative voices in multiple contexts. Access to data gives malicious state and nonstate actors the ability to manipulate and utilize it to their benefit. We see considerable evidence of how data has been abused and misused to use the democratic process in the 2016 US elections.

We also see evidence of how facial-recognition surveillance and policing disproportionately harm people of color and marginalized communities (Crockford 2020). Privacy has been foundational in the history of LGBTQ+ rights (Crockford 2020). States passed invasive laws and policies violating the privacy of individuals to suppress and stigmatize them due to their sexual preferences and gender expressions for decades (Ringrose 2020). For instance, in the US, "LGBTQ+ individuals in the US were subject to immense amounts of surveillance and were systematically removed from public servant roles due to fear and stigma of 'sexual perversion'" (Crockford 2020; also see Gleason 2017). People of color are also subject to extreme and unwarranted surveillance compared to white people. Surveillance disproportionately affected the Muslim community after 9/11 after the signing of the USA PATRIOT Act (2001). The act expanded law enforcement agencies' ability to conduct surveillance on anyone suspected of involvement in terrorism (Council on American-Islamic Relations 2004; Ibish 2003; O'Connor 2014). However, the surveillance efforts have been mainly directed at several people, specifically Muslims, with no connection to terrorism (Ibish 2003). For instance, in 2012, it was revealed that the New York Police Department built a comprehensive surveillance program of Muslim student organizations on campuses all over the Northeast (Ebadolahi 2012; O'Connor 2014).

Similarly, the Federal Bureau of Investigation (FBI) surveillance programs were later revealed in other regions in the US (ACLU 2012). Moreover, the emergence and advancement of AI technologies such as facial recognition, digital surveillance, and automated decision-making algorithms have exacerbated and increased the tools of oppression available in the hands of governments and other groups. Data retention and anti-encryption policies further entrench the harm caused by privacy-invasive technologies.

The advancements in internet censorship technology and Edward Snowden's revelations about the NSA's global surveillance exposed the weakness of internet freedom, privacy, and data protection (MacAskill et al. 2013). Government surveillance violates privacy and the human rights of anyone perceived in opposition to the state (Mhajne 2021). For example, the UAE hired hackers to collect data to help make a case against Emirati activist Ahmed Mansoor who critiqued the country's engagement in the war in Yemen (Bing and Schectman 2019). He also criticized the treatment of migrant workers in the UAE and its suppression of the opposition (Bing and Schectman 2019). Saudi Arabia was able to execute Jamal Khashoggi, a Saudi journalist, in Turkey after relying on hackers to collect information on his work (Mhajne 2021). China (see Richardson 2016), Russia (see Human Rights Watch 2018), and Vietnam (see Human Rights Watch 2019) weaponize cybersecurity threats to magnify their control over the internet and limit some rights (Mhajne 2021).

Feminism has generally pushed to challenge the public/private dichotomies, which traditionally organized social relations and contributed to the subordination of women (Olsen 1985). Men usually controlled the public sphere, which included work, governance, and civil society, whereas women were tied to the private sphere of the family and home (Gilman 2021). However, feminists such as Anita Allen (1988) and Linda McClain (1998) argued that privacy is essential for women to "live out their disparate, nonconforming preferences" because it gives women space to develop and carry out their ends (Allen 1988, 86–87). In cyberspace, women experience several gendered harms, including online harassment, digital discrimination, and sexual surveillance (Gilma 2021). For instance, automated digital profiles used to regulate the access of individuals to jobs and other benefits "raise issues of digital discrimination based on gender (as well as other identities)" (Gilman 2021, 18; See also Madden et al. 2017). For example, until they were faced with a lawsuit in 2019, Facebook enabled advertisers to target job ads at only men (Gilman 2021). Also, Amazon tested a hiring algorithm for technical jobs but abandoned it because it suggested men over equally competent women (Dastin 2018).

Nonetheless, there is a lack of work applying a feminist lens to data protection. "Data privacy" refers to protocols for collecting and handling "sensitive" data. However, "data protection" refers to a set of technical mechanisms you can use to protect your data's privacy, availability, and integrity. Data protection is focused on preventing the unauthorized use of your data, while data privacy defines who has authorized access. Feminists can start addressing data protection by analyzing and questioning governments' and private institutions' power over users' data collection and distribution. These bodies can collect data without users' full knowledge or understanding of how their data is used once collected. Privacy systems currently in place are based on notice and consent. However, this idea is flawed because it is difficult for users to read long, vague, and confusing privacy policies (Gilman 2021). They cannot also negotiate its terms (Gilman 2021). This generates risks for everyone, specifically from communities already living and experiencing multiple inequalities (Noble 2018; Gandy 2010; Guzik 2009; de Vries 2010). Similar to the central goal of feminism, the push for data protection aspires to address structural inequalities and power hierarchies on the local, state, and global levels.

The Protection of Data Privacy HRL, and IHL

Human rights law (HRL) and IHL are two laws applicable to examining the right to privacy and its development in international law. Both IHL and HRL apply in armed conflict (ICRC 2010). However, a state can suspend several human rights under HRL if it deals with "a situation of emergency" (ICRC 2010), while the state cannot append IHL "(except as provided in Article 5 to the Fourth Geneva Convention)" (ICRC 2010).

HRL

The right to privacy is recognized and protected in Article 12 of the Universal Declaration of Human Rights (UDHR) and Article 17 of the International

Covenant on Civil and Political Rights (ICCPR). Various tools, such as the ICCPR, the European Convention on Human Rights, and the Human Rights Act, play a critical role in establishing a person's right to privacy. HRL safeguards both online and offline communications.

In Article 12 of the Universal Declaration of Human Rights (UDHR), privacy was initially acknowledged as a right in international law. It was afterward included in the ICCPR and regional mechanisms (Woods 2019). Article 12 of UDHR (Diggelmann 2014) and Article 17 of the ICCPR state that no individual should be subjected to the indiscriminate and illegal violation of their privacy. HRLs tools such as the ICCPR, the European Convention on Human Rights, and the Human Rights Act were critical in establishing a person's right to privacy (Woods 2019). However, with the internet becoming both omnipresent and progressively intimate, the borders between private and public domains are not clearly defined (Woods 2019; see UN High Commissioner for Human Rights 2014). However, this does not undermine the right to privacy (Woods 2019). The right to privacy has been understood to include informational privacy in the General Comment on the right to privacy (UDHR, Article 17), which speculates that "the gathering and holding of personal information on computers, data banks, and other devices, whether by public authorities or private individuals or bodies, must be regulated by law" (UNHRC 1988, Section 10) (see Mathiesen 2014). Therefore, online and offline communications are safeguarded under HRL.

Article 12 of the UDHR and Article 17 of the ICCPR establish that no one shall be subjected to arbitrary or unlawful interference with their privacy. This obligation has been understood to include informational privacy in General Comment 16 of the Human Rights Committee from 1988 (Lubin 2020). There, individual online and offline communications are protected under HRL from indiscriminate interception (Lubin 2020).

In addition, the right to privacy has been addressed in multiple international and regional human rights treaties (Lubin 2020). Toward the end of the 1960s, data protection regulations have become the center of a continuing debate within the international community (Lubin 2020).[1] As the International Law Commission has stated:

> A variety of binding and non-binding instruments, national legislations and judicial decisions regulate this area. Earlier efforts within the United Nations, the Council of Europe and the [Organization for Economic Co-operation and Development (OECD)] culminated in the adoption of "first

generation" instruments and provided synergies at the domestic level in the promulgation of "first generation" legislation, beginning in the 1970s. (See United Nations 2006)

These tools were incorporated in the Council of Europe Convention for the Protection of Individuals Concerning Automatic Processing of Personal Data (No. 108), the OECD Guidelines on the Protection of Privacy and Transborder Data Flows of Personal Data, and the UN Guidelines for the regulation of computerized personal data files (Lubin 2020). However, these instruments did not create universally accepted data protection procedures (Kriangsak and Kuner 2015; Lubin 2020). For example, in contrast to the right to privacy, the right to data protection is not recognized in HRL (Kriangsak and Kuner 2015).

IHL

On the other hand, IHL specifically applies in armed-conflict situations. Data protection and the right to data privacy do not find explicit mention or specific protection in the treatises of IHL (Lubin 2020). Under IHL, civilian items are safeguarded from attack and excessive accidental damage, "but States take different views on whether data benefits from the same protection" (Gisel and Rodenhäuser 2019). The ICRC Customary IHL Database does not have a significant mention of privacy within the 161 rules it identifies as the common core of humanitarian law binding on all entities to all recent armed conflicts (Lubin 2020). According to Rodenhäuser (2021), some questions remain extremely debated among states and some IHL experts; for example, does civilian data have the same protection as civilian objects? There were a few incidents where data protection was mentioned during armed conflict (Lubin 202). For instance, the International Court of Justice (ICJ), in the 2004 Palestinian Wall Advisory Opinion, recognized that the right to privacy in Article 17 of ICCPR pertained to the occupied Palestinian territory (oPt) (Lubin 2020; also see *Legal Consequences of the Construction of a Wall in the Occupied Palestinian Territory* 2004). However, the court did not clarify why and how it applied or assess the implications of such an application (Lubin 2020).

The Edward Snowden revelations in 2013 of the invasiveness of US intelligence surveillance and the Cambridge Analytica scandal in 2018, when the firm used data inappropriately attained from Facebook to build voter profiles, were seminal points in the debate around data protection (Woods 2019). They resulted in various international and regional human rights treaties dealing with protection against surveillance from state and nonstate actors (Lubin 2020). For instance, starting in 2014, the UN Human Rights Committee has begun regularly dealing with surveillance regulation in its final comments to states parties' reports (Lubin 2020). Regionally, the European Court of Human Rights (ECtHR), the Court of Justice of the European Union (CJEU), the Inter-American Commission, and the Court on Human Rights have advanced extensive jurisprudence on surveillance and privacy (Lubin 2020).

Despite the progress, these initiatives are insufficient because they viewed data protection as an extension of the right to privacy (Woods 2019; Lubin 2020). These instruments do not create general agreed-upon data protection rules (Woods 2019; Lubin 2020). Data protection extends data privacy (Woods 2019; Lubin 2020). Unlike the right to privacy, there is no standalone right to data protection, which could be applied to private and public data. Therefore, these instruments do not deliver adequate regulations and guidance for data protection (Woods 2019; Lubin 2020).

Despite the lack of universal data protection regulation, we are witnessing local and regional shifts toward developing legal procedures recognizing data protection that is separate from the right to privacy. A good example is the European Union's General Data Protection Regulation (GDPR) of 2018, which covers data processors outside the EU handling EU subjects' data (Lubin 2020). In addition, several countries have implemented legal procedures for data protection. According to the UN Conference on Trade and Development, as of November 15, 2023, 137 out of 194 countries have legislation to protect data and privacy. These local and regional steps should serve as a basis for international recognition of the right to data protection.

These initiatives do not address the right to data protection during occupation or armed conflict. More academic and legal literature is needed for managing wartime informational privacy and data protection. This is a significant issue because it leaves too much power to a few security institutions and professionals who are not interested in assessing the humanitarian cost of their surveillance and data manipulation (Rodenhäuser 2021). This is especially concerning since there is an increased risk for the civilian population through the (mis)use of data by warring parties and the spread of misinformation, disinformation, and hate speech (Rodenhäuser 2021). Feminist engagement in this literature is essential for centering human security and guaranteeing data protection, justice, and equality. One way feminists can contribute to the debate is by highlighting the importance of developing legal protections in IHL for civilian data.

Additionally, they can challenge the concept of necessity outlined in Article 53 of the Fourth Geneva Convention. The article establishes that "any destruction by the Occupying Power of real or personal property belonging individually or collectively to private persons . . . is prohibited, except where such destruction is rendered necessary by military operations." This leaves it in the hands of the occupying power to decide what constitutes a "legitimate" threat authorizing abuse of physical and data property as well as abuse of data privacy. Feminists could also highlight how the violence of the occupation in the physical realm translates into discrimination and violence in the virtual realm. Israel's occupation of the Palestinians is a prominent example of such abuses.

The Applicability of IHL to Palestine

IHL applies to Israel's conduct in the Palestinian territories due to the military nature of the occupation. IHL considers occupation a warfare tool to control a foreign territory after an armed conflict. The purpose of IHL is to regulate the Occupying Power's administration of the occupied territory, balancing between the security of the occupying forces and the welfare of the local population (ICRC 2023). In this context, IHL outlines the primary responsibility of the occupying power to provide for the needs and ensure the welfare of the occupied population (ICRC 2023). In addition, the occupier must ensure public life and order while respecting the country's laws (ICRC 2023). IHL strictly prohibits collective punishment and demolishing private property outside of military operations. In 1967, the Israeli Defense Forces (IDF) gained effective control over the Palestinian territories, encompassing the West Bank, East Jerusalem, and the Gaza Strip (ICRC 2023). These areas constitute the occupied Palestinian territory (oPt). Hence, IHL governs Israel's engagement and conduct in the oPt and its relationship with the Palestinians (ICRC 2023). As mentioned, Article 53 of the Fourth Geneva Convention establishes that "any destruction by the Occupying Power of real or personal property belonging individually or collectively to private persons . . . is prohibited, except where such destruction is rendered necessary by military operations." Customary IHL further prohibits an invading army's forcible taking of private property. Protecting private property should be extended to civilian digital data protection and safe civilian access to information technology under IHL.

Surveillance of the Palestinians

Surveillance has played an essential role in maintaining Israel's occupation of the Palestinians. However, before the surveillance of the internet and social media sites became prominent, Israel attempted to restrict and control Palestinian access to the internet. As Weidmann et al. (2016) demonstrate, politically marginalized communities have lesser internet access rates than the dominant group. Their findings show that since states play a central role in distributing internet access, they can sabotage its liberating effects (Weidmann et al. 2016). Two mechanisms can explain this conclusion (Weidmann et al. 2016). First, the government develops "ethnic favoritism," meaning it mainly promotes economic and technological development in regions where their ethnic group is the majority (Weidmann et al. 2016). Second, some governments, who are worried about the capacity of communication technology to facilitate protests and organize the opposition, will strategically prevent specific groups from access to communication technology (Weidmann et al. 2016). This results in digital discrimination, which refers to lower access of marginalized groups to up-to-date information and communication technology (ICT) (Weidmann et al. 2016). If this digital inequality is alleviated, we expect these modern channels to empower people and societies to foster lasting political and economic development.

Internet access in the Palestinian territories was illegal until 1993 when the Oslo Accords permitted the Palestinians to own and construct their individual telecommunications infrastructure (Tawil-Souri and Aouragh 2014). However, the Accords stipulated that Israel would control all frequencies and determine where Palestinians could build new infrastructure (Tawil-Souri and Aouragh 2014). Additionally, the Oslo Accords fragmented the West Bank into three areas. The first is Area A, which contains about 18% of the West Bank. This area was supposed to be under the Palestinian Authority's (PA) complete control (Tawil-Souri and Aouragh 2014). The second is Area B. It includes 20% of the West Bank and is intended to be under PA civil jurisdiction and combined Israeli and Palestinian security control (Tawil-Souri and Aouragh 2014). Finally, Area C, which encompasses 62% of the West Bank, was under complete Israeli civil and security management (Tawil-Souri and Aouragh 2014). As a result, infrastructure is typically allowed in Area A but rarely in Area B and never in Area C (Tawil-Souri and Aouragh 2014).

Moreover, Israel forbade Palestinians from installing infrastructure buffer zones along the separation wall (Tawil-Souri and Aouragh 2014). Thus,

Palestinian internet traffic relies on fragmented infrastructure dependent on Israeli networks. According to a 2016 World Bank report, on top of having complete control of the core network, Israel frequently blocks importing ICT equipment to Palestinian-controlled areas of the West Bank (AbuShanab 2019). Israel's cyberspace dominance in the Palestinian territories hampers service delivery similar to Israeli roadblocks, checkpoints, and Kafkaesque permit systems (Berda 2017). Since the Gaza blockade, Palestinian internet service providers (ISPs) have needed permits to enter the Gaza Strip to maintain infrastructure (Tawil-Souri and Aouragh 2014).

Nonetheless, these permits are frequently denied (Abou Jalal 2017). Israel's kinetic attacks on Palestinian ICTs and consistent power cuts hinder infrastructure and service delivery (Weinthal and Sowers 2019). The IDF has jammed and hacked telephone, internet, and broadcast signals. Moreover, the army destroyed network infrastructure even when violence was absent. For example, in 2012, the IDF deliberately and continually cut the sole landline connection between southern and northern Gaza (Tawil-Souri and Aouragh 2014). Moreover, "it digs up fiber-optic cables in parts of the West Bank, uproots transmission towers, confiscates equipment, and holds up multimillion-dollar purchases while charging Palestinian firms' storage' fees" (Tawil-Souri and Aouragh 2014, 117).

This contrasts with Israel's internet penetration rates and advancement in cyberspace, which could be credited to their occupation of the Palestinians. Israel's cybersecurity exports constitute about 5% to 10% of the international cybersecurity market (Tsipori 2016). The IDF has created two spillover effects, contributing to Israel's high-tech and cybersecurity success. First, Unit 8200 is famous for initiating the tech careers of several of its alumni, with companies founded by former soldiers, including NYSE-listed, US-based Palo Alto Networks Inc.; Nasdaq-listed Check Point; and NICE Systems Ltd. (Ravet 2019). Second, Unit 8200 specializes in intelligence gathering. It precedes the foundation of Israel in 1948 (Behar 2016). The Unit's work started during the British Mandate period of the 1930s when it bugged the phone lines of Arabs to acquire information about planned riots (Behar 2016). Therefore, you cannot separate Israel's cyber capability from its occupation of the Palestinian territories. Israel has used the conflict with Palestinians to test its conventional weapons and cyber tools.

Following the occupation of the West Bank and Gaza Strip in 1967, Israel increased its reliance on surveillance, especially during unrest such as the first (1987) and second Palestinian Intifadas (2000). After the outbreak of the second Intifada in 2000, Israel subjected the Palestinians in the oPt to severe movement restrictions, influencing all their daily activities, including the installment of checkpoints (B'tselem 2017). Today, these physical checkpoints serve a purpose beyond the physical control of Palestinians. It became a site for data collection through the installment of facial-recognition technology to verify Palestinians' identities as they cross into Israel.

This heritage of surveillance has been continually upgraded and technologized. The developments in digital technology and biometric surveillance—such as facial, voice, and iris recognition, as well as thumbprinting—have been adopted to monitor Palestinians. Like the old technologies, these new ones have been employed to deepen Israeli state surveillance of the Palestinians. Now, video surveillance and facial-recognition software are daily realities for Palestinians. Since 2000 when several hundred closed-circuit television cameras (CCTVs) were placed in Jerusalem as part of Mabat 2000 ("gaze" in Hebrew), Israel's massive network of CCTV, license plate recognition, and internet protocol cameras have existed throughout the city (Doris 2013). There is approximately one camera per 100 people out of the total population of 40,000, covering only 0.9 square kilometers. Some CCTVs are positioned so that they can see into private homes, leading some women to sleep in their hijabs (Goodfriend 2021), while other families are hesitant about allowing their children to play outside due to the cameras.

In 2015, Israel considerably expanded its surveillance system (Goodfriend 2021). Facial-recognition technology has become pervasive enough to make Palestinians feel unsafe in their cities, towns, and homes (MEE Staff 2021). In 2019, AnyVision, an Israeli facial-recognition firm, began installing automated checkpoints between the occupied West Bank and Israel. Palestinians are electronically registered by tapping an ID card onto a sensor and staring into a small camera that scans their face to be granted access. This technology has advanced to include smartphone technology called Blue Wolf. According to a November 2021 *Washington Post* report, the technology captures photos of Palestinians' faces and matches them to an extensive database of images (Dwoskin 2021). The app helps soldiers decide which Palestinians to detain. The report also stated that to create the database for Blue Wolf, soldiers "competed in photographing Palestinians, including children and the elderly, with prizes for the most pictures collected by each unit." Israel has also been known to use drones at Palestinian protests as surveillance or drop large amounts of tear gas.

The limited and regulated access the Palestinians have to the internet has given the Palestinians a tool to transcend territorial fragmentation and aided the unification of Palestinian voices worldwide (Tawil-Souri and Aouragh 2014). Moreover, the internet emerged as an economic development instrument and a site of transnational political activism surpassing borders, checkpoints, and blockades. Cyber activism may provide a level of virtual mobility. However, it also makes them an easy target of state control and surveillance. Israel has intensified its crackdown on Palestinian digital users after the October 2015 uprising (Taha 2020). It has arrested hundreds of Palestinian activists, students, artists, and journalists "under the pretext of 'incitement' over social media platforms" (Taha 2020, 3). Israel's security establishment has also seized Palestinians' communications to blackmail them into collaborating with the state (Taha 2020).

Social Media

Social media made it much easier for the state to suppress and monitor Palestinian voices and narratives globally (Fatafta 2019). Digital surveillance and control of Palestinians have become a foundational strategy for the Israeli government in the information age, with new institutions and policies emerging to carry out these goals (7amleh 2018). This surveillance is now being done through collaboration between Israeli security units and social media platforms (Fatafta and Nashif 2017).

Israel hacks social media accounts to access information such as sexual orientation, medical and mental conditions, and marital and financial status. According to a public letter signed in 2014 by 43 veterans from Unit 8200, often compared to the US National Security Agency, explaining their refusal to serve in operations involving oPt, the officers stated that Unit 8200 uses such surveillance methods to find "pressure points" to turn Palestinians into informants (Beaumont 2014). The letter highlighted that many Palestinians under Israeli surveillance "are innocent people unconnected to any military activity" (Beaumont 2014). It also explained how harmful personal information about adultery, sexual orientation, and other things deemed controversial in Palestinian society were "used to extort/blackmail the person and turn them into a collaborator" (Beaumont 2014).

Israel created, in 2015, a Cyber Unit in the attorney general's office. The unit pressures Meta (previously known as Facebook), X (formly know as

Twitter), and other social media companies to censor pro-Palestinian content Israel deems offensive, incites violence, or praises terrorism, especially when posted by Palestinians. In 2019, the Israeli Cyber Unit submitted 19,606 requests for content removal to social media platforms (Osman 2021). Sada Social (2021), another Palestinian digital rights organization, documented about 1,000 violations against Palestinian social media users in 2019 by removing public pages, accounts, posts, publications, and access restrictions. In 2020, the Cyber Unit submitted more than 20,000 requests for content moderation (Brem 2021). Social media companies comply with a high percentage of requests for content removal from Israel. 7amleh reported that in 2020, social media companies complied with 81% of Israel's requests to remove Palestinian online content (Carmel et al. 2021).

The extent of the collaboration between social media companies and the Israeli government was further revealed in May 2021, when peaceful demonstrations erupted in the East Jerusalem neighborhood of Sheikh Jarrah against forced expulsions of Palestinians by Israeli authorities. These protests triggered an upsurge of support on social media platforms resulting in thousands of tweets, Facebook posts, and TikTok videos citing hashtags such as #savesheikhjarrah to be shared (Siddiqui and Suleymanova 2021). However, according to 7amlah, the Arab Center for Social Media Advancement, numerous users have reported their Facebook or Instagram posts in solidarity with Sheikh Jarrah residents were blocked, hidden, or deleted. This collaboration to suppress and erase Palestinian voices online effectively extends Israel's colonial practices from the physical to the digital realm, creating a form of digital colonialism.

Additionally, Israel has created a legal structure to prosecute individuals who allegedly published "incitement and hostile propaganda" (Sa'di 2021). To do so, Israel employs predictive algorithmic scanning of Palestinians' social media contents, including statuses, comments, and pictures, to recognize contents the state deems critical of Israel or a form of "incitement to violence," loosely defined (Fatafta and Nashif 2017). The algorithm looks for words such as shaheed (martyr), Zionist state, Al Quds (Jerusalem), or Al Aqsa. It also sweeps for social media accounts containing posts of photos of Palestinians killed or imprisoned by Israel (Nashif 2017). The algorithm flags posts critical of the Israeli occupation and detects "suspects" based on the likelihood of violence. For instance, in 2018 an Israeli court sentenced poet Dareen Tatour to five months in prison for "inciting terrorism" in a poem she posted on social media about Palestinian resistance to the occupation

(Noy 2017). This comes after she spent three years under house arrest and was barred from publishing her work (Al Jazeera 2018). Tatour recited the poem in a video of herself on Facebook and YouTube reading a poem titled "Resist, My People Resist Them" as the soundtrack to images of Palestinians resisting Israeli troops.

Pegasus

In 2010, the NSO Group, an Israeli technology company, was founded to sell a cyber-surveillance product called Pegasus, supposedly intended to mitigate terrorism and serious crime to promote (as it proclaims on its website) global security and stability (see https://www.nsogroup.com/) (Marczak and Scott-Railton 2016). As documented by researchers at the University of Toronto's Citizen Lab and Amnesty International and initially broken by journalists with Forbidden Stories, Pegasus has mainly been used to surveil journalists, civil society activists, and human rights advocates who engage in activities critical of the government in the states that have purchased Pegasus, including in Israel, which tracks Palestinian activists (Human Rights Watch 2022). In November 2021, it was publicized that six Palestinian human rights advocates had been hacked with Pegasus (Kirchgaessner and Safi 2021). These activists worked for organizations categorized by Israel as "terrorist organizations" (Associated Press 2021), including Defense for Children-Palestine and Al-Haq. Al-Haq has been active in Palestine since 1979. International and Israeli human rights groups and the UN rebuked this classification (Lieblich and Shinar 2022). Moreover, the US State Department requested Israel to provide explanations for this move.

Conclusion

Surveillance is a powerful method Israel utilizes to maintain its occupation of the Palestinians. Israel has a known history of using the occupied West Bank as a place to develop and test new technologies. This history is traced to its founding days, especially with its plan to control the Palestinian population, which stayed within its formal territory after 1948. During the Military Regime (1948–1966), the Palestinian population in Israel was put under a comprehensive disciplinary surveillance system characterized by movement restrictions and aggressive policing and monitoring. The advancement of digital technologies and the increased reliance of Palestinians on it has enabled the state to strengthen and optimize its surveillance to penetrate every aspect of Palestinians' daily lives. As Tawil-Souri states, "The mechanisms of digital occupation are exercised through the disruption of everyday life, not simply during exceptional moments of violence" (2012, 36). Thus, Israel's control of Palestinian communication infrastructure extends its occupation to cyberspace and should constitute a violation of IHL. Universal regulations of cyber surveillance at the international level in cases of occupation are needed. Digital data protection and privacy frameworks that promote, respectively, collecting only legitimate data and then housing that data safely (data protection) and the right to privacy in cyberspace (data privacy) can go far in addressing surveillance and other infringements on human rights (General Assembly Resolution 73/179 2018).

However, any practical international legislation needs to be based on a comprehensive understanding of the impact of surveillance on activists. This is where an intersectional postcolonial feminist analysis is essential for shedding light on how various vulnerable groups and individuals are impacted during war and conflict settings by surveillance technology. Feminist and postcolonial scholarship focus on intersectionality and are critical of power hierarchies, colonialism, and violence in all its forms. It puts the experiences of marginalized communities and identities at the center of its analysis of international politics. As the chapters in this volume show, the Palestinian case is only one case where questions of power, intersectionality, data protection, data privacy, and human rights in the digital realm emerge. The new cyber tools and weapons Israel exports to the international community have a more comprehensive global implication on human rights.

Note

1. For more see United Nations (2006).

References

Abou Jalal, Rasha. 2017. "How Gazans Are Dealing with Internet Crisis." *Al-Monitor*, July 9. https://www.al-monitor.com/pulse/originals/2017/07/gaza-power-cuts-electricity-crisis-internet-israel.html.

AbuShanab, A. 2019. "Hashtag Palestine 2018: An Overview of Digital Rights Abuses of Palestinians." 7amleh—The Arab Center for the Advancement of Social Media.
ACLU. 2012. "ACLU EYE on the FBI" [bulletin]. March 2. http://www.aclu.org/files/assets/aclu_eye_on_the_fbi_-_mosque_outreach_03272012_0_0.pdf.
Allen, Anita L. 1988. *Uneasy Access: Privacy for Women in a Free Society*. New Jersey: Rowman & Littlefield.
Al Jazeera. 2018. "Palestinian Poet Jailed over Social Media Post." Conflict News, Al Jazeera, July 31. https://www.aljazeera.com/news/2018/7/31/dareen-tatour-sentenced-to-five-months-in-prison-over-poem.
Al Jazeera. 2019. "Twitter Suspends Accounts of Palestinian Quds News Network." Censorship News, Al Jazeera, November 2. https://www.aljazeera.com/news/2019/11/2/twitter-suspends-accounts-of-palestinian-quds-news-network.
Associated Press. 2021. "Israel Designates 6 Palestinian Human Right Groups as Terrorist Organizations." NPR, October 23. https://www.npr.org/2021/10/23/1048690050/israel-palestinian-human-right-groups.
B'tselem. 2017. "Restrictions on Movement." November 11, 2017. https://www.btselem.org/freedom_of_movement.
Behar, Richard. 2016. "Inside Israel's Secret Startup Machine." *Forbes*, May 12. https://www.forbes.com/sites/richardbehar/2016/05/11/inside-israels-secret-startup-machine/?sh=173e01221a51.
Berda, Yael. 2017. *Living Emergency: Israel's Permit Regime in the Occupied West Bank*. Palo Alto, CA: Stanford University Press.
Beaumont, Peter. 2014. "Israel's Unit 8200 Refuseniks: 'You Can't Run from Responsibility.'" *The Guardian*, September 12. https://www.theguardian.com/world/2014/sep/12/israel-unit-8200-refuseniks-transcript-interview.
Bing, Christopher, and Joel Schectman. 2019. "Exclusive: Ex-NSA Cyberspies Reveal How They Helped Hack Foes of UAE." Reuters, January 30. https://www.reuters.com/investigates/special-report/usa-spying-raven/.
Brem, Hannah. 2021. "Palestine Rights Groups Warn Against Proposed Israel Facebook Law." JURIST, December 30. https://www.jurist.org/news/2021/12/palestine-rights-groups-warn-against-proposed-israel-facebook-law/.
Carmel, Alison, Rahaf Salahat, and Sarah Abu Alrob. 2021. "#Hashtag Palestine 2020: An Overview of Digital Rights Abuses of Palestinians During the Coronavirus Pandemic." 7amleh—The Arab Center for the Advancement of Social Media. May. https://7amleh.org/2021/05/10/hashtag-palestine-2020-an-overview-of-digital-rights-abuses-of-palestinians-during-the-coronavirus-pandemic.
Charlesworth, Hilary. 1999. "Feminist Methods in International Law." *American Journal of International Law* 93, no. 2: 379–394.
Council on American-Islamic Relations. 2004. *Unpatriotic Acts* [Annual Report of the Status of Muslim Civil Rights in the United States]. Washington, DC.
Crockford, Kade. 2020. "ACLU News & Commentary." American Civil Liberties Union, June 16. https://www.aclu.org/news/privacy-technology/how-is-face-recognition-surveillance-technology-racist/.
Dastin, Jeffrey. 2018. "Amazon Scraps Secret AI Recruiting Tool That Showed Bias Against Women." Reuters, Oct. 9.
De Vries, Katja. 2010. "Identity, Profiling Algorithms and a World of Ambient Intelligence." *Ethics and Information Technology* 12, no. 1: 71–85.

Diggelmann, Oliver, and Maria Nicole Cleis. 2014. "How the Right to Privacy Became a Human Right." *Human Rights Law Review* 14, no. 3: 441–458.

Droege, Cordula. 2012. "Get Off My Cloud: Cyber Warfare, International Humanitarian Law, and the Protection of Civilians." *International Review of the Red Cross* 94, no. 886: 533–578.

Durham, Helen, and Katie O'Byrne. 2010. "The Dialogue of Difference: Gender Perspectives on International Humanitarian Law." *International Review of the Red Cross* 92, no. 877: 31–52.

Dwoskin, Elizabeth. 2021. "Israel Escalates Surveillance of Palestinians with Facial Recognition Program in West Bank." *Washington Post*, November 8. https://www.washingtonpost.com/world/middle_east/israel-palestinians-surveillance-facial-recognition/2021/11/05/3787bf42-26b2-11ec-8739-5cb6aba30a30_story.html.

Ebadolahi, M. 2012. "Associated Press Report Confirms Widespread Secret NYPD Surveillance of Innocent Muslims." ACLU National Security Project, February 24. http://www.aclu.org/blog/national-security-religion-belief/associated-press-report-confirms-widespread-secret-nypd.

Fatafta, Marwa. 2019. "'Incitement' and 'Indecency': How Palestinian Dissent Is Repressed Online." *+972 Magazine*, December 4. https://www.972mag.com/censorship-online-palestinians/.

Fatafta, Marwa, and Nadim Nashif. 2017. "Surveillance of Palestinians and the Fight for Digital Rights." Al-Shabaka, October 23. https://al-shabaka.org/briefs/surveillance-palestinians-fight-digital-rights/.

Floreani, Samantha. 2021. "Why Digital Privacy Is a Feminist Issue." *Overland Literary Journal*, February 16. https://overland.org.au/2021/02/why-digital-privacy-is-a-feminist-issue/.

Gandy, Oscar H. 2010. "Engaging Rational Discrimination: Exploring Reasons for Placing Regulatory Constraints on Decision Support Systems." *Ethics and Information Technology* 12, no. 1: 29–42.

Gardam, Judith G., and Michelle J. Jarvis. 2001. "A Final Word." In *Women, Armed Conflict and International Law*, ed. Judith G. Gardam and Michelle J. Jarvis, 263–264. The Hauge: Kluwer Law International.

Gilman, Michele E. 2021. "Feminism, Privacy and Law in Cyberspace." University of Baltimore School of Law Legal Studies Research Paper, February 4. https://ssrn.com/abstract=3779323.

Gisel, Laurent, and Timan Rodenhäuser. 2019. "Cyber Operations and International Humanitarian Law: Five Key Points." Humanitarian Law and Policy. https://blogs.icrc.org/law-and-policy/2019/11/28/cyber-operations-ihl-five-key-points/.

Gleason, James. 2017. "LGBT History: The Lavender Scare." NGLCC, October 3. https://www.nglcc.org/blog/lgbt-history-lavender-scare.

Goodfriend, Sofia. 2021. "The Expansion of Digital Surveillance in Jerusalem and Impact." 2021. 7amleh—The Arab Center for Social Media Advancement. https://7amleh.org/storage/Digital%20Surveillance%20Jerusalem_7.11.pdf.

Guzik, Keith. 2009. "Discrimination by Design: Predictive Data Mining as Security Practice in The United States' 'War on Terrorism.'" *Surveillance & Society* 7, no. 1: 3–20.

Human Rights Watch. 2018. "Russia: Assault on Internet Freedom, Cybersecurity." April 30. https://www.hrw.org/news/2018/04/30/russia-assault-internet-freedom-cybersecurity.

Human Rights Watch. 2019. "Vietnam: Intensifying Rights Crackdown." January 17. https://www.hrw.org/news/2019/01/17/vietnam-intensifying-rights-crackdown

Human Rights Watch. 2022. "Human Rights Watch Among Pegasus Spyware Targets." https://www.hrw.org/news/2022/01/26/human-rights-watch-among-pegasus-spyware-targets.

Ibish, I. 2003. *Report on Hate Crimes and Discrimination Against Arab Americans: The Post September 11 Backlash, September 11, 2001–October 11, 2002*. Washington, DC: American-Arab Anti-Discrimination Committee.

International Committee of the Red Cross. (ICRC). 2004. "What Is International Humanitarian Law?" July 2004. https://www.icrc.org/en/doc/assets/files/other/what_is_ihl.pdf.

International Committee of the Red Cross. (ICRC). 2010. "IHL and Human Rights Law." October 29. https://www.icrc.org/en/document/ihl-human-rights-law.

Kempinski, Yoni. 2021. "Benny Gantz to Facebook and TikTok Executives: You Must Take Action." Israel National News, May 14. https://www.israelnationalnews.com/News/News.aspx/306224.

International Committee of the Red Cross. (ICRC). 2023. "What Does the Law Say about the Responsibilities of the Occupying Power in the Occupied Palestinian Territory?" March 28. https://www.icrc.org/en/document/ihl-occupying-power-responsibilities-occupied-palestinian-territories

Kirchgaessner, Stephanie, and Michael Safi. 2021. "Palestinian Activists' Mobile Phones Hacked Using NSO Spyware, Says Report." *The Guardian*, November 8. https://www.theguardian.com/world/2021/nov/08/palestinian-activists-mobile-phones-hacked-by-nso-says-report.

Kittichaisaree, K. 2017. "Application of the Law of Armed Conflict, Including International Humanitarian Law, in Cyberspace." In *Public International Law of Cyberspace*, 201–231. Cham, Switzerland: Springer.

Kittichaisaree, Kriangsak, and Christopher Kuner. 2015. "The growing importance of data protection in public international law." *EJIL: Talk* 14.

Legal Consequences of the Construction of a Wall in the Occupied Palestinian Territory. 2004. International Court of Justice Reports 136, Advisory Opinion of July 9.

Lieblich, Eliav, and Adam Shinar. 2022. "Counterterrorism off the Rails: Israel's Declaration of Palestinian Human Rights Groups as 'Terrorist' Organizations." Just Security, June 9. https://www.justsecurity.org/78732/counterterrorism-off-the-rails-israels-declaration-of-palestinian-human-rights-groups-as-terrorist-organizations/.

Lubin, Asaf. 2020. "The Rights to Privacy and Data Protection Under International Humanitarian Law and Human Rights Law." In *Research Handbook on Human Rights and Humanitarian Law: Further Reflections and Perspectives*, ed. Robert Kolb, Gloria Gaggioli, and Pavle Kilibarda, 462–491. Northampton: Edward Elgar.

MacAskill, Ewen, Gabriel Dance, Feilding Cage, Greg Chen, and Nadja Popovich. 2013. "NSA Files Decoded: Edward Snowden's Surveillance Revelations Explained." *The Guardian*, November 1. https://www.theguardian.com/world/interactive/2013/nov/01/snowden-nsa-files-surveillance-revelations-decoded#section/1.

Madden, Mary, Michele Gilman, Karen Levy, and Alice Marwick. 2017. "Privacy, Poverty, and Big Data: A Matrix of Vulnerabilities for Poor Americans." *Washington University Law Review* 95: 53.

Marczak, Bill, and John Scott-Railton. 2016. "The Million Dollar Dissident: NSO Group's iPhone Zero-Days Used Against a UAE Human Rights Defender." Citizen Lab. https://citizenlab.ca/2016/08/million-dollar-dissident-iphone-zero-day-nso-group-uae/.

Mathiesen, Kay. 2014. "Human Rights for the Digital Age." *Journal of Mass Media Ethics* 29, no. 1: 2–18. doi:10.1080/08900523.2014.863124.

McClain, Linda C. 1998. "Reconstructive Tasks for a Liberal Feminist Conception of Privacy." *William & Mary Law Review* 40: 759.

MEE Staff. 2021. "Israeli Press Review: Police Promote Nationwide Facial Recognition System." Middle East Eye, July 16. https://www.middleeasteye.net/news/israel-facial-recognition-cameras-police-press-review.

Mhajne, Anwar. 2021. "A Human Rights Approach to U.S. Cybersecurity Strategy." Carnegie Council for Ethics in International Affairs, February 17. https://www.carnegiecouncil.org/publications/articles_papers_reports/a-human-rights-approach-to-us-cybersecurity-strategy.

Nashif, Nadim. "Surveillance of Palestinians and the Fight for Digital Rights." Al-Shabaka, IFEX, October. https://ifex.org/images/israel/2017/10/26/israel-surveillance-palestinians-alshabaka-7amleh.pdf.

Noble, Safiya Umoja. 2018. *Algorithms of Oppression*. New York: New York University Press.

Noy, Orly. 2017. "Meet the Palestinian Israel Put on Trial for Her Poetry." *+972 Magazine*, August 28. https://www.972mag.com/meet-the-palestinian-israel-put-on-trial-for-her-poetry/.

O'Connor, Alexander J., and Farhana Jahan. 2014. "Under Surveillance and Overwrought: American Muslims' Emotional and Behavioral Responses to Government Surveillance." *Journal of Muslim Mental Health* 8, no. 1, 95–106.

Office of the UN High Commissioner for Human Rights. 2014. *The Right to Privacy in the Digital Age*. A/HRC/27/37. New York: United Nations, para. 1.

Olsen, Frances. 1985. "From False Paternalism to False Equality: Judicial Assaults on Feminist Community, Illinois 1869–1895." *Michigan Law Review* 84: 1518.

Osman, Nadaa. 2021. "Sheikh Jarrah: Activists Raise Concerns over Deleted Social Media Content." Middle East Eye, May 7. https://www.middleeasteye.net/news/sheikh-jarrah-israel-palestine-activists-social-media-deleted-content-concerns?fbclid=IwAR09p5mXGDsMDDeMCi45sWEov0RFbNycIlKShnMuNmUkuTj8vn-xP1noY5E.

Ravet, Hagar. 2019. "Unit 8200 Commander Attacks Cybersecurity Startup That Tried to Poach Soldiers." CTECH. December 30. https://www.calcalistech.com/ctech/articles/0,7340,L-3776723,00.html.

Richardson, Sophie. 2016. "China: Abusive Cybersecurity Law Set to Be Passed." Human Rights Watch, October 28. https://www.hrw.org/news/2016/11/06/china-abusive-cybersecurity-law-set-be-passed.

Ringrose, Katelyn. 2020. "A Look Back at the Role of Law and the Right to Privacy in LGBTQ+ History." Future of Privacy Forum, October 22. https://fpf.org/blog/a-look-back-at-the-role-of-law-and-the-right-to-privacy-in-lgbtq-history/.

Rodenhäuser, Tilman. 2021. "Cyber Warfare: Does International Humanitarian Law Apply?" International Committee of the Red Cross, September 6. https://www.icrc.org/en/document/cyber-warfare-and-international-humanitarian-law.

Sada Social. 2021. "Sada Social Center Documented Nearly 50 Violations against Palestinian Content." Sada Social | صدى سوشال, September 8. http://sada.soc ial/%D8%B5%D8%AF%D9%89-%D8%B3%D9%88%D8%B4%D8%A7%D9%84-%D8%AA%D9%88%D8%AB%D9%82-%D9%85%D8%A7-%D9%8A%D9%82%D8%A7%D8%B1%D8%A8-50-%D8%A7%D9%86%D8%AA%D9%87%D8%A7%D9%83%D8%A7-%D9%84%D9%84%D9%85%D8%AD%D8%AA/.

Sa'di, Ahmad H. 2021. "Israel's Settler-Colonialism as a Global Security Paradigm." *Race & Class* 63, no. 2: 21–37.

7amleh. 2018. "Facebook and Palestinians: Biased or Neutral Content Moderation Policies?" 7amleh—The Arab Centre for Social Media Advancement, October. https://7amleh.org/wp-content/uploads/2018/10/booklet-final2-1.pdf.

Siddiqui, Usaid, and Radmilla Suleymanova. 2021. "Israel, Social Media Groups Cooperating Against Palestinians: NGO." Israel-Palestine Conflict News, Al Jazeera, May 21. https://www.aljazeera.com/news/2021/5/21/close-cooperation-between-israel-and-social-media-companies-ngo.

Taha, Suhail. 2020. "The Cyber Occupation of Palestine: Suppressing Digital Activism and Shrinking the Virtual Sphere."

Tawil-Souri, Helga, and Miriyam Aouragh. 2014. "Intifada 3.0? Cyber Colonialism and Palestinian Resistance." *The Arab Studies Journal* 22, no. 1: 102–133.

Tsipori, Tali. 2016. "Israeli Cyber Security Exports Grew 10% in 2015." GLOBES, January 14. https://en.globes.co.il/en/article-israel-solidifies-its-standing-as-cyber-power-1001095258.

UN Conference on Trade and Development. 2023. "Data Protection and Privacy Legislation Worldwide." https://unctad.org/en/Pages/DTL/STI_and_ICTs/ICT4D-Legislation/eCom-Data-Protection-Laws.aspx.

UN Human Rights Committee (HRC), CCPR General Comment No. 16: Article 17 (Right to Privacy), The Right to Respect of Privacy, Family, Home and Correspondence, and Protection of Honour and Reputation, 8 April 1988, available at: https://www.refworld.org/docid/453883f922.html [accessed 3 January 2024].

United Nations. 2006. *Report of the International Law Commission on the Work of its Fifty-Eighth Session, Annex IV: Protection of Personal Data in Transborder Flow of Information.* UN Doc Supplement No. 10 (A/61/10). New York. https://legal.un.org/ilc/reports/2006/english/annexes.pdf.

General Assembly Resolution 73/179. 2018. *The Right to Privacy in the Digital Age*, A/73/589/Add.2, December 17. https://digitallibrary.un.org/record/1661346?ln=en

Weidmann, Nils B., Suso Benitez-Baleato, Philipp Hunziker, Eduard Glatz, and Xenofontas Dimitropoulos. 2016. "Digital Discrimination: Political Bias in Internet Service Provision Across Ethnic Groups." *Science* 353, no. 6304: 1151–1155.

Weinthal, Erika, and Jeannie Sowers. 2019. "Targeting Infrastructure and Livelihoods in the West Bank and Gaza." *International Affairs* 95, no. 2: 319–340. https://blogs.icrc.org/law-and-policy/2019/11/28/cyber-operations-ihl-five-key-points/.

Woods, Lorna. 2019. "Digital Privacy and Article 12 of the Universal Declaration of Human Rights." *The Political Quarterly* 90, no. 3: 422–429.

7
Capacity Building and Cyber Insecurity in Latin America

Geopolitics, Surveillance, and Disinformation

Alexis Henshaw

Given its large population and high level of internet and mobile phone connectivity, Latin America represents an important context in which to apply a critical lens to cybersecurity. On the one hand, it is a highly connected region where—in part because of the COVID-19 pandemic—we have seen a rapid movement of public discourse and government services to the online space. At the same time, it represents a context in which increases in connectivity unfold alongside government corruption, high levels of gender-based violence, and heightened risks to journalists and human rights defenders.

This chapter makes three key arguments about cyber (in)security in Latin America. The first is that patterns in the region reveal how the state remains an unreliable provider of cybersecurity. While technology is often touted as a force for greater accountability or transparency, examples from across Latin America demonstrate how state agents extend harmful practices into cyberspace in the absence of efforts to challenge cultures of abuse. Related to this, the chapter also argues that Latin America shows concerning examples of how cyber capacity-building efforts enable this shift in abusive practices. This is especially true where technical assistance and aid is provided by outside actors in the name of security, without corresponding measures for oversight. Finally, the chapter argues that critical insight brings to light how abuses are gendered, classed, and racialized.

The foundations of this chapter rest in feminist international relations (IR) theory, but the analysis also highlights the important contributions of other schools of thought. Feminist IR has long sought to call attention to the gendered experience of security while highlighting how such concerns are overlooked by institutions concerned with traditional security interventions

(Cohn 2014). Central to this critique is the role of the state. Feminist researchers have pointed out that, while traditional IR theory envisions the state as provider and/or referent of security, states have generally failed to offer security to women and other marginalized groups (Tickner 2001). Quite the contrary, states have retained a vested interest in managing sexual and gender politics in ways that reinforce and project national power and identity (Peterson 1999; True 2018).

This has especially been the case in Latin America, where institutionalized anti-leftist views have meshed with the desire of religious institutions to advance conservative gender politics. In recent years, this alliance of conservative interests has manifested as moral panic in response to developments such as abortion rights campaigns, LGBTQI+ rights movements, and the election of leftist governments. Though gender and politics scholars have found that leftist governments of the so-called Pink Tide era were relatively unprepared to tackle issues of gender politics, domestic and regional feminist organizing has created momentum for change (Blofield et al. 2017). Contrary to research showing the domestic roots of change, anti-feminist backlash has painted progressive social movements as a type of outsider threat. Drawing on Cold War era tropes of leftist internationalism, conservative and populist leaders have advanced platforms that position women's and LGBTQI+ rights as threats to religious freedom and national identity (Bohn 2022; Payne and Santos 2020).

These contested portrayals of security, identity, and gender politics have moved into the online space along with the larger political discourse. Here, a feminist IR perspective can engage with other views that more directly address digital politics and cybersecurity. Though Peterson (2003) warned two decades ago of the coming virtual economy and the politics of data commodification, feminist work in IR and security studies has been somewhat slow to engage with the digital space (Henshaw 2023). Critical work in surveillance studies and the study of race and technology can help fill this gap. Briefly put, work in these areas shares several common themes relevant to feminist IR:

1. Both surveillance studies and work in race and technology studies see continuities between current deployments of technology by governments and historical deployments of technology for colonial governance and social control. These theories see technologies past and present as important tools for reinforcing and policing gender

and racial hierarchies (Benjamin 2019; Karimi 2019; Pugliese 2012; Smith 2015).
2. Both schools of thought argue that the biases of dominant social groups are encoded in systems of governance and surveillance in ways that create new insecurities. In the modern era, specific examples include the biases encoded in facial-recognition systems (which, based on their programming, are more likely to misidentify women and people of color) and the stereotyped and/or sexualized results of search engine queries, which promote derogatory views toward women and people of color (Abu-Laban 2015; Benjamin 2019; Magnet and Dubrofsky 2015; Magnet and Rodgers 2012; Noble 2018; Noble and Tynes 2016).
3. These scholars argue that systems of surveillance and security place greater burdens on members of marginalized groups or ignore threats affecting these groups entirely. Examples include systems designed to combat violence against women, which have sometimes imposed invasive data collection requirements as a prerequisite for accessing these systems (Armstrong and Norris 1999; Browne 2012; Mason and Magnet 2012).

In general, it can be fairly said that work throughout the landscape of critical surveillance and technology studies shares the assumption that more interaction with technology should not be perceived as a normative good (Henshaw 2023). These discussions about the inherent risks and biases associated with security in the digital space can be carried into an analysis of cybersecurity in Latin America. With many countries having contentious histories of racial/ethnic inequality and violence against women and LGBTQI+ populations, there is space to explore where these biases continue to be encoded.

This chapter offers a transnational overview of the cybersecurity landscape in Latin America. This begins with a critical assessment of the state of digital politics and the region's emerging definitions of "cybersecurity," as seen in national cyber strategies. It then proceeds to look at two key issues where cybersecurity efforts collide with social hierarchies: disinformation campaigns and surveillance via cyberweapons. In each case, I argue that evidence of harm accruing to marginalized social groups reveals the shortcomings of current cybersecurity strategies. I further point out how, in each case, state agents are engaged in the perpetration of abuse, casting doubt on the ability of states to act as guarantors of cybersecurity. In the case of cyberweapons especially, I point out how abuses are further linked to capacity-building initiatives supported by external actors. This calls for greater attentiveness to how geopolitics influences online security.

The Digital Landscape of Latin America

It may be possible to say that Latin America, on the whole, is the most connected part of the Global South. The Inclusive Internet Index places six Latin American states (Chile, Brazil, Mexico, Argentina, Peru, and Colombia) among the world's 50 most inclusive countries (Economist Impact/Meta 2022). These states rank highly on a combination of affordability, local-language content, domestic sites for news and other information, digital literacy, and cultural acceptance of the internet. In terms of affordability and relevance, some Latin American states outrank peers in the Global North. In the longer term, the picture this data presents is one of a region making rapid advances in connectivity and acceptance of new technologies. In an executive summary of the 2022 data, analysts noted that close to three-quarters of Latin Americans surveyed believed that increased internet use during the COVID-19 pandemic was likely to constitute a "new normal," persisting into post-pandemic life (Economist Impact/Meta 2022). This further bolsters the claims of cultural acceptance.

At the same time, questions about freedom, safety, and accessibility persist. These concerns to some extent map onto regional divides in economic prosperity and the quality of governance. Data from Freedom House demonstrates this: among the nine Latin American countries included in their 2021 Freedom on the Net data, just two (Argentina and Costa Rica) ranked as "free." Two other states (Cuba and Venezuela) ranked as "not free," while a further five states ranked as "partly free." Significant issues of concern have been racial/ethnic inequalities in access and politically motivated takedowns of information. While censorship is endemic to Cuba and Venezuela, Freedom House also notes that even some countries that enshrine freedom of speech in national law—like Mexico and Colombia—routinely engage in filtering or removal of online content (Freedom House 2021).

This raises questions of disparities between the policies and practices of cybersecurity in Latin America. Regional approaches to cybersecurity continue to emerge, with many countries only recently developing national cyber strategies. Perhaps unsurprisingly, global reports rank some of the region's wealthier countries (including Brazil, Mexico, and Uruguay) highly on the provision of cybersecurity, while poorer states (such as Nicaragua and Haiti) rank extremely low (ITU 2020). The existence and quality of national policies are reflected in these scores. The Organization of American States (OAS) has, as a regional player, been instrumental in helping states develop their national cyber policies.[1] A closer assessment of these efforts reveals the roles played by the United States and Canada in shaping regional policy. Norms espoused by the US and Canada—including concepts of rights-based cybersecurity and multistakeholder approaches to cybersecurity—are reflected in many strategies throughout the Americas (Organization of American States/Global Partners Digital 2022). At the same time, many strategies within the region lack strong provisions for data protection. This, too, potentially reflects U.S. interests, as it is also seen as a weakness of U.S. cyber strategy (ITU 2020).

Another limitation of regional approaches to cybersecurity is that it is not always clear how cybersecurity ideals are being translated into specific, enforceable laws and policies. For example, Mexico's 2017 cyber strategy takes "a human rights perspective" as one of its guiding principles. This is defined as including freedom of expression, access to information, respect for privacy, and the protection of personal data (Parraguez Kobek 2018). However, the country has drawn criticism for politically motivated takedowns of information as well as the surveillance and harassment of journalists and human rights defenders by government parties (a topic explored further below) (Freedom House 2021). International ratings note that the country's progress on digital literacy, open data, and affordability/accessibility has stagnated in recent years, while gender gaps in internet access have actually grown (Economist Impact/Meta 2022). Such issues are not unique to Mexico. The following two sections discuss two areas in which threats to rights-based cybersecurity map onto persistent social inequalities.

Disinformation

The spread of disinformation online demonstrates the shortcomings of existing efforts to ensure information access while implicating institutional actors as parties to information insecurity. Trends in disinformation further point to the transnational nature of the problem, with linguistic and cultural ties promoting the spread of harmful narratives.

As a region that was hit particularly hard by the COVID-19 pandemic,[2] online responses to the coronavirus and COVID-19 vaccinations serve as an example of how mis/disinformation can have devastating consequences. In Brazil, campaigns to circulate misinformation were aided and abetted by figures at the highest levels of the government of Jair Bolsonaro. Ricard and Medeiros (2020) outline linkages between the president's supporters and disinformation campaigns intended to minimize the severity of the disease; promote pseudo-scientific information on treatments and cures; and de-legitimize political rivals, international organizations, and foreign governments that advocated more aggressive action. While it is unclear the extent to which these campaigns represent a coordinated effort, Ricard and Medeiros (2020, 3) call the president himself "one of the main vectors of misleading content." This included the advertisement of sham treatments or "cures" for the novel coronavirus.

Later, as COVID-19 vaccines became available, vaccine skepticism became another conduit for politically charged mis- and disinformation. In one study on the global spread of the QAnon movement,[3] authors identified Portuguese as one of the top-five languages in use on QAnon Telegram channels. Around the onset of the COVID-19 pandemic, authors note that Portuguese surpassed English to (briefly) become the most spoken language in the QAnon sphere. Brazilian politics, correspondingly, became a top topic of discussion (Hoseini et al. 2021). Commentators have noted that QAnon discourse in Brazil is not only fervently pro-Bolsonaro, but also it is visible and normalized in right-wing politics. Examples include the use of QAnon quotes and hashtags by political candidates and the display of QAnon symbols at political rallies (Muggah 2021).

Authors have linked the spread of COVID-19 mis/disinformation in Brazil to the country's high-mortality rate and to high rates of vaccine hesitancy (Muggah 2021; Ricard and Medeiros 2020). However, elements of this so-called infodemic are not new—nor are they limited to Brazil. Ricard and Medeiros (2020) note that misinformation in Brazil made use of the same networks and channels previously used by Bolsonaro and his supporters to discredit political rivals. This network was, in turn, developed with assistance from corporate allies and partners outside of Brazil. Similar coalitions have been observed in other Latin American countries.

Regionally, a major focus of political disinformation prior to COVID-19 was the notion of "gender ideology." Broadly defined, these anti-gender campaigns represent backlash against women's rights, reproductive rights, and/or LGBTQI+ rights movements in Latin America. As is the case with QAnon, the movement to fight gender ideology is loosely organized, has a conspiratorial element, and feeds off misinformation. It has also become entrenched in regional politics with the support of powerful institutional actors and foreign interests. The notion of campaigning against the use of the term "gender" by governmental and intergovernmental agencies can be traced back to the 1990s, when Catholic groups in the United States rallied against the work of UN agencies. Eventually, influential figures in both the clergy and lay religious communities would present the language of gender as one move in a larger effort to subjugate religious populations (Corrêa 2017).

In Latin America, discourse around gender ideology has been deployed by figures across the political spectrum in order to stoke fears about religious freedom, neocolonialism, the welfare of children, and the sanctity of culture and family structures (Biroli and Caminotti 2020; Rousseau 2020). Though these concerns most closely align with right-wing interests, some leaders from the center and left have likewise deployed anti-gender sentiments in an opportunistic way (Corrêa 2017). In the case of Peru, an anti-gender movement became nationally salient in 2016. Led by religious communities, the proximate focus of the group's activism was initially to oppose a sex education curriculum that incorporated discussions of gender diversity and equality. In time, though, they articulated a broader agenda that sought to de-legitimize feminist and LGBTQI+ activist groups through misinformation. Among the various claims the movement circulated were accusations of Marxist indoctrination, of children being exposed to pornography in schools, and of a broader neocolonial plot by transnational organizations to undermine Latin American family structures (Biroli and Caminotti 2020; Rousseau 2020).

Though authors have noted the transnational nature of the anti-gender movement in Latin America,[4] surprisingly little attention has been given to the role of information and communication technology in spreading anti-gender messaging. Authors have noted that offline activism including demonstrations, the spread of books and pamphlets, and travel/tours by anti-gender leaders have been instrumental to the development of cross-border activism (Biroli and Caminotti 2020; Corrêa 2017; Rousseau 2020). Yet the fact that one of the movement's main slogans, #ConMisHijosNoTeMetas (Don't mess with my children) is styled as a hashtag indicates the importance of social media messaging. Ferré-Pavia and Sambuceti (2022) find anti-gender activists from over a dozen Latin American and Spanish-speaking countries interacting on Twitter (now X) through hashtags. Dominant themes in these conversations included personal attacks on politicians and attempts to de-legitimize feminist activism and/or pro-choice movements. Bonet-Martí (2020) sees social media as a space in which religious anti-feminism combines with far-right populist sentiments to create a more aggressive and misinformation-driven campaign.[5]

These movements deserve attention because the political consequences in Latin America have been real. In Peru, anti-gender activists used the court system to hinder the implementation of sex education programming. Politicians also capitalized on anti-gender sentiment by trying to exclude transgender and nonbinary populations from national policies on gender-based violence (Rousseau 2020). In Colombia, anti-gender campaigns mobilized against the 2016 peace agreement between the government and the Revolutionary Armed Forces of Colombia (FARC). Campaigners online and offline linked the draft peace agreement to fears of Marxist indoctrination and opposed the implementation of gender provisions. The anti-gender movement in Colombia has been discussed as an important part of a coalition that initially rejected the peace deal in a referendum (Bohórquez Oviedo 2021; Gómez and Montealegre 2021).

As has been the case with COVID-19 disinformation, the use of ICTs and social media platforms allows outside actors to exert influence over domestic political discourse. This seems especially ironic in the case of anti-gender movements, as the movement sustains itself in part by stoking fears of neocolonial or cosmopolitan influence. Developing effective responses to mis- and disinformation in Latin America has been a struggle. On the one hand, as the case of Brazil demonstrates, governments and political officeholders can benefit from these campaigns in ways that create disincentives for action. This means the state cannot always be relied upon to create good-faith responses. ICT platforms, too, have shown a lack of interest and/or a lack of capacity to respond to disinformation. While events in several liberal democratic states have prompted more aggressive action by platforms to flag misinformation and de-platform those who commit abuse,[6] social media companies struggle with meaningful content moderation in non-English-language spaces. Research in Spanish-speaking communities on Facebook suggests that misinformation is missed on the vast majority of occasions (Avaaz 2020). Former Facebook employees have further admitted that spending on non-English language content moderation is paltry at best. In the United States, Latino populations spend more time online than other ethnic groups and are more likely to view social media sites as a primary source of information.

With misinformation easily spreading across borders, the lack of oversight sets the stage for serious problems (Valencia 2021).

In this environment, where both states and technology companies have largely abdicated their responsibilities to regulate the online space, who is left to push back on misinformation? Civil society becomes the obvious alternative, but civil society actors in Latin America are themselves embattled. The tide of violence throughout the region that impacts peacebuilders, journalists, environmental advocates, Indigenous leaders, and other activists is a well-known phenomenon that crosses international borders. These threats also cross borders into cyberspace. The following section addresses how electronic surveillance has rendered these groups more vulnerable, reducing their ability to counter misinformation and act as a force for Internet freedom.

Surveillance

The examination of surveillance as a threat in Latin America is a story of state abuse and overpolicing, as well as one of cyber-capacity building. Specifically, it shows how powers outside of Latin America can influence domestic events (often, in unanticipated ways) while using the region as a market and/or laboratory for new technological interventions. In this sense, there are two dimensions of surveillance worth exploring. The most obvious is the use of surveillance in the service of security, that is, how police and security forces deploy technology in abusive ways.

The security dimensions of surveillance speak to how cyber-capacity building has occurred in Latin America and to the unanticipated consequences of security cooperation. In particular, financial and technical support from the United States has been instrumental to some Latin American countries. Two major security cooperation initiatives show these forces at work: Plan Colombia and the Merida Initiative.

Plan Colombia, in effect from 2000 to 2015, was primarily aimed at combating drug trafficking and insurgency in Colombia. The Merida Initiative, in place from 2008 through the time of this writing,[7] is aimed at combating drug trafficking, organized crime, and money laundering in Mexico and some Central American states. Each of these initiatives has brought US aid, technical assistance, and security cooperation to the region in the name of law enforcement and/or counterinsurgency efforts. Some of the most well-known (and oft-criticized) expenditures associated with these plans include the purchase of military equipment, including large aircraft, helicopters, and firearms. However, technological-capacity building was a key element of each plan (Marra and Bennett 2020; Seelke and Finklea 2018). Examples of technology-related expenditures during Plan Colombia included the purchase of computers and related equipment for professional military education (PME) institutions, the purchase of video equipment for recording the depositions of demobilized combatants, and the funding of a "logistics command and control" system to manage material and human resources (GAO 2009). In the case of the Merida Initiative, expenditures included software systems and a biometric system "to help agencies collect, store, and share information on criminals and migrants" (Seelke and Finklea 2018).

Both plans sought to empower law enforcement and military agencies through technological-capacity building and other means. However, both resulted in abuses of power. In Colombia, the "False Positives" scandal resulted in the deaths of thousands of people (many of them young men from lower economic classes) at the hands of Colombian soldiers. In an attempt to present the appearance of success in military operations (and in an attempt to gain a variety of incentives), military officers ordered subordinates to kill civilians and then stage the bodies, reporting the deaths as deaths of insurgent combatants (Asmann 2021; Gordon 2017; Wood 2009). While these operations were themselves relatively low tech, observers have noted that an uptick in the apparent number of False Positives cases occurred around the time that the US Congress was trying to draw down spending for Plan Colombia. This suggests that anxieties about the reduced flow of aid put pressure on military leaders to appear more "successful" (FCR/CCEEU 2014). Surveillance abuses also reportedly accompanied Plan Colombia, as it was revealed in 2009 and 2014 that internal security forces and Colombian Army intelligence officials, respectively, were engaged in extensive campaigns of wiretapping, email monitoring, and surveillance against members of civil society, journalists, politicians, and even other members of the government (WOLA 2016).

The Merida Initiative, similar to Plan Colombia, was created in response to drug trafficking and drug-related violence. While offering assistance to multiple countries in Latin America and the Caribbean, Mexico has received the largest share of aid from the program—a reflection of US anxieties about the possibility of cross-border violence (Seelke and Finklea 2018).

Though there was some attempt to link aid offered through Merida to human rights conditions, aid generally repeated the patterns established by Plan Colombia. That is to say, the provision of military equipment, surveillance technologies, and training were focal to the program; at times, this had the effect of militarizing law enforcement (Abu-Hamdeh 2011; Arteaga 2009; Seelke and Finklea 2018). By comparison, less attention or assistance was devoted to the social problems underlying the growth of drug violence or to the North-South dimensions of the problem, that is, US demand for drugs and the flow of small arms from the US to Mexico (Abu-Hamdeh 2011; Seelke and Finklea 2018).

Seelke and Finklea (2018) note that some initiatives supplementing Merida aid *were* intended to address cross-border issues involving the United States. This includes Project Gunrunner, a Bureau of Alcohol, Tobacco, and Firearms program designed to track and disrupt the flow of small arms, and other programs run through the Department of Homeland Security (DHS). Greater surveillance at the US border has been a keystone of these programs. Technological solutions have been deployed to enhance surveillance of those crossing the US border, like the use of electronic license plate readers (Seelke and Finklea 2018). US law enforcement agencies have also benefited by harvesting data from the countries to which it provides law enforcement aid. Police in Arizona, for example, have incorporated all Honduran driver's license photos and mugshots into their facial-recognition databases with assistance from the Honduran government (Garvie et al. 2016).[8]

The expansion of surveillance technologies along the border is one area of concern for privacy advocates in Latin America and the US. In the case of facial-recognition software, the racialized and gendered algorithmic biases in such systems are well-established (Buolamwini and Gebru 2018; Garvie et al. 2016; Jones 2021). That these technologies continue to be deployed along the border and within the United States remains concerning; yet these are not the only technologies currently in use. Drones, motion sensors, and AI-enhanced surveillance tools are also currently in use along the US-Mexico border. At least some of these technologies were initially developed for use in war zones and contested border regions, like the West Bank (Ghaffary 2019). Observers have noted that these technologies are not only unreliable, but they also pose humanitarian risks (Chambers et al. 2021; Ghaffary 2019). Deployments of surveillance towers during the George W. Bush and Obama administrations were connected with increased migrant deaths, as migrants became increasingly reliant on trafficking networks and/or more likely to attempt crossing via dangerous routes to avoid detection (Chambers et al. 2021). Moreover, the increased demand for surveillance technologies along the border has come with pressure to lessen the human oversight required, especially the rote work of image processing. This has led to growth in AI-enhanced systems, which purport to reduce the need for human monitoring (Ghaffary 2019). Yet the deployment of these systems seems at odds with best practices recommended by the US government, which suggests that human oversight of automated processes is an essential right and a safeguard against algorithmic bias (White House 2022).

Political expediency has been a force in building support for building a "smart wall" along the border—despite the concerns about ethics and efficacy (Ghaffary 2019; Misra 2019). In July 2022, Mexico and the US announced a $1.5 billion dollar agreement for the purchase of border surveillance technologies by Mexico (Weissert and Miller 2022). Though it appears much of this spending is meant to further securitize the US-Mexico border, it seems likely that efforts will eventually turn to Mexico's southern border, where economic and human rights concerns have led to an influx of asylum seekers coming from (or through) Central America.[9]

Apart from the moral and ethical concerns associated with these technologies themselves, there is an attendant concern about the ethics of cyber-capacity building in a context where state actors have revealed themselves to be agents of insecurity. The misuse of cyberweapons by Latin American countries against dissidents, journalists, and human rights defenders is just the latest example of abusive practice by state agents and security forces. Perhaps the most well-publicized example of such abuse has been the deployment of Pegasus and related spyware tools in Latin American countries including Mexico and El Salvador.

Pegasus, which has been called "the world's most powerful cyberweapon,"[10] is a tool developed by the Israeli firm NSO Group. Originally developed for counterterrorism purposes, it is a tool capable of breaking encryption on Android handsets and iPhones. It allows users to access a target's data including contacts, messages, and emails; calendar appointments; and the GPS location of the phone. It also allows access to the camera and microphone of targeted devices (Bergman and Mazzetti 2022; Perlroth 2016). Because of the potential risk associated with this tool, the NSO Group itself states that it will only license Pegasus to "select approved, verified and authorized states and state agencies," which includes law enforcement, militaries, and state intelligence (NSO Group 2021a). The licensing process is also meant to include measures for due diligence, to prevent it from ending up in the hands of human rights abusers. Independent investigations have, however, found that process to be seriously flawed. Pegasus is now known to have been licensed to a number of authoritarian states, likely as a result of pressures from the US and/or Israeli governments (Bergman and Mazzetti 2021, 2022). Documented abuses of the cyberweapon worldwide include its deployment against journalists, student organizers, labor union leaders, women's rights and minority rights activists, and other human rights defenders (Access Now/Front Line Defenders 2022; Bergman and Mazzetti 2022; NSO Group 2021b; Priest et al. 2021; Walker et al. 2021).

Though the deployment of Pegasus and related tools (such as Kismet, The Trident, and ForcedEntry, which are also manufactured by the NSO Group and licensed to government agencies for surveillance) are discussed elsewhere in this volume, of particular interest to this chapter is how these tools have been used in Latin America. Mexican government agencies including the Mexican Army have engaged in abusive forms of surveillance using these tools. The University of Toronto's Citizen Lab, which investigates these cases, found that Mexico targeted one human rights activist who was reporting on extrajudicial executions and forced disappearances involving the army (R3D 2022). Mexico has also used spyware against journalists investigating corruption including Carmen Aristegui, whose family members and friends were harassed over a prolonged period with aggressive attempts to trick them into downloading spyware (Ahmed and Perlroth 2017; Priest et al. 2021). Abuses by Mexico were documented from 2015 up to 2020 and included attacks on minor children and US citizens living in Mexico (Scott-Railton et al. 2017a). Some attacks further suggest gendered motivations. In addition to the targeting of women journalists and anti-corruption activists, a 2017 investigation found that Mexico had targeted lawyers representing the family of a slain women's rights activist, who was murdered along with a journalist and three others in 2015. The lawyers had questioned official accounts of the crime, which portrayed it as a random attack, and called attention to the possibility of an official coverup (Scott-Railton et al. 2017b).

Abuses in El Salvador are notable for the fact that they were documented months after the NSO Group had promised to improve transparency and oversight of its systems. This probably underscores the lack of oversight of existing NSO Group clients (rather than new purchases of its systems), but it nonetheless sheds light on the difficulty of ensuring ethical uses of cyberweapons once they are deployed. Citizen Lab investigators, through a collaborative effort, confirmed 35 instances where journalists and civil society activists were targeted using NSO Group tools between mid-2020 and late 2021 (Scott-Railton et al. 2022). The targets include more than a half-dozen women. Though it is unclear whether or how gender might have impacted target selection, the Citizen Lab reports that documented cyberattacks coincided with an uptick in threats against women journalists nationwide (Scott-Railton et al. 2022).

Deployments of Pegasus and related tools, which continue to come to light throughout Latin America, hearken back to the themes introduced earlier in this chapter. First, in some cases they do appear to be gendered—especially where they have targeted figures calling attention to violence against women. Aside from that, though, they also show that the state cannot be considered a reliable guarantor of cybersecurity to its citizens. Moreover, although this has not been conclusively proven, there is some suggestion that political pressure or intervention from the United States allowed Latin American countries to obtain these tools, even though there were valid concerns about potential misuse. The possible role the US may have played certainly deserves more scrutiny, as this would fit within a larger pattern of the US enhancing cyber capacity within the region without effective intervention to ensure human rights are protected.

Conclusion: The Need for a Human Cybersecurity in Latin America

This chapter has offered a broad and transnational overview of current cybersecurity challenges in Latin America. A key takeaway of this analysis is that despite an emerging discourse about rights-based cybersecurity within the region, many countries are still plagued by state-sponsored abuses and a crisis of misinformation that threatens to destabilize democracies. National cyber strategies that are in place or in development across the region tend to focus on concerns about cybercrime—and for good reason. However, the human dimension of cybersecurity also requires more focus and efforts to translate ideals into practice. The impact of the COVID-19 pandemic should underscore the potential human cost of ignoring how people's lives may be impacted where information, systems, and services are not secure.

A discussion of the future of cybersecurity in Latin America must also include the role that external actors play in capacity building. While the

US, Canada, and international agencies have supported the development of rights-based cybersecurity plans, the US has also been a major force in supplying governments with surveillance tools that some deploy against their own citizens. Democratic backsliding is a substantial concern within the region. Abusive practices in Latin America are also not without consequences for the United States. US citizens in Latin America have also been targeted by spyware, as noted above, and the size of the Latin American diaspora in the United States raises concern over transnational flows of mis/disinformation (Valencia 2021).

Similarly, advocates for privacy and human security in the United States and other parts of the Global North may learn something from emerging forms of resistance taking place across Latin America. As this chapter was being drafted, over a dozen journalists from El Salvador's *El Faro* newspaper sued NSO Group over the abusive use of its spyware. In an opinion piece for *The Guardian*, one of these journalists made clear the quality-of-life impacts that journalists had suffered due to the spying. He also clarified that Salvadorean journalists were interested in suing not just for themselves but also on behalf of hundreds of other hacked journalists worldwide, who may have had no recourse to justice in their own national courts (Rauda Zablah 2022). Elsewhere in Latin America, we see the emergence of a counter-data movement aimed at bringing attention to the underreporting and undercounting of gender-based violence and using data to call law enforcement agencies into account. D'Ignazio (2022), writing on the emergence of a network of groups recording and reporting data on femicide, notes that advocates "don't imagine data as a 'solution' but rather see data as one tactic in a larger, networked movement of social and political actors." That network now includes groups across not only Latin America but also in the US and Canada—countries where violence against women is common, but where the legal concept of femicide/feminicide does not yet exist.[11]

A critical analysis of the issues discussed in this chapter calls upon us to see how current patterns of online insecurity map onto existing longstanding sources of inequality in the region. The targeting of feminist movements and activists by spyware and misinformation campaigns points to historical opposition to women's rights and leftist political movements. Yet we must also appreciate that these issues are transnational in nature. We can see neocolonial or geopolitical forces at work in the strategic deployments of technology across the Latin American region. While the US role in cyber-capacity building extends longstanding concerns about US imperialism in the region, other geopolitical actors are extending their influence as well. Freedom House has implicated Russia in denial-of-service attacks against media outlets in Venezuela, while Cuba is believed to employ Chinese technology for the filtering and censorship of online content (Freedom House 2021). These examples show how Latin America may be becoming a site of geopolitical contestation over cyber norms. Thus any attempt to adopt a more human security-focused approach to cybersecurity should take into account the need not only to address offline inequalities but also to resist new forms of digital colonialism.

Notes

1. A report from the OAS notes that, as of 2022, 14 out of 17 member states that have national cyber strategies in place developed their plans with technical support from the OAS (Organization of American States/Global Partners Digital 2022).
2. As of mid-2022, Peru has been identified as the country with the world's highest mortality rate due to COVID-19. Peru reports 657 deaths per 100,000 people. Brazil rates 16th in the world in mortality rates, Chile 18th, and Argentina 23rd. In absolute terms, Brazil is second in the world in the number of COVID deaths, with Mexico fifth and Peru sixth (*New York Times* 2020). It has been noted, however, that official statistics likely represent a significant undercount of deaths in India, where deaths likely surpassed totals in the US and Brazil (Cohen 2022).
3. QAnon is a far-right, conspiracy-based movement that emerged online in 2017. It has most closely been linked to conspiratorial views about US politics, claiming the existence of a secret satanic and/or pedophilia-perpetrating cabal operating behind the scenes of international politics. While discourse in the movement sought to promote US President Donald Trump, over time it has become significantly more internationalized (GNET Team 2020; Hoseini et al. 2021).
4. Rousseau (2020), e.g., directly links leaders in Peru's anti-gender movement to leaders in Bolivia, Ecuador, Colombia, Mexico, and Argentina. Ferré-Pavia and Sambuceti (2022) find related social media discourse extending beyond Central and South America to Spain and the Dominican Republic.
5. Among other things, Bonet-Martí (2020) highlights the coexistence and intermingling of anti-feminist and COVID-19 misinformation.
6. For example, the 2016 and 2020 US presidential elections, the rise of QAnon, and the spread of COVID-19-related conspiracies.
7. Mexico announced its intent to withdraw from the Merida Initiative in 2019. At the time of this writing, plans were underway to replace the agreement with a more comprehensive, binational pact.
8. Private companies have also enabled this data harvesting, e.g. through the sale of cell phone location data (Ghaffary 2019).

9. International Crisis Group (2018) notes that Mexico's southern border is already heavily militarized, though the use of surveillance technologies in these areas seems limited.
10. See Bergman and Mazzetti (2022). For further discussion on Pegasus, see Chapter 6 of this volume.
11. Puerto Rico became the first US territory to pass a law related to femicide in 2021.

References

Abu-Hamdeh, Sabrina. 2011. "The Merida Initiative: An Effective Way of Reducing Violence in Mexico?" *Pepperdine Policy Review* 4, no. 5: 37–54. https://digitalcommons.pepperdine.edu/cgi/viewcontent.cgi?article=1004&context=ppr.

Abu-Laban, Yasmeen. 2015. "Gendering Surveillance Studies: The Empirical and Normative Promise of Feminist Methodology." *Surveillance & Society* 13, no. 1: 44–56.

Access Now/Front Line Defenders. 2022. "Women Human Rights Defenders Speak out About Pegasus Attacks." Access Now. https://www.accessnow.org/women-human-rights-defenders-pegasus-attacks-bahrain-jordan/.

Ahmed, Azam, and Nicole Perlroth. 2017. "Using Texts as Lures, Government Spyware Targets Mexican Journalists and Their Families." *New York Times*, June 16. https://www.nytimes.com/2017/06/19/world/americas/mexico-spyware-anticrime.html.

Armstrong, Gary, and Clive Norris. 1999. *The Maximum Surveillance Society: The Rise of CCTV*. New York: Routledge. https://www.amazon.com/Maximum-Surveillance-Society-Rise-CCTV-dp-1859732267/dp/1859732267/ref=mt_other?_encoding=UTF8&me=&qid=.

Arteaga, Nelson. 2009. "The Merida Initiative: Security-Surveillance Harmonization in Latin America." *European Review of Latin American and Caribbean Studies/Revista Europea de Estudios Latinoamericanos y del Caribei*, no. 87 (October): 103–110. http://www.jstor.org/stable/25676378.

Asmann, Parker. 2021. "Colombia Report Triples Number of Known False Positives Victims." *InSight Crime*. https://insightcrime.org/news/report-colombia-false-positives/.

Avaaz. 2020. *How Facebook Can Flatten the Curve of the Coronavirus Infodemic*. New York: Avaaz. https://secure.avaaz.org/campaign/en/facebook_coronavirus_misinformation/.

Benjamin, Ruha. 2019. *Race After Technology: Abolitionist Tools for the New Jim Code*. Medford, MA: Polity.

Bergman, Ronen, and Mark Mazzetti. 2021. "Israeli Companies Aided Saudi Spying Despite Khashoggi Killing." *New York Times*, July 17. https://www.nytimes.com/2021/07/17/world/middleeast/israel-saudi-khashoggi-hacking-nso.html.

Bergman, Ronen, and Mark Mazzetti. 2022. "The Battle for the World's Most Powerful Cyberweapon." *New York Times*, January 28. https://www.nytimes.com/2022/01/28/magazine/nso-group-israel-spyware.html.

Biroli, Flávia, and Mariana Caminotti. 2020. "The Conservative Backlash Against Gender in Latin America." *Politics and Gender* 16, no. 1: 1–7.

Blofield, Merike, Christina Ewig, and Jennifer M Piscopo. 2017. "The Reactive Left: Gender Equality and the Latin American Pink Tide." *Social Politics: International Studies in Gender, State & Society* 24, no. 4: 345–369.

Bohn, Simone. 2022. "Advancing Gender Claims in Post-Pink Tide Brazil: Bolsonaro's Project for Women." *Politics, Groups, and Identities* 10, no. 1: 166–170.

Bohórquez Oviedo, Ángela María. 2021. "Weaponizing Gender: The Campaign Against 'Gender Ideology' in the Colombian Peace Plebiscite." (PhD diss., University of Delaware.)

Bonet-Martí, Jordi. 2020. "Análisis de las estrategias discursivas empleadas en la construcción de discurso antifeminista en redes sociales." *Psicoperspectivas. Individuo y Sociedad* 19, no. 3 (online). https://www.psicoperspectivas.cl/index.php/psicoperspectivas/article/view/2040.

Browne, Simone. 2012. "Race and Surveillance." In *Routledge Handbook of Surveillance Studies*, ed. Kirstie Ball, Kevin Haggerty, and David Lyon, 72–80. Florence, KY: Taylor & Francis Group. http://ebookcentral.proquest.com/lib/troy/detail.action?docID=957182.

Buolamwini, Joy, and Timnit Gebru. 2018. "Gender Shades: Intersectional Accuracy Disparities in Commercial Gender Classification." *Proceedings of Machine Learning Research* 81: 1–15.

Chambers, Samuel Norton, Geoffrey Alan Boyce, Sarah Launius, and Alicia Dinsmore. 2021. "Mortality, Surveillance and the Tertiary 'Funnel Effect' on the U.S.-Mexico Border: A Geospatial Modeling of the Geography of Deterrence." *Journal of Borderlands Studies* 36, no. 3: 443–468.

Cohen, Jon. 2022. "COVID-19 May Have Killed Nearly 3 Million in India, Far More Than Official Counts Show." *Science*, January 6. https://www.science.org/content/article/covid-19-may-have-killed-nearly-3-million-india-far-more-official-counts-show.

Cohn, Carol. 2014. "Women and Wars: A Conceptual Framework." In *Women and Wars*, ed. Carol Cohn, 1–35. Cambridge: Polity Press.

Corrêa, Sonia. 2017. "Gender Ideology: Tracking Its Origins and Meanings in Current Gender Politics." *Engenderings*, November 12. https://blogs.lse.ac.uk/gender/2017/12/11/gender-ideology-tracking-its-origins-and-meanings-in-current-gender-politics/.

D'Ignazio, Catherine. 2022. *Counting Feminicide: Data Feminism in Action*. Cambridge, MA: MIT Press. https://mitpressonpubpub.mitpress.mit.edu/counting-feminicide.

Economist Impact/Meta. 2022. "Economist Impact: The Inclusive Internet Index (2022)." https://impact.economist.com/projects/inclusive-internet-index.

FCR/CCEEU. 2014. *The Rise and Fall of "False Positive" Killings in Colombia: The Role of U.S. Military Assistance, 2000–2010*. Nyack, NY: Fellowship of Reconciliation/Coordinación Colombia-Europa-Estados Unidos. https://static1.squarespace.com/static/54961aebe4b0e6ee1855f20a/t/5bcb47b68165f55241ef07d4/1540048846084/Rise-Fall-False-Positives-US-Military-Assistance.pdf.

Ferré-Pavia, Carme, and Maria Fe Sambuceti. 2022. "El Neoconservadurismo Religioso En Twitter: La Campaña #ConMisHijosNoTeMetas y El Discurso Contra La Igualdad de Género." *Teknokultura* 18, no. 1: 55–66.

Freedom House. 2021. "Freedom on the Net 2021 (Country Reports)." https://freedomhouse.org/countries/freedom-net/scores.

GAO. 2009. *Plan Colombia: Drug Reduction Goals Were Not Fully Met, but Security Has Improved; U.S. Agencies Need More Detailed Plans for Reducing Assistance*. Washington, DC. https://www.gao.gov/assets/a282521.html.

Garvie, Clare, Alvaro Bedova, and Jonathan Frankle. 2016. "Perpetual Line Up—Unregulated Police Face Recognition in America." Georgetown Center on Privacy and Technology. https://www.perpetuallineup.org/.

Ghaffary, Shirin. 2019. "The 'Smarter' Wall: How Drones, Sensors, and AI Are Patrolling the Border." *Vox.* https://www.vox.com/recode/2019/5/16/18511583/smart-border-wall-drones-sensors-ai.

GNET Team. 2020. "What Is QAnon?" GNET. https://gnet-research.org/2020/10/15/what-is-qanon/.

Gómez, Diana Marcela, and Diana María Montealegre. 2021. "Colombian Women's and Feminist Movements in the Peace Negotiation Process in Havana: Complexities of the Struggle for Peace in Transitional Contexts." *Social Identities* 27, no. 4: 1–16.

Gordon, Eleanor. 2017. "Crimes of the Powerful in Conflict-Affected Environments: False Positives, Transitional Justice and the Prospects for Peace in Colombia." *State Crime Journal* 6, no. 1: 132–155.

Henshaw, Alexis. 2023. *Digital Frontiers in Gender and Security.* Bristol, UK: Bristol University Press.

Hoseini, Mohamad et al. 2021. "On the Globalization of the QAnon Conspiracy: Theory Through Telegram." arXiv. https://arxiv.org/pdf/2105.13020.pdf.

International Crisis Group. 2018. "Mexico's Southern Border: Security, Violence and Migration in the Trump Era." https://www.crisisgroup.org/latin-america-caribbean/mexico/66-mexicos-southern-border-security-violence-and-migration-trump-era.

ITU. 2020. *Global Cybersecurity Index 2020.* Geneva, Switzerland. https://www.itu.int/epublications/publication/D-STR-GCI.01-2021-HTM-E.

Jones, Christopher. 2021. "Law Enforcement Use of Facial Recognition: Bias, Disparate Impacts to People of Color, and the Need for Federal Legislation." *North Carolina Journal of Law & Technology* 22, no. 4: 777–815.

Karimi, Ali. 2019. "Surveillance in Weak States: The Problem of Population Information in Afghanistan." *International Journal of Communication* 13: 4778–4793.

Magnet, Shoshana, and Rachel E. Dubrofsky. 2015. "Introduction." In *Feminist Surveillance Studies*, 1–20. Durham, NC: Duke University Press,.

Magnet, Shoshana, and Tara Rodgers. 2012. "Stripping for the State." *Feminist Media Studies* 12, no. 1: 101–118.

Marra, Michael A., and Douglas W. Bennett. 2020. "PLAN COLOMBIA: Learning from a Light-Footprint 'America Second' Military Strategy." *Small Wars Journal.* https://smallwarsjournal.com/jrnl/art/plan-colombia-learning-light-footprint-america-second-military-strategy.

Mason, Corinne, and Shoshana Magnet. 2012. "Surveillance Studies and Violence Against Women." *Surveillance & Society* 10, no. 2: 105–118.

Misra, Tanvi. 2019. "The Problem with a 'Smart' Border Wall." Bloomberg.com. https://www.bloomberg.com/news/articles/2019-02-12/the-problem-with-a-smart-border-wall.

Muggah, Robert. 2021. "In Brazil, QAnon Has a Distinctly Bolsonaro Flavor." *Foreign Policy*, October 2. https://foreignpolicy.com/2021/02/10/brazil-qanon-bolsonaro-online-internet-conspiracy-theories-anti-vaccination/.

New York Times. 2020. "Coronavirus World Map: Tracking the Global Outbreak." Accessed June 29, 2022. https://www.nytimes.com/interactive/2021/world/covid-cases.html.

Noble, Safiya Umoja. 2018. *Algorithms of Oppression: How Search Engines Reinforce Racism.* Illustrated edition. New York: New York University Press.

Noble, Safiya Umoja, and Brendesha M. Tynes, eds. 2016. "Introduction." In their *The Intersectional Internet: Race, Sex, Class, and Culture Online*, 1–19. New York: Peter Lang International Academic.

NSO Group. 2021a. "Cyber Intelligence Sector Leader NSO Group Unveils the Industry's First 'Transparency and Responsibility Report.'" NSO News. https://www.nsogroup.com/Newses/cyber-intelligence-sector-leader-nso-group-unveils-the-industrys-first-transparency-and-responsibility-report/.

NSO Group. 2021b. *Transparency and Responsibility Report 2021*. Hersliya, Israel. https://www.nsogroup.com/wp-content/uploads/2021/06/ReportBooklet.pdf.

Organization of American States/Global Partners Digital. 2022. *National Cybersecurity Strategies: Lessons Learned and Reflections from the Americas and Other Regions*. https://www.oas.org/en/sms/cicte/docs/National-Cybersecurity-Strategies-Lessons-learned-and-reflections-ENG.pdf.

Parraguez Kobek, Luisa. 2018. *Quo Vadis? Mexico's National Cybersecurity Strategy*. Washington, DC: Wilson Center. https://www.wilsoncenter.org/sites/default/files/media/documents/publication/quo_vadis_mexicos_cybersecurity_strategy.pdf.

Payne, Leigh A., and Andreza Aruska de Souza Santos. 2020. "The Right-Wing Backlash in Brazil and Beyond." *Politics & Gender* 16, no. 1: E6.

Perlroth, Nicole. 2016. "How Spy Tech Firms Let Governments See Everything on a Smartphone." *New York Times*. https://www.nytimes.com/2016/09/03/technology/nso-group-how-spy-tech-firms-let-governments-see-everything-on-a-smartphone.html.

Peterson, V. Spike. 1999. "Political Identities/Nationalism as Heterosexism." *International Feminist Journal of Politics* 1, no. 1: 34–65.

Peterson, V. Spike. 2003. *A Critical Rewriting of Global Political Economy: Integrating Reproductive, Productive and Virtual Economies*. New York: Routledge.

Priest, Dana, Craig Timberg, and Souad Mekhennet. 2021. "Private Israeli Spyware Used to Hack Cellphones of Journalists, Activists Worldwide." *Washington Post*. https://www.washingtonpost.com/investigations/interactive/2021/nso-spyware-pegasus-cellphones/.

Pugliese, Joseph. 2012. *Biometrics: Bodies, Technologies, Biopolitics*. London: Taylor and Francis. http://www.123library.org/book_details/?id=59542.

R3D. 2022. "Ejercito Espía." *Ejército Espía*. https://ejercitoespia.r3d.mx/.

Rauda Zablah, Nelson. 2022. "Pegasus Spyware Was Used to Hack Reporters' Phones. I'm Suing Its Creators." *The Guardian*, December 5. https://www.theguardian.com/commentisfree/2022/dec/05/pegasus-spyware-journalists-phone-hacking-lawsuit.

Ricard, Julie, and Juliano Medeiros. 2020. "Using Misinformation as a Political Weapon: COVID-19 and Bolsonaro in Brazil." *Harvard Kennedy School Misinformation Review* 1, no. 3 (online). https://misinforeview.hks.harvard.edu/article/using-misinformation-as-a-political-weapon-covid-19-and-bolsonaro-in-brazil/.

Rousseau, Stéphanie. 2020. "Antigender Activism in Peru and Its Impact on State Policy." *Politics & Gender* 16, no. 1 (online). https://www.cambridge.org/core/journals/politics-and-gender/article/abs/antigender-activism-in-peru-and-its-impact-on-state-policy/2A6396F98EC482ED4F1307D09BAA5940.

Scott-Railton, John et al. 2017a. *Reckless Exploit: Mexican Journalists, Lawyers, and a Child Targeted with NSO Spyware*. University of Toronto. https://citizenlab.ca/2017/06/reckless-exploit-mexico-nso/.

Scott-Railton, John et al. 2017b. *Reckless IV: Lawyers for Murdered Mexican Women's Families Targeted with NSO Spyware*. University of Toronto. https://citizenlab.ca/2017/08/lawyers-murdered-women-nso-group/.

Scott-Railton, John et al. 2022. *Project Torogoz: Extensive Hacking of Media & Civil Society in El Salvador with Pegasus Spyware.* University of Toronto. https://citizenlab.ca/2022/01/project-torogoz-extensive-hacking-media-civil-society-el-salvador-pegasus-spyware/.

Seelke, Clare Ribando, and Kristin Finklea. 2018. *U.S.-Mexican Security Cooperation: The Mérida Initiative and Beyond.* Washington, DC: Congressional Research Service. https://web.archive.org/web/20181018022356/https://fas.org/sgp/crs/row/R41349.pdf.

Smith, Andrea. 2015. "Not-Seeing: State Surveillance, Settler Colonialism, and Gender Violence." In *Feminist Surveillance Studies*, ed. Shoshana Magnet and Rachel E. Dubrofsky, 21–38. Durham, NC: Duke University Press.

Tickner, J. Ann. 2001. *Gendering World Politics.* New York: Columbia University Press.

True, Jacqui. 2018. "Bringing Back Gendered States: Feminist Second Image Theorizing of International Relations." In *Revisiting Gendered States: Feminist Imaginings of the State in International Relations*, ed. Swati Parashar, J. Ann Tickner, and Jacqui True, 33–48. New York: Oxford University Press.

Valencia, Stephanie. 2021. "Misinformation Online Is Bad in English. But It's Far Worse in Spanish." *Washington Post.* https://www.washingtonpost.com/outlook/2021/10/28/misinformation-spanish-facebook-social-media/.

Walker, Shaun, Stephanie Kirchgaessner, Nina Lakhani, and Michael Safi. 2021. "Pegasus Project: Spyware Leak Suggests Lawyers and Activists at Risk across Globe." *The Guardian.* https://www.theguardian.com/news/2021/jul/19/spyware-leak-suggests-lawyers-and-activists-at-risk-across-globe.

Weissert, Will, and Zeke Miller. 2022. "Mexico Agrees to Invest $1.5B in 'Smart' Border Technology." AP NEWS. https://apnews.com/article/russia-ukraine-biden-immigration-climate-and-environment-120f8a3fc440e3b2cccce6100e65b912.

White House. 2022. "Blueprint for an AI Bill of Rights." https://www.whitehouse.gov/ostp/ai-bill-of-rights/.

WOLA. 2016. "15th Anniversary of Plan Colombia: Learning from Its Successes and Failures." https://www.wola.org/files/1602_plancol/content.php?id=us_aid.

Wood, Rachel Godfrey. 2009. "Understanding Colombia's False Positives." Oxford Transitional Justice Working Paper Series.

Conclusion

Anwar Mhajne and Alexis Henshaw

In a 2018 speech at the World Economic Forum Annual Meeting in Davos, Switzerland, Professor Yuval Harari stated, "Those who control the data control the future not just of humanity, but the future of life itself. Because today, data is the most important asset in the world" (see Dickson 2018).

Various actors, including democratic and nondemocratic states, as well as corporations, have used data as a weapon to consolidate their power. These actors have used data and statistics as tools to preserve an unequal status quo (D'ignazio and Klein 2020). The reliance on the internet and intelligent technologies to perform personal daily tasks and interact with state bureaucracies and institutions, which became even more consolidated during COVID lockdowns, makes it almost impossible for us to escape surveillance. The actors engaged in surveillance vary from governments to corporations, to criminal groups, to individuals, among others.

Surveillance practices are heavily data driven. They are not exclusive to oppressive or authoritarian regimes. As the cases in the book show, surveillance technologies have also been used by democratic governments to control and "manage" minority communities and groups deemed a threat to national security. These tools allow states to control communities within their borders and, as Yılmiz's chapter shows in the case of China, diaspora communities. Surveillance technologies and practices have multiplied in scale, quantity, and quality. We see these technologies used as leverage to achieve national and international gains and increase cooperation between different surveillance states, such as in the case of Israel's normalization agreements with the UAE. A 2022 *New York Times* investigation revealed "how sales of Pegasus played an unseen but critical role in securing the support of Arab nations in Israel's campaign against Iran and even in negotiating the Abraham Accords, the 2020 diplomatic agreements that normalized relations between Israel and some of its longtime Arab adversaries" (Bergman and Mazzetti 2022).

Similarly to feminist critiques of traditional international relations approaches to security and understanding international politics, international relations scholarship on cybersecurity lacks a discussion around intersectionality, and it overwhelmingly focuses on state security at the expense of human security. This scholarship marginalizes the stories and needs of individuals and groups inhabiting the virtual realm. This includes data privacy and protection during periods of conflict and the absence of conflict. As the chapters in this volume show, this is especially problematic when the marginalized stories are stories of vulnerable groups who experience violence daily inside and outside the cyber realm. Surveillance capabilities and technologies have made this violence invisible yet more potent. Even though some use surveillance as a form of deterrence and a tool for conflict prevention and management, it has been abused by various democratic and nondemocratic countries to silence minority groups, opposition groups, and anything they deem a "security threat."

The advancement in digital and surveillance technologies directly impacts conflict dynamics, enabling governments and other conflict parties with potent instruments to perpetrate invisible violence and suppress opponents. Cyber technologies have extended violence, conflict, oppression, and occupation into the cyber domain. For instance, as Mhajne's chapter showed, Israel's cyber capability cannot preclude discussing Israel's occupation and surveillance of the Palestinians. One of the themes the chapter explored is emerging geographical divides in how nation-states and regions apply regulations, policies, and protections to internet users and their data. Authoritarian governments tend to focus on information security, which focuses on controlling and managing users' data in the name of security, versus cybersecurity, which focuses on data protection. Surveillance technology, especially tools focused on collected biometric data, is creating opportunities for oppressive regimes, democratic (such as the case of Israel) and nondemocratic (such as the case of China), to engage in digital authoritarian practices such as using personal data as a tool for suppressing, managing, weakening, and attacking vulnerable communities in the name of national security.

Additionally, current attempts at regulating cyberspace still need to consider human rights issues caused by overreaching cybersecurity policies. For instance, the Anti-Cyber Crime Law of Saudi Arabia has a vague clause on the "protection of public interest, morals, and common values." This clause has been "used to crack down on online speech and freedom of expression by imprisoning bloggers and others for voicing different opinions, insulting public officials, or supporting forces other than the government in power" (Rossini and Green 2015). Also, as Monyani and Wefwafwa argue in Chapter 5, this is present in Kenya, where the government and society established regulatory regimes of online and offline female nudity to protect public morals. Moreover, the lack of regulations for using cyberweapons increases the chances of human rights abuses in conflict settings and situations of relative peace ("peace" here is defined as the absence of visible violence rather than the presence of sustainable peace). When governments use cyberattacks or hack into an opposition leader's or journalist's phone, human rights are at stake.

Even though feminist work on surveillance and data is emerging academically (see Dubrofsky and Magnet 2015) and in activist circles, sufficient feminist situated and contextual discussions of data privacy and surveillance in different contexts, such as armed conflict and under different regimes, are still lacking. As the chapters in this volume show, an intersectional postcolonial and feminist analysis are essential for shedding light on how power dynamics and conflicts in the physical world bleed into cyberspace. It is also essential for showing how power dynamics in cyberspace shape the lived experiences of different individuals, groups, communities, and states. The insistence of feminists that power relations matter, that situated knowledge is essential, and that objectivity is questionable give feminists practical tools to comprehensively analyze the colonial, gendered, racialized, and classed effects of cybersecurity practices directly tied to data privacy and digital surveillance. These tools enabled feminist scholars to understand and address human rights violations in cyberspace. For example, human rights activists, journalists, and individuals from vulnerable communities, due to their religion, ethnicity, sexual orientation, or gender, are more likely to be targeted by government surveillance (Brown and Esterhuysen 2019). Moreover, "the consequences of more broad threats like data breaches or network shutdowns are often more severe for them because of their location within society" (Brown and Esterhuysen 2019).

This book adds to works such as Catherine D'ignazio and Lauren F. Klein's (2020) work on data feminism and Rachel E. Dubrofsky and Shoshana Amielle Magnet's intervention on feminist surveillance studies. D'ignazio and Klein (2020) define "data feminism" as "a way of thinking about data, both their uses and their limits, that is informed by direct experience, by a commitment to action, and by intersectional feminist thought" (8). They add: "The starting point for data feminism is something that goes mostly unacknowledged in data science: power is not distributed equally in the world. Those who wield power are disproportionately elite, straight, white, able-bodied, cisgender men from the Global North" (8).

The chapters in the book took the available feminist and postcolonial literature. They expanded it to help us understand how cybersecurity shapes politics and international relations while focusing on digital and human rights. The chapters assessed the implications of existing cybersecurity concerns on individuals from various communities and highlighted how the lack of international consensus on regulations is also concerning. It has been well documented that "race, ethnicity, religion, gender, location, nationality, socio-economic status ... determine how individuals become administrative and legal subjects through their data and, consequently, how those data can be used to act upon them by policymakers, commercial firms and both in combination" (Taylor 2017, 3). The more categories an individual belongs to, the more likely they will be identified as targets of surveillance (Taylor 2017).

The chapters also analyzed data protection and privacy regimes from a colonial lens. In doing so, they ask us to consider whose data is worthy of being protected and whose is worthy of having agency over who accesses their data, how it is being shared, when it is being shared, and by whom. As Hofstetter reminds us in Chapter 3, "The colonial logic legitimizes international actors to prioritize the collection of vast amounts of data and the deployment of invasive surveillance technologies to assert control in crisis situations over local populations' rights to data privacy and agency." On the other hand, Saltman and Hussein remind us in Chapter 2 that in addition to the majority of major tech companies with access to users' data globally being located in the West, especially in the US, current data protection legislations such as GDPR are meant to protect the data privacy of citizens of counties located in the Western Hemisphere. As a result, we see a rise in inequalities between users with protected digital rights in the West and users in the Global South lacking such protections and living under constant state-corporate surveillance.

Most important, some of our authors moved beyond critiquing current cybersecurity regulations to provide a human rights framework for devising and implementing cybersecurity laws and policies (see Whetstone and K.C.'s chapter, Mhajne's chapter, as well as Saltman and Hussein's chapter). Intelligent services and the military have dominated debates on cybersecurity under the guise of national security. As a result, cybersecurity laws, practices, and policies do not pay serious attention to human's and women's rights. It is essential to ask who/what the security in cybersecurity stands for—often, cybersecurity policies, like national security policies, define security as the state rather than the people (and the infrastructure needed). This is why it is essential to create an international legal framework to protect human rights in cyberspace and apply international human rights laws to the conduct of states in the cyber domain. When assessing a cybersecurity framework, the chapters in this volume remind us to ask, Whose security are we talking about? Security from what? And security by what means?

A cybersecurity framework not centered on protecting digital human rights must be revised. They remind us that cybersecurity processes must be inclusive, multidisciplinary, context specific, and intersectional. These processes must de-center the state's narrow definition of cybersecurity as national security. They need to consider human rights and pay attention to the stories and advice of marginalized individuals, activists, and civil society groups. Finally, they need to include guidelines for data protection and privacy, the protection of digital identity, restrictions on the use of surveillance technologies by state actors in the context of war as well as peace, and international guidelines on how to combat online violence and harassment against women and vulnerable groups. This is why a feminist framework is essential for any discussion on (in)security and rights in cyberspace.

References

Bergman, Ronen, and Mark Mazzetti. 2022. "The Battle for the World's Most Powerful Cyberweapon." *New York Times*, January 28. https://www.nytimes.com/2022/01/28/magazine/nso-group-israel-spyware.html.

Brown, Deborah, and Anriette Esterhuysen. 2019. "Why Cybersecurity Is a Human Rights Issue, and It Is Time to Start Treating It like One." Association for Progressive Communications, November 28. https://www.apc.org/en/news/why-cybersecurity-human-rights-issue-and-it-time-start-treating-it-one.

Dickson, Ben. 2018. "AI, Big Data and the Future of Humanity." TechTalks, January 31. https://bdtechtalks.com/2018/01/31/yuval-harari-wef-ai-big-data-digital-dictatorship/.

D'ignazio, Catherine, and Lauren F. Klein. 2020. *Data Feminism*. Cambridge, MA: MIT Press.

Dubrofsky, Rachel E., and Shoshana Amielle Magnet, eds. 2015. *Feminist Surveillance Studies*. Durham, NC: Duke University Press.

Kirchgaessner, Stephanie, and Michael Safi. 2021. "Palestinian Activists' Mobile Phones Hacked Using NSO Spyware, Says Report." *The Guardian*, November 8. https://www.

theguardian.com/world/2021/nov/08/palestinian-activists-mobile-phones-hacked-by-nso-says-report.

Rossini, Carolina, and Natalie Green. 2015. "Cybersecurity and Human Rights." Global Partners Digital. https://www.gp-digital.org/wp-content/uploads/2015/06/GCCS2015-Webinar-Series-Introductory-Text.pdf.

Taylor, Linnet. 2017. "What is Data Justice? The Case for Connecting Digital Rights and Freedoms Globally." *Big Data & Society* 4, no. 2: 2053951717736335.

Index

For the benefit of digital users, indexed terms that span two pages (e.g., 52–53) may, on occasion, appear on only one of those pages.

Tables are indicated by *t* following the page number

abortion, 4, 17n.4, 117, 138–39, 174
Afghanistan, 15–16, 81–109
algorithmic bias, 5, 155–56, 183–84
algorithmic surveillance, 165–66
Amazon, 121, 155–56
anti-gender movement. *See* gender ideology
Apple, 121, 184–85
Argentina, 38, 176

biometrics
   in Afghanistan, 81, 83–84, 88–94
   in China, 116–17
   Israeli-Palestinian conflict and, 163
   migration and, 181–82
Bolsonaro, Jair, 178
border surveillance, 182–84
Brazil
   counterterrorism legislation, 56*t*, 67–69
   COVID-19 and, 177–81
   data breaches in, 17–18n.8
   misinformation in, 177–81
   National Action Plan of, 38

Canada, 56*t*, 66, 176–77
capacity building, 181–86
China
   cybersecurity norms and, 7–8
   digital authoritarianism and, 115–18, 119–24, 126–27
   social media and, 70–71
   surveillance and, 120–22, 195
Citizen Lab, 166
civil society
   feminist advocacy and, 29, 36–37

   international law and, 13, 16, 71, 84–85, 181
   LGBTQ+ rights advocacy and, 98–99
   privacy advocacy, 81, 101, 106
   surveillance of, 92, 93–94, 166, 182, 198
Colombia, 176, 181–83
colonialism, 154, 165, 179
content removals, 54, 56*t*, 66–67, 69, 101, 137, 164–65, 176
counterdata, 187
counterterrorism, 5–6, 52, 55, 56*t*, 70–71, 116
COVID-19, 4, 8–9, 118, 173, 176, 178–79
Cuba, 175, 187–88
cyberattacks, 1, 4, 16, 33–34, 84–85, 93, 126, 128–29, 152–53, 195–96
cyberbullying, 30–31, 126–27, 134, 142–44, 147–49
cyber-capacity building, 181–86
cybercrime, 9–10, 11, 13–14, 30, 35, 43–46, 186
cyber domain, 1, 6, 13, 14, 195
cyberfeminism, 27, 29, 30–32
cyberstalking, 29
cybersurveillance. *See* surveillance
cyberwar, 1–2, 4, 16, 84–85
cyberweapons, 1, 5–7, 184–86
   See also Pegasus

data governance, 83–84, 100, 103–6, 108
data harvesting, 10, 183
data privacy, 10, 13, 16, 42, 73–74, 122
   in Afghanistan, 83–84, 86–87, 91, 98–99, 104, 107
   Israeli-Palestinian conflict and, 154–60, 166–67

deepfakes, 13–14
digital authoritarianism, 7, 82–85, 87–88, 107, 114–18, 119–29, 195
digital divide, 8–10, 34, 41–42, 161
digital ethnography, 120–21
digital literacy, 105–6, 176
digital politics, 2–3, 5, 174
digital rights, 5, 13, 33–34, 164–65, 197, 198
in Afghanistan, 86, 101, 105, 107
digital violence, 39–43
disinformation, 4, 56*t*, 82–83, 159, 177–81, 186–87
doxxing, 13–14, 28–29, 30–31
drones, 163, 183–84

Egypt, 82–83, 122–23, 135–36
El Salvador, 17–18n.8, 184, 185–86, 187
espionage, 1, 152
ethics, 5–7, 32, 103–4, 184
ethnic minorities, 16, 41–42, 56*t*, 121–22, 128, 161, 175, 180–81, 196–97
ethnic studies, 5
ethnic violence, 13, 56*t*
European Union (EU), 6–7, 9–10, 11, 158–59
legislation in, 52, 53–54, 56*t*, 66–68
See also General Data Protection Regulation (GDPR)

Facebook, 17n.4, 40, 42, 180–81
in Afghanistan, 81–82, 92, 93–94, 100–1
Israeli-Palestinian conflict and, 155–56, 158–59, 164–65
in Kenya, 136*t*, 142–43, 144–45
facial recognition, 10, 15, 116–17, 154–55, 162–63, 175, 183–84
feminist activism, 139–41, 142–44, 148–49, 179–80, 187–88
France, 9–10, 56*t*, 66, 67, 68–69

Gaza Strip, 160, 161–63
Gender-based violence (GBV), 13, 25–26, 27–32, 33, 84–85, 95–96, 108, 187
gender ideology, 178–80
gender inequality, 37–38, 41–42, 86–87, 123, 177
See also digital divide
gender mainstreaming, 3
gender trolling, 30–31, 40

General Data Protection Regulation (GDPR), 10, 52, 56*t*, 67–68, 159, 197
Geneva Conventions, 152, 153–54, 156, 158, 160
genocide, 56*t*, 115, 128, 153–54
Global Positioning System (GPS), 184–85
Google, 10–11, 100, 101, 121

hacking, 13–14, 92–93, 97–98, 155, 164, 166, 187, 195–96
humanitarian law, 152–54, 156–60
human rights, 5–6, 11–12, 31, 32–35, 67, 156–60, 197–98
in Afghanistan, 91–92, 101, 105–6, 108
in China, 115, 125
in Latin America, 176–77, 184
of Palestinians, 152, 155
human rights defenders, 5–6, 66–67, 82–83, 94–95, 166, 177, 184–85

India, 56*t*, 66, 67–69
infertility, 126–27
Instagram, 136*t*, 142–43, 165
International Committee of the Red Cross (ICRC), 93, 152
internet access, 7–10, 15, 27–32, 94, 99, 161–64
internet shutdowns, 56*t*, 96
iPhone. *See* Apple
Iran, 92–93, 194
Islamophobia, 27, 31–32, 123
Israel
censorship and, 164
cybersurveillance, 161–66, 195
international law and, 160
trade in cyberweapons, 5–6, 184–85, 194
use of cyberweapons, 166

journalists
in Afghanistan, 91–92, 96–97, 101–2
censorship and, 66–67, 164
in China, 125
gender issues and, 14
Pegasus and, 5–6, 166, 184–86, 187
in Russia, 121

Kenya
censorship in, 134–35, 137–39

counterterrorism legislation, 56t, 67–68, 69
cyberbullying in, 144–49
cybercrime in, 35
internet access in, 136–39
labor force of, 17n.6
Khashoggi, Jamal, 119, 155, 195–96

legislation
  censorship and, 137–38
  counterterrorism and, 56t, 66–69
  gender-based violence and, 41
  regionally, 54–55, 157–58
  user protection and, 52, 159, 197
LGBTQ+ populations
  censorship and, 82–83
  conspiracy theories and, 174, 178–79
  rights of, 154–55, 174
  targeting of, 40, 95–96, 161–62
LinkedIn, 93–94, 100–1, 136t

malware, 13–14, 126, 128–29
Meta, 164–65
  See also Facebook; Instagram; WhatsApp
Mexico
  border security and, 183–84
  censorship in, 176
  cybersecurity policy, 177
  internet access in, 176
  Merida Initiative, 181–83
  Pegasus and, 184–85
Microsoft, 10–11
misinformation, 45, 187–88
  in Brazil, 178
  counterterrorism and, 55, 56t
  in United States, 17n.3, 180–81
misogyny
  ideologically, 30, 39–40
  harassment and, 40, 123, 127–28
  pornography and, 29
  Taliban and, 87–88
  violence and, 28
mobile phones
  internet access and, 27, 136–37
  surveillance of, 93–94, 97, 102, 166, 184–86
  women and, 35, 90

Myanmar, 40, 83

neoliberalism, 1, 2–3
neorealism, 1
Nigeria, 35, 56t, 135–36
non-governmental organizations (NGOs)
  in Afghanistan, 83–84, 90, 93–94, 100–1
  digital rights and, 5
  humanitarian efforts, 32, 103–4
  Women, Peace, and Security efforts, 36–37, 42
  See also International Committee of the Red Cross (ICRC)
norms, 7–12, 34, 176–77
North Atlantic Treaty Organization (NATO), 3, 89–90
NSO Group, 5–6, 166, 184–86, 187
nude photography, 134, 138–49

OpenAI, 17n.6
Organization of American States (OAS), 11, 176–77
Organisation for Economic Co-operation and Development (OECD), 70–71, 157–58

Pakistan, 14, 56t, 66, 67–69, 90, 93
Palestine/occupied Palestinian territories
  internet access in, 161–62, 164
  legal status of, 158, 160
  social media access, 164–66
  surveillance of, 161–66
  See also Gaza; West Bank
Pegasus, 5–6, 166, 184–86
Peru, 176, 179–80, 194
Poland, 56t, 67–68
pornography, 29–30, 56t, 179
  See also revenge pornography
post-conflict states, 37–43, 44, 45
privacy rights, 9–10, 42, 56t, 67, 122, 195
  in Afghanistan, 91, 96, 98–99, 107
  Israeli-Palestinian conflict and, 154–60, 166–67

QAnon, 178

racism, 31, 43, 121–22, 123
rape, 35, 40, 128–29, 153–54
revenge pornography, 13–14, 29–30

Russia
 capacity building and, 187–88
 counterterrorism legislation, 56t, 67–69
 cybersecurity norms and, 7–8, 11–12
 murders of dissidents, 119
 online propaganda, 121
 surveillance and, 92–93, 155

Saudi Arabia, 119, 155, 195–96
securitization, 26, 91, 105
Singapore, 56t, 66, 67
smartphone, 140–42, 145, 163
Snapchat, 136t
social media
 activist use of, 99, 118, 179–80
 censorship of, 92
 counterterrorism and, 39–40, 56t
 cybercrime and, 13–14
 economic impact, 141–42
 harassment and, 9–10, 14, 40
 misinformation and, 180–81
 surveillance of, 82–84, 93–94, 97, 120–22, 124–26, 164–66
 usage statistics, 27, 70–71, 135–39
 women and, 35, 95, 102, 140–42, 144–49
spyware, 5–7, 184, 185, 186–88
surveillance studies, 118–19, 121, 174–75
surveillance systems, 16–17, 146–47, 194–95
 in Afghanistan, 83, 92, 97–98, 104
 in China, 115–16, 121–22
 historical development, 154–55
 Israeli-Palestinian conflict and, 161–67
 in Latin America, 181–87
 legality of, 158–59
Switzerland, 93, 194

Taliban, 81, 87–88, 91–96, 99, 100–1, 106–9
technology companies
 as actors in governance, 10–11
 censorship and, 66–67, 164–65
 collaboration with authoritarian governments, 121
 content moderation and, 180–81
 data harvesting and, 13, 67–68, 86, 94, 101

 regulation of, 10, 52–53, 54, 56t, 69
 surveillance and, 81
telecommunications companies, 94, 161
Telegram, 120, 178
Tibet, 116
Tik Tok, 42, 165
transgender persons, 180
transnational authoritarianism, 114–15, 118–22, 123–29
Turkey, 56t, 66, 67–69, 118, 155
Twitter, 14, 81, 100–1, 137, 142–43, 164–65, 179–80

United Kingdom, 56t
United Nations, 72–73, 88–89, 157–58
United States
 Afghanistan and, 89
 border security and, 183–84
 capacity building and, 176–77
 counterterrorism legislation, 56t
 cybersecurity norms and, 3, 7–9
 data breaches in, 13–14
 disinformation in, 9–10, 180–81, 186–87
 role in Internet development, 6–7
Universal Declaration of Human Rights, 156–57
UNSCR 1325. *See* Women, Peace, and Security Agenda
Uyghurs, 115–19, 124–29

vaccine misinformation, 4, 178
Venezuela, 176, 187–88

West Bank, 161–62
WhatsApp, 136–37, 136t, 142–43
Women, Peace, and Security Agenda, 3, 25–27, 35–46
 National Action Plans, 25–26, 36–38, 45
Women's rights. *See* feminist activism

X
 See Twitter
Xinjiang, 115–18. *See also* China

Yahoo, 9–10, 136t
YouTube, 136t, 165–66

Printed in the USA/Agawam, MA
August 2, 2024

870361.015